D1601267

Covered Wagon Women

Diaries and Letters from the
Western Trails
1862–1865

Volume 8

Edited and compiled by
KENNETH L. HOLMES

Introduction to the Bison Books Edition
by María E. Montoya

University of Nebraska Press
Lincoln and London

⊗

First Bison Books printing: 1999
Most recent printing indicated by the last digit below:
10   9   8   7   6   5   4   3   2   1

Library of Congress Cataloging-in-Publication Data
The Library of Congress has cataloged Vol. 1 as:
Covered wagon women: diaries & letters from the western trails, 1840–1849 / edited and compiled by Kenneth L. Holmes; introduction to the Bison Books edition by Anne M. Butler.
p. cm.
Originally published: Glendale, Calif: A. H. Clark Co., 1983.
"Reprinted from volume one . . . of the original eleven-volume edition"—
T.p. verso.
"Volume 1."
Includes index.
ISBN 0-8032-7277-4 (pa: alk. paper)
1. Women pioneers—West (U.S.)—Biography.   2. West (U.S.)—History.   3. West (U.S.)—Biography.   4. Overland journeys to the Pacific.   5. Frontier and pioneer life—West (U.S.)   I. Holmes, Kenneth L.
F591.C79   1996   978—dc20   95-21200   CIP

Volume 2 introduction by Lilian Schlissel
ISBN 0-8032-7274-X (pa: alk. paper)
Volume 3 introduction by Susan Armitage
ISBN 0-8032-7287-1 (pa: alk. paper)
Volume 4 introduction by Glenda Riley
ISBN 0-8032-7291-X (pa: alk. paper)
Volume 5 introduction by Ruth B. Moynihan
ISBN 0-8032-7294-4 (pa: alk. paper)
Volume 6 introduction by Linda Peavy and Ursula Smith
ISBN 0-8032-7295-2 (pa: alk. paper)
Volume 7 introduction by Shirley A. Leckie
ISBN 0-8032-7296-0 (pa: alk. paper)
Volume 8 introduction by María E. Montoya
ISBN 0-8032-7297-9 (pa: alk. paper)

Reprinted from volume eight (1989) of the original eleven-volume edition titled *Covered Wagon Women: Diaries and Letters from the Western Trails, 1840–1890*, published by The Arthur H. Clark Company, Glendale, California. The pagination has not been changed and no material has been omitted in this Bison Books edition.

Introduction the Bison Books Edition

María E. Montoya

> If I were only a word painter I would try to give you
> a description of it but Nature has blessed me with no
> such gift & so I can give you no idea of it but only
> tell you that it was grand splendid & magnificent.
> —Louisa Cook

So why publish or read another collection of trail diaries from White, relatively middle-class women? It has been over twenty years since John Mack Faragher published *Women and Men on the Overland Trail* and opened up an unexamined world of relationships between families as they traveled West. Since then, the field of western women's history has blossomed and produced some of the most interesting and provocative work in the fields of women's history, history of the American West, and labor history. So to publish yet another volume of diaries and letters, which seemingly reiterate and cover ground already well trod upon by historians, seems redundant or at the very least boring. Yet, one can not pick up this collection of women's writings and not be drawn into the drama of their everyday lives as they struggled to maintain a family, some sense of home, and their own identities as they persevered in the West. These writings offer fresh and personal insight into familial relations, national politics, and race relations on the Great Plains and in the Far West. In the words of Louisa Cook above, these are "grand splendid & magnificent."

The diaries and letters that appear in this collection from the University of Nebraska Press offer a rare and important window into the feelings and lives of nine women who shared relatively little in common with one another before they left their homes to travel west. One of the great assets of these collections is that they remind us of the individuality of the real humans who lived these experiences: few generalizations can be made about this cohort. Aside from their similar experience of traveling overland during the early 1860s, their worlds differed tremendously and consequently they experienced the trail in ways unique to their own personal situations. Some, like Ellen Tootle, were wealthy and traveled in relative luxury, while others, like Mary Ringo, barely made financial ends meet and had spent their family's life savings to make this trip and a new start in the Far West. These women also represent a variety of ages and life experiences. A couple of the women made the trip West for pleasure and returned within the year to their homes back East: Harriet Hitchcock was fourteen and on a short family trip to prospect for gold and Ellen Tootle was on her honeymoon with her husband who was looking into expanding his business west. The majority of these women, however, were making permanent moves that would change the course of their lives as they took themselves and their families to a new environment and a whole new set of experiences.

Each woman was quite diverse and unique in the choices she made about what to tell and her feelings about the move. As you read through the entries you will be charmed by their individuality in prose style and personality. Some of the women, in particular Louisa Cook and Harriet Hitchcock, exhibit a wonderful sense of humor. Hitchcock sees the world from her naive vantage point of fourteen years, and while she parrots the ugly racism of her parents regarding Indians, she also makes wonderfully insightful and funny comments about the odd characters she encounters in the mining fields of Colorado. Louisa Cook, a single mother traveling west to make a new life for herself and her child, writes home to her family, "if you do not hear from me for a long time you must not think I am dead or married (might as well be one or the other) but keep writing   Direct to Portland" (55). This woman has taken control of her "unfortunate" position and even finds levity in her situation. When she arrives in Oregon, she again writes her family to tell them of the bright prospects for single women like herself, as there is but one available lady for every one hundred men, and she soon takes advantage of the gender imbalance and finds herself a suitable mate (57). Like all of the women in this collection, Louisa Cook is an active participant in the world around her and creates opportunities for herself.

Other woman, particularly the ones with large families, find little amusing as they make the difficult trip. You can feel the exhaustion that must have racked these women's bodies as they did the difficult work of maintaining a family on the trail. Mary Lightner, a Morman woman, traveling with her husband and seven children to settle in Utah wrote in the middle of the trip, "Camped in dust as if in the middle of the street in the States. Baked a shortcake, fried some bacon and had tea for supper after dark. Tired almost to death—lost the children's pet rabbit today" (103). Just the normal day of cooking, cleaning, dressing children, and keeping them from harm's way was more than enough for any woman, but the added stress of the lost pet rabbit with all of its attendant whining and worrying about leaving it behind was more than most of us can bare in the comfort of our own modern homes, much less in the middle of nowhere with few basic comforts.

Some of the writings are just downright gloomy. One cannot read Mary Ringo's diary without the eerie feeling that this woman had a premonition that disaster was about to befall her family. Throughout the diary she seems depressed, overwhelmed, and anxious. Two weeks before her husband accidentally shot himself, leaving her eight months pregnant and with five children, she came across the grave of a man who had accidentally shot himself and later wrote, "I pray God we may get along safely" (216). The despair and loneliness that she endured after her husband's tragic and sudden death is difficult to read as she left her husband buried along the trail and pushed on with her young family. As Mary Ringo moved farther West she became less self-absorbed dealing with the very public world of concerned emigrants who help her move her wagon and the merchants to whom she wants to sell her possessions so that she can take the stagecoach west with her family. Since Mrs. Ringo does not have enough possessions to sell in order to pay for their passage, she has to continue the trip and drive her family all the way to Oregon, but not before another disaster visits her family.

Despite the dissimilarity in what they chose to write down, there are themes that appear in all of the women's writings. First, each of these women is extremely private and reserved. For example, we do not know that Mary Ringo is pregnant until we read her daughter's postscript to her mother's unfinished diary. Lucretia Epperson is also pregnant but makes no mention of her condition except for her recurring fatigue. Moreover, none of the women discuss their personal relationships with their husbands. To our twentieth-century sensibilities, too used to "tell-all" narratives, the lack of intimate details may be surprising, if not troubling. Only Ellen Tootle, the newlywed, hints at the possibility of sexual relations on the trail. She boasted of her feather bed, the attentiveness of her husband, and wrote one unusual passage, "We undress at night though it is not customary on such trips" (65). Her diary is almost frivolous as she soaks in the newness of being married, being out on the trail, and seeing a new world.

The most common theme that runs through all of the letters and diaries is fear. When Harriet Loughary penned the words, "leaving not one to tell the tale," she voiced the overwhelming concern that all of these women shared: the possibility of their own death or the death of a family member (152). Mrs. Loughary had come upon Massacre Creek where a large emigrant train had been murdered. Her company assumed that Indians had killed the emigrants, but the group soon learned that the depredations were committed by a band of "destroying angels" from the Mormon Church. In fact, as the diaries and letters reveal, there was little reason to fear Indians. Not one woman in this book has a direct violent encounter with Native Americans, although they hear rumors and stories about Indian massacres and depredations. As this case demonstrates and as the diaries and letters themselves reveal over and over again, emigrants had much more to fear from their fellow white travelers. So while these memoirs are not necessarily accurate depictions of the reality of trail life, in particular of Indian/white relations, they do reveal the concerns that plagued these women as they made their way west at the height of the Civil War.

Mrs. Loughary's words also suggest another common strain that runs throughout these diaries and letters: the desire to be heard and remembered. Each of the nine diarists and letter writers in this collection of essays write quite self-consciously and know that someone—a family member, an ancestor, or perhaps a larger impersonal audience—will read their story and judge them and their lives. Some, such as Louisa Cook, blatantly acknowledge that their letters are the public recordings of the trip. "I hope you will save my letters as I have written a great deal that I have not in my journal & when I come back I should like to have them to refer to or look over" (38). Most others do not explicitly make the connection between writing and public persona, but as you will see, the generality of the context and the formality reveal little of what we would consider today to be the modern habit of "journaling."

One of the most curious aspects of these diaries is that we get relatively little sense of the historical era in which they lived. All of these diaries and letters were written during the American Civil War and yet only two of the women, Louisa Cook and Harriet Loughary, make direct mention of the national events and upheaval that surrounds them. Cook wrote, "No thundering of cannon rattling to & fro of carriages filled with pleasure seekers or attractive displays announced to us that to day is the anniversary of our national independence & yet not unfit is it that quiet & stillness should reign when we realize at what fearful cost our Government is struggling to maintain those rights which our ancestors have handed down to their posterity" (46). All of the women were from Union states, none came from the deep South, and only Harriet Loughary mentioned the presence of "Copperheads" or Confederate sympathizers. Of all the women, Mrs. Loughary was the one who most closely followed the progress of the Civil War, reporting the news she received about Grant's victories. She also had a verbal, almost physical, violent confrontation with a group of southern men who did not appreciate her hanging of the Union flag from her wagon. Only the cooler demeanor of her husband averted a fight within the camp (134). I have no good answer for why, in the midst of the greatest political and miliary conflict in the nation's history today, these women were not commenting on the Civil War. Were they trying to escape the horror and disruption of war? Were they unconcerned about what they had left behind, too overwhelmed with the day-to-day work? Did they just not consider this appropriate journal and letter material? No matter what the explanation, their silence reminds us of the isolation that these women faced as relatively little news reached them as they drove into the Far West.

These diaries usually have been read as the stories of women moving from the East to create their new homes, and hence civilization, in the American West: a gendered female version of Manifest Destiny. As the reader situates himself or herself in the East watching the seemingly inevitable march of progress westward, we cannot help but project the end of the story onto these historical texts. Can we set aside our knowledge and try to experience the trail as they would have in the early 1860s? Moreover, can we use these texts in a very different way than they have previously been read? For example, what would it have been like to be the people already in the West, watching this movement of outsiders and interlopers moving into their homeland? For as these documents all make clear, these women and their families were not moving into empty space. Indeed these women traveled over well-worn, if not overused, trails that moved alongside the telegraph lines. Furthermore, the U.S. federal government had established trade stations and forts to ease the difficulty of the trip. So this landscape was marked not only by the presence of the government and white settlers, but it was also home to the Native Americans and Mexican-Americans who had been living here prior to Euro-American incursions.

By the time the women in this collection were traveling west, there had been twenty years of continuous travel across these trails. Indians had become accustomed to the presence of whites within their homelands, and as these diaries and letters reveal, they relied upon the wagon trains for trade and acquisition of goods. On the other hand, these women were still intrigued and in many cases disgusted by the perceived "otherness" of the Indians along the trail. Only Lucretia Epperson's discussion of Indians is at all sympathetic to their plight as they struggled for survival in the midst of this onslaught of settlers. Most of the women use words such as "dirty," "eery," and "degraded" to describe the various Native Americans they encounter. Louisa Cook for example wrote, "I have been much disappointed in what I have seen of the Indians I thought when I got away from the white mans settlements where they could roam at will & live uncontaminated by society that we should see some of those noble qualities that have been attributed to them by so many writers but O dear what a contrast filthy degraded deceitful & treacherous they seem to me to be but a little above the brute creation" (54). As mentioned earlier, none of these women had a violent or even a hostile confrontation with any Native American, and yet all of these women treated the Indians with contempt and fear. Harriet Loughary summed up the feelings of these women best when she wrote, "We have found that all the harmless Indians so far are the dead ones" (150). This, of course, was simply untrue as she had traded with the Indians and given them food on occasion. These women had preconceived notions of who they thought Indians were and how they supposedly acted. Even the day-to-day interactions with individual Indians could not dissuade these women from their simplistic and racist attitudes. So imagine the difficulty Native Americans faced in losing control of their landscape, their inability to communicate with these interlopers, and the hostility of the transgressors.

As twentieth-century readers it is important not to lose sight of the fact that in the early 1860s this was still a contested landscape. The Civil War raged in the eastern United States and its outcome would determine who would settle the West and what type of labor system they would bring with them. In the Far West, despite historical hindsight, White settlers did not have control over the land and its resources. Native Americans still believed they controlled vast tracts of the Great Plains and were still decades away from complete removal. So, as you read these diaries and letters try to let go of your twentieth-century sensibilities and place yourself in the position of these women as they faced new lives on the western landscape. More importantly perhaps, also try to imagine what it would have been like to already be sitting in the American West and seeing these women and their families moving towards you and your own family. This collection offers the rare glimpse into the world of nineteenth-century trail life in the American West: enjoy and learn from their lives!

Contents

Illustrations

Introduction to Volume VIII

In the introduction to Volume VII (1854-1860) we pointed out that the overland trails in those years differed greatly in conditions of travel from what they had been in the earlier years. This was even more true as to conditions in the 1860s. The overland stage with its need for stations every 10 to 20 miles was a major factor in this change. Frank A. Root and William Connelley in their classic book, *The Overland Trail to California* (Topeka, KS, 1901, pp. 102-03) listed 150 of these stations (*see* supplement following this introduction). These stage stations had to be supplied with feed for the journey using horse power. This meant that the overlanders now could obtain oats for their horses and mules which could not live off grass alone as could oxen. Great freight wagons kept the stations supplied with good feed and other supplies as well. Now the time needed for the journey was much less. The rapid movement of the stages meant a much more reliable United States mail service. In the fall of 1864 the overland telegraph made its appearance. From the east it followed the Platte River route to Salt Lake City. There it was linked with a line from California. A branch was soon added from the Platte River to Denver.

With the coming of the Civil War volunteer army units were stationed at strategic forts and cities aborning along the overland route. Their main purpose was to guard against Indian attack. Our women mention units at such forts as Kearny, Laramie, Bridger and Walla Walla. And there were new posts as well.

It is noteworthy that in the diaries and letters of this

volume there is so little made of the Civil War. One might even be led to think that they were turning their backs to the conflict and trying to forget that it was happening.

Only Harriet Loughary made much of the Fourth of July in her journal:

> This morning was a lovely one, which we hailed with joy notwithstanding we were cuddled down in a lone valley, far from home and all great national festivities. Yet some recognition of a patriotic nature must be observed. The few stars and stripes were raised on top of our tents, a line of men drawn up, and a salute fired from a hundred little guns and pistols. Three cheers were lustily given for "Our Country," "The Soldiers in the field" and last though not least "The Captains new Grand baby." After an extra dinner made of the same kind of provisions, baked beans, & soup, instead of burned hoe cake, was our bill of fare. All had a "go as you please time" Some hunted or fished, others lounged around camp, while the children had a picnic under the bows of a large pine tree. Two more trains came up today and camp with us greatly enjoying our celebration.

There are sparse references to the great war, usually made on the Fourth, but Harriet wrote more than all the others put together.

The 1860s were years of active engagement of the emigrants with the Plains Indians. The women report on what they heard along the way from contacts with other wagon trains, and they were constantly in fear of Indian attack; however, none of them were among those who experienced warfare.

They reported all kinds of rumors, and the wagon trains often drew together to make a target too large for Indian attack. Several of the women reported they had heard of Indian attacks ahead of their caravans. They also added that it was feared that renegade white men were involved in such raids, and the Indians were not to be blamed entirely.

One particularly poignant description of Indian affairs is

that told by Harriet Hitchcock as she recorded what she had learned about the Sand Creek Massacre. She wrote on December 22, 1864:

> The third Col[orado] came into Denver riding four abreast displaying their flags of honor of their great victory over the Indians in the late battle at Sand Creek. The band rode out a few miles to meet them. It was quite a sight.

She goes on to tell of the fight itself and its baleful results:

> At the late battle at Sand Creek Col Shivington [Chivington] destroyed a village of 1000 Cheyennes   The next day while the soldiers were burning the wigwams three little Indian children were found hidden under some Buffalo robes. They were nearly frightened to death. The soldiers brought them here and are getting clothes made for them. Bell has made a dress for the little girl and I have made her an apron. She is very shy and afraid of white people but seems much pleased with her new clothes. The man who took her intends sending her to the states to be educated.

For those who have not read the introduction to the first volume of this series, we reiterate some salient points which have been used to guide the editorial hand. It is a major purpose to let the writers tell their own story in their own words with as little scholarly trimming as possible. The intent in this publication of primary sources is to transcribe each word or phrase as accurately as possible, leaving misspellings and grammatical errors as written in the original.

Two gestures have been made for the sake of clarity:

1. We have added space where phrases or sentences ended and no punctuation appeared in the original.

2. We have put the daily journals into diary format even though the original may have been written continuously line by line because of the writer's shortage of paper.

There are numerous geographic references that are mentioned over and over again in the various accounts. The final volume in the series will include a geographical gazeteer, in addition to an index and bibliography to aid the reader.

The scarce and unusual in overland documents have been sought out. Readily available accounts are not included, but they will be referred to in the final volume along with the bibliography. If the reader knows of such accounts written while on the journey, please let us know. Our goal is to add to the knowledge of all regarding this portion of our history — the story of ordinary people embarked on an extraordinary experience.

KENNETH L. HOLMES

Monmouth, Oregon, 1989

TABLE OF DISTANCES BETWEEN ATCHISON, KAN., AND PLACERVILLE, CAL.

Between Stations	NAMES OF STATIONS	From Atchison	Between Stations	NAMES OF STATIONS	From Atchison
----	ATCHISON . . . . Kan.	----	20	Bijou . . . . Colo.	553
10	Lancaster . . . . "	10	16	Fremont's Orchard, ... "	569
14	Kennekuk . . . . "	24	11	Eagle's Nest . . . . "	580
12	Kickapoo . . . . "	36	12	Latham . . . . "	592
13	Log Chain . . . . "	49	15	Big Bend . . . . "	607
11	Seneca . . . . "	60	17	Fort Lupton . . . . "	624
12	Laramie Creek . . . . "	72	15	Pierson's . . . . "	639
12	Guittard's . . . . "	84	14	DENVER . . . . "	653
10	Oketo . . . . "	94	11	Child's . . . . "	664
11	Otoe . . . . Neb.	105	12	Boon's . . . . "	676
11	Pawnee . . . . "	116	18	Little Thompson . . . . . . "	694
14	Grayson's . . . . "	130	8	Big Thompson . . . . "	702
10	Big Sandy . . . . "	140	16	Laporte . . . . "	718
14	Thompson's . . . . "	154	10	Boner . . . . "	728
14	Kiowa . . . . "	168	12	Cherokee . . . . "	740
12	Little Blue . . . . "	180	12	Virginia Dale . . . . "	752
13	Liberty Farm . . . . "	193	15	Willow Springs . . . . Wyo.	767
15	Lone Tree . . . . "	208	15	Big Laramie . . . . "	782
10	32-Mile Creek . . . . "	218	14	Little Laramie . . . . "	796
12	Summit . . . . "	230	17	Cooper Creek . . . . "	813
13	Hook's . . . . "	243	11	Rock Creek . . . . "	824
10	Fort Kearney . . . . "	253	17	Medicine Bow . . . . "	841
10	Platte Station . . . . "	263	8	Elk Mountain . . . . "	849
11	Craig . . . . "	274	14	Pass Creek . . . . "	863
15	Plum Creek . . . . "	289	16	North Platte . . . . "	889
15	Willow Island . . . . "	304	14	Sage Creek . . . . "	903
14	Midway . . . . "	318	10	Pine Grove . . . . "	913
15	Gilman's . . . . "	333	9	Bridger's Pass . . . . "	922
17	Cottonwood Springs . . . . "	350	10	Sulphur Springs . . . . "	932
15	Cold Springs . . . . "	365	11	Waskie . . . . "	943
14	Fremont Springs . . . . . . "	379	13	Duck Lake . . . . "	956
11	Elkhorn . . . . "	390	12	Dug Springs . . . . "	968
14	Alkali Lake . . . . "	404	15	Laclede . . . . "	983
12	Sand Hill . . . . "	416	12	Big Pond . . . . "	995
11	Diamond Springs . . . . . . "	427	14	Black Buttes . . . . "	1009
15	South Platte . . . . "	442	14	Rock Point . . . . "	1023
14	Julesburg . . . . Colo.	456	14	Salt Wells . . . . "	1037
12	Antelope . . . . "	468	14	Rock Spring . . . . "	1051
13	Spring Hill . . . . "	481	15	Green River . . . . "	1066
13	Dennison's . . . . "	494	14	Lone Tree . . . . "	1080
12	Valley Station . . . . "	506	18	Ham's Fork . . . . "	1098
15	Kelly's . . . . "	521	12	Church Buttes . . . . "	1110
12	Beaver Creek . . . . "	533	8	Millersville . . . . "	1118

TABLE OF DISTANCES BETWEEN ATCHISON, KAN., AND PLACERVILLE, CAL. — *concluded.*

Between Stations	NAMES OF STATIONS	From Atchison	Between Stations	NAMES OF STATIONS	From Atchison
13	Fort Bridger .... Wyo.	1131	15	Butte .... "	1506
12	Muddy .... "	1143	11	Mountain Spring ...... Nev.	1517
10	Quaking Asp Spr'gs .... "	1153	9	Ruby Valley .... "	1526
10	Bear River .... "	1163	12	Jacob's Wells .... "	1538
10	Needle Rock .... Utah	1173	12	Diamond Springs ...... "	1550
10	Echo Cañon .... "	1183	12	Sulphur Springs .... "	1562
10	Hanging Rock .... "	1193	13	Robert's Creek .... "	1575
10	Weber .... "	1203	13	Camp Station .... "	1588
12	Daniel's .... "	1215	15	Dry Creek .... "	1603
11	Kimball's .... "	1226	10	Cape Horn .... "	1613
15	Mountain Dell .... "	1241	11	Simpson's Park .... "	1624
14	GREAT SALT LAKE		15	Reese River .... "	1639
	CITY .... "	1255	12	Mount Airey .... "	1651
9	Travellers' Rest .... "	1264	14	Castle Rock .... "	1665
11	Rockwell's .... "	1275	12	Edward's Creek .... "	1677
9	Joe Dug Out .... "	1284	11	Cold Spring .... "	1688
10	Fort Crittenden .... "	1294	10	Middle Gate .... "	1698
10	No Name .... "	1304	15	Fair View .... "	1713
10	Rush Valley .... "	1314	13	Mountain Well .... "	1726
11	Point Lookout .... "	1325	15	Still Water .... "	1741
15	Simpson's Springs ..... "	1340	14	Old River .... "	1755
8	River Bed .... "	1348	14	Bisby's .... "	1769
10	Dug Way .... "	1358	11	Nevada .... "	1780
12	Black Rock .... "	1370	12	Desert Wells .... "	1792
11	Fish Springs .... "	1381	13	Dayton .... "	1805
10	Boyd's .... "	1391	13	Carson .... "	1818
10	Willow Springs .... "	1401	14	Genoa .... "	1832
15	Cañon Station .... "	1416	11	Friday's .... "	1843
12	Deep Creek .... "	1428	10	Yank's .... Cal.	1853
8	Prairie Gate .... Nev.	1436	12	Strawberry .... "	1865
18	Antelope Springs ...... "	1454	12	Webster's .... "	1877
13	Spring Valley .... "	1467	12	Moss .... "	1889
12	Schell Creek .... "	1479	12	Sportsman's Hall ...... "	1901
12	Gold Cañon .... "	1491	12	PLACERVILLE ..... "	1913

From Frank A. Root and William E. Connelly, *The Overland Stage to California* (Topeka, KS, 1901, and reprint Glorieta, NM, 1970).

The Diaries Letters, and Commentaries

NANCY C. GLENN
Courtesy of Woodrow Glenn, Libby, Montana

A Letter from La Grande Ronde, 1862

✤ Nancy Glenn

INTRODUCTION

In the spring of 1862 when Nancy Cordelia and her husband
William Stone Glenn, of Pleasantville, Iowa, were packing
wagons for the long journey to Oregon — along with a host of
their neighbors — little did they think that they would spend
most of the rest of their lives within a few miles of the Oregon
Trail in that far-off land. After a long tedious trip the Pleasantville
wagon train arrived in what the French Canadian voyageurs had
named *La Grande Ronde* at an altitude of 2788 feet amidst the
Blue Mountains, in the state of Oregon. The valley was then and
is now a thing of beauty, a round alpine meadow twenty miles
across surrounded by towering fault block mountains.

When Nancy Beckwith had met William Glenn, he was a
widower, his first wife having been Maria Yates Glenn. There was
one son by that marriage: Tolbert, who was 18-years-old at the
time of the 1862 journey. The wedding of William and Nancy
took place in 1851. She was 20 years old, having been born in
Lake County, Ohio, on November 24, 1831. The new husband
was born in Barron County, Tennessee, on March 4, 1815. He
was an energetic merchant, established general stores wherever
they settled. On the journey west there were five other children:
Amanda M., age 10; Emma A., 8; William R., 6; Arthur W., 3;
and Charles, one-year-old. There would be five more born in
Oregon.

The Pleasantville wagon train, of which William Glenn was
elected captain, traveled the usual route over the Platte road to
Oregon. In Wyoming they took the newly surveyed Landers

cutoff. Although they had no troubles with the Indians, there was Indian-white conflict just ahead of them in southern Idaho.

Upon arrival in the Grande Ronde valley, they settled near Summerville just north of present La Grande. They lived there until they moved to the mining town of Eldorado in Malheur County in 1868. There William opened another store; he did the same in a brand new town which he named Glennville — now a ghost of its former self. The Glenns moved once more to the new town of Vale on the Malheur River. The little town was literally astride the Oregon Trail, and was the county seat of the huge new Malheur County. Vale's main center of business was really Boise, Idaho, some 75 miles to the southeast.

So it was that for the rest of their lives William and Nancy Glenn's activities centered in Vale, a focal point of huge ranges and ranches, with livestock as the principal source of wealth. William died there and was buried in the Vale cemetery on May 7, 1890, at age 75. After his death "Mother Glenn" as she was fondly called, moved to Portland, there to stay with her oldest daughter, Mrs. Amanda Rinehart. The Portland *Oregonian* published her obituary in its April 18, 1909, edition, saying she died surrounded by four of her children on April 15th. The final words of the obituary read "The remains were taken to Vale on yesterday's train and the funeral will be held at Vale this afternoon, when she will be laid to rest beside her husband."

Decendants of William and Nancy Glenn have treasured the letter printed below and have been most cooperative in supplying information about Nancy and her family.

Woodrow Glenn of Libby, Montana, has supplied us with several pictures of members of the family. We have used one of the portraits of Nancy Glenn from this collection. He has also sent us photocopies of some of her other letters. This made possible comparison and verification of her handwriting.

Rod Linkous of Seattle has the precious original letter and provided us with a photocopy of the handwritten document.

We appreciate also the help given us by John W. Evans, librarian of Eastern Washington State College in La Grande,

Oregon, in our pursuit of information about the Glenn family.

The letter was published in 1950 by Jacob Ray Gregg in his book, *Pioneer Days in Malheur County*. It was in the following up on information in this rare book that we were led over a devious trail to the original letter. The published letter was mainly faithful to the document, but there were several words left out and mis-copied passages.

PERSONS NAMED IN NANCY GLENN'S LETTER

(Note: Others are mentioned, but the references are so meager — usually a surname only — that we cannot identify them)

David Cassidy was a 23-year-old single man, oldest son of Samuel and Mary Cassidy of Marion Co., Iowa. They had moved from Ohio to Iowa when David was in his teens and had farmed there over the years. *U.S. Census, 1860*, Marion Co., Iowa.

Jefferson and Esther Hilles are listed in the 1860 census of Marion Co., Iowa, also five children. He was a physician. The Glenn letter tells of the death of the youngest child, probably a 4-year-old girl named Sylvia.

William Kincaid was living in LaGrande, Oregon, when the 1870 census was compiled. He was a 33-year-old farmer, a single man.

John and Susanna Lewis had farmed in Iowa for several years. They were the parents of six children. The 1870 census taker listed them as 55 years old, farming in Summerville precinct, north of LaGrande in Union Co. Oregon. There were two sons, J.A., 19, a "teamster," and John, Jr., 22, a "hostler." One daughter, Jane, was the wife of Alpheus Terwillger; the second daughter, Maria, was the wife of Terry Tuttle. They are listed under their husbands' surnames below.

"The Logans" were members of a large clan of that name living in Marion Co., Iowa, according to the 1860 census. The older ones had been born in Kentucky and emigrated northward, leaving the old South behind. They went first to Indiana, then to Iowa, from which place numerous members of the families migrated to northeastern Oregon.

Fletcher Pitman is so-far unidentified. He was one of a large clan of well-off farm families in the Pleasantville region of Marion Co., Iowa. The 1860 census lists them all, but there is no Fletcher Pitman among them. Probably he was a young single man, footloose and free, not staying in one place long enough for the census to catch up with him. Toward the western end of the Oregon Trail he might end up in the Idaho or Montana mines or in any of the western slope territories or states.

Alpheus and Jane Terwilliger were traveling over the trail with their three children. The family had followed the usual trek for residents of Iowa. From Kentucky they had moved north to Ohio, then to Indiana, and on to Pleasantville, where they farmed. When citizens of that town took the trail to eastern Oregon, they joined the caravan. Jane Terwilliger was the daughter of John and Susanna Lewis, listed above. *An Illustrated History of Union and Wallowa Counties*, (n.p., 1902), pp. 449-50. They settled near Summerville north of La Grande in Union Co., Oregon.

Andres F. (age 31) and Mary C. (age 29) Titus were not well-off farmers like the other families. They were a young couple with three children, William L., age 7; George, 5; and Margaret, 3. According to the 1860 census of Marion Co., Iowa, they had no property in land and only $150 in personal property. They disappear from view after their mention in 1862 by Nancy Glenn.

Terry and Maria Tuttle were traveling west with their four children. Maria was the daughter of John and Susanna Lewis, listed above. their children were John, age 8; Adin R., 3; and a younger child, whose name we don't know, who died and was buried along the trail. They settled in Union Co., Oregon, near Summerville, on 320 acres. There they lived out their lives. Terry Tuttle was also a school teacher. He was Union County's Superintendent of Schools for a period. Later on in life he was county assessor. In 1880 he was elected as State Representative for the county. *An Illustrated History of Union and Wallowa Counties* (n.p., 1902) pp. 345-46.

John Vallet, whom Nancy referred to as "Mr. Vollett," was a single man who settled in Marion Co., Oregon, near the town of Silverton.

THE LETTER

Grand Round Valley   Oregon
Oct the 8   62[1]

Dear Father Mother sisters, and brothers   after so
long a silence I am again permitted to write a few lines to you
to let you know that we are all yet upon the land among the
liveing   I doubt not but you have had many fears concerning
our safety crossing the plains if you have heard of the many
deprodations committed by the Indians, but we are all here
but Wm and Tolbert   they started day before yesterday
down to the dalls [The Dalles] 180 miles after a load of
provision, and all well except myself   I have the summer
complaint   We arrived at the upper end of this Valley the
first day of this month   the next day we went acrost over to
a little town called Grand Round City[2] not knowing where
we would stoop [sic] or where we would spend the
winter.   we stopped there hearing that Fletcher Pittman
and John Lewis had stopped about 15 miles below us   The
next day Robert Logan, Isaac Glenn and Wm went down
to see them   Found that Fletcher had gone after provision   the rest of his folks have gone to Wilamet
Valley   he staid on account of wintering his cattle   Pitt-
mans lost a great many of their cattle   had to by about $300
worth on the road   when They got here Fletcher bought
the rest out and halled them down to the dalls where they

---

[1]The date of arrival is given as October 1 in Jacob Ray Gregg, *Pioneer Days in Malheur County* (Los Angeles, 1950), p. 103.

[2]The full name of the valley is *La Grande Ronde*. It is an attractive, grass covered valley in present Union Country, Oregon, right on the old Oregon trail. It was named by French Canadian trappers of fur trade days. The city of La Grande is in about as scenic a locale as any town in northeastern Oregon. A post office was established there on May 28, 1863. Lewis A. McArthur, *Oregon Geographic Names* (Portland, 1982), 5th edition, revised and enlarged by Lewis L. McArthur, pp. 327 and 426. The pioneer Oregonians were very ingenious at mis-spelling this French name as will be seen in Nancy Glenn's letter.

would take a boat for Portland. We received your kind letter
at Ft Larimie and were truly glad to hear from you but sorry
to hear of the deaths among our old neighbors   We also sent
you a letter from there and expected to have an opportunity
of sending one every week or two but were disappointed in
that as in many other things as they moved the stage stock
from there on another road and immediately after we passed
there   We start from there out into the black hills and I
thought they were the most beautiful of any thing I had seen
on the road. They reminded me of the dear old home of my
childhood[3] and soon the unbidden tear was finding its way
down my cheek.   yes I do often think of that place and
some dear ones there. But not so often as I do of my once
happy home in Iowa and the dear ones there that such a short
time ago could sooth and cheer my heart by their presence.   but now what a change   No Father nor Mother
sister nor brother to cheer my home. Think of me when you
enjoy each others society and think also what a blessing it is
to be where you can see each other often but I do not despair
I hope to meet you all again this side of the grave if the Lord
will but if not I hope we may be able to say his will be
done   When we left Sweetwater we took Landerses[4] cut off
represented to be a saving of about 100 miles and a good road
which we found to be so except where the high water had
washed and spoiled the road. We had not traveled more than
50 or 60 miles on this road until we came up to where the
Indians had stolen some emigrants horses and in trying to
get them back the Indians had killed one man and badly

---

[3]Lake Co., Ohio.

[4]See the diary of Martha Missouri Moore, Volume VII above, p. 282, fn. 11.
Colonel Frederick West Lander surveyed this cutoff in 1857-8. W. Turrentine
Jackson, *Wagon Roads West* (Berkeley, 1952) pp. 207-8; also E. Douglas Branch,
"Frederick West Lander, Road-Builder," *Mississippi Valley Hist. Rev.*, XVI (Sept.
1929), pp. 172-87.

wounded two more   this was done but a few days before we got there   You nor any one else would have thought that there could ever have been such a good road made over such a country but there has been a great deal of work done on Landerses cut off   I wish I could have had a chance to wrote some more on the road as I cannot recollect exactly every place that I want to tell you about — Well we came on and one day we had just got up a big hill and there was buried a man found by some of the emigrants supposed to be killed by the Indians   he was buried but six inches under ground for they could not move him he had been dead so long but we believed he had been killed by white men as the ferrymen at Ft Hall[5] could tell all about him and how much money he had   they said he had five thousand dollars and his name was Camel from Denver but he was killed by the Indians as there was a company of emigrants crossed at Ft Hall and came down on the north side of snake river and saw an Indian with a nice gold watch and it had Camels name inside of it and one of them traded something to the Indian and got the watch   he has since came to powder river[6] where he met with Camels brother and let him have the watch   they said also that the Indians had plenty of twenty dollar gold pieces coined at Denver and plenty of treasury notes   they do not know any thing about the value of money   they would give a $20 gold piece for a blanket or any thing of that kind so the Indians likely killed him but no doubt in my mind but there are a plenty of white men on the plains that are as bad as an Indian dare be and I think some of them were there at the

[5]Jennie Broughton Brown, *Fort Hall on the Oregon Trail* (Caldwell, Id.), says this was named "Gibson's Ferry," but she tells nothing of his given name. She quotes Alexander Toponce, *Reminiscences* (Ogden, 1923), p. 346, as saying Gibson was "afterwards a great prize fighter."

[6]The Powder River gold rush began in 1862 when James W. Virtue discovered the precious metal about 12 miles east of present Baker, Oregon. Thousands of miners rushed in. This area was a major gold producer well into the 20th century. Howard M. Corning, *Dictionary of Oregon History* (Portland, 1956), p. 203.

snake river ferry near Ft Hall   Well we came on and before
we got to Ft Hall we came to where some men from Denver
had been attacked by the Indians   there was but six men
and it seems to me they said there was 30 or 40 Indians   they
killed 4 of the men and badly wounded another so badly that
he soon died   one man alone made his escape went on and
overtook a train and some of them went back and found the
dead bodies of those 4 men that had been killed   they were
all scalped   they buried them all in one grave but the men
that had been wounded they could not find   they were
killed on saturday   we passed there the tuesday following
we had a company of about 40 wagons and some of our men
were walking all the time   sometimes they would be out a
half mile from the road   this morning as they were walking
along about a quarter of a mile from the road they discovered
the dead body of a man   they sent to have the captain that
was William come down and say what they should do with
him   they brought him up near the road where his clothes
were searched to see if they could discover what his name was
but they could find nothing here   they buried him leaving
his coat and boots I think on the grave thinking perhaps
some one might recognize them   I told you there was but
one escaped but as we afterwards found out this man that we
buried had his wife with him   she got away and those
ferrymen at Ft Hall were mormons   they said they sent her
to Salt lake telling her they had found her husband and
buried him
as we were traveling along on burnt river we met a large
train of packers going to Boise river prospecting   they said
there had been a company there and had been driven off by the
Indians   they think there will be as rich mines discovered
there as on Salmon river   Well among this train was the
man that had made his escaped from the Indians   he

told Wm, all about it[7]   he had heard that our co had found
and buried that man   he thanked them very much   said he
would write to the mans wife and tell her about it   He said
he thought they killed twelve or 14 of the Indians but they
had taken them all away before they got back and every thing
they had in their wagons that they wanted and one
wagon   Well we came on and between Ft Hall and Salmon
falls we came to where a company of 13 wagons had been
attacked by the savages   we thought by that they had run
and left their wagons and the Indians had taken what they
wanted for from the quantity of feathers there they must
have emptied as much as 6 or seven good beds and there was
lots of things scattered around   I tell you some of our
women began to be a little frightened   Well 4 or 5 miles
from here we came to where there was five men buried that
they had killed out of the same train and soon where a
woman was buried that was wounded at the same time.
Saturday the 11 [of October]   Well I will now tell you
something about the old neighbors that left Iowa last
spring   Uncle Alonzo Harry Dr. Williams Mr. Vollett A
Terwilegar [Terwilliger] Terry Tuttle Harrison Logan
stopped up at the powder river mines about 50 miles from
where we are now — about 30 miles from the upper end of
this Valley   P. M Logan Uncle Mc Mr Lefolet [La-
Follette] Mr Titus Mr Rhodes Thomas Glenn R. Glenn S
Glenn have started for Wilamet valley   He left his loos

[7]This Indian attack happened a few miles northeast of present-day "Massacre
Rocks," so-named in the 1920's for the event of August 9-10, 1862. Although the rock
structures look as if they might have been ideal for a sneak attack, the event did not take
place at the rocks. The area is today an Idaho State Park of 566 acres, about ten miles
southwest of American Falls. Most of the park is sandwiched between U.S. Highway
30 and the Snake River. The most even-handed treatment of the event is in the
National Park Service's *Comprehensive Management and Use Plan of the Oregon
National Historic Trail*, Appendix III (Washington, D.C., Aug. 1981), pp. 258-9,
which reports that the number of whites killed by Indians was 10.

cattle here and calculates to send his work cattle back to have
them wintered here   Mr Coon I Glen and our selves are
here   Tell Mrs Casady or Rachiel that David is with them
and they are all well   They had bad luck with their
stock   lost all they started with but one yoke of cattle and
one cow — we lost 2 steers   This is one of the most
beautiful valleys in the world surrounded by high mountains
William thinks it the most beautiful valley he ever saw and a
plenty of the nicest timber and the best springs in the world
almost   I wish you were all here and had provision enough
to last until you could raise some   But nearly all the
emigrants that has went down into Oregon this year intend
coming back as soon as they can get back in the spring and I
expect the land will then all be claimed up   there is a real
good valley on powder river   we thought some of stopping
there but concluded it would be to cold there this
winter there is also a good valley on the Umatilla
river   Wm liked the country down where Pittman and
lewis was so well that he sent us down the day he started   we
are all camped close together and have not one of us got a
house put up yet   Wm Kinkaid is at work for us and Mr
Coon was going down with John to bring back his cattle so
Tol went in his place and Bill and him have been putting up
hay   they say cattle will not need any hay but we thought we
had rather not risk it.   girls I have got to be quite a mule
driver   I drove a good deal on the road   I will now tell you
a little about what I have heard of the Salmon river gold
mines   we concluded not to go there this fall as we heard at
Ft hall that we could not get there only by comeing down
past Ft Wal lah Wal lah and then we must pack 30
miles   Well I saw a woman that had just come from
there   I saw her in Powder river valley   she said she lived
in Wilamet valley when she was at home   her and her

husband was packing to powder river mines   she said the
mines were as rich there as had ever been reprisented to
be   she said she had seen them get from one pan of dirt 30 or
40 dollars   she told me also that there was a man went there
that had lived 3 years with them in oregon and he had sent a
good deal of gold dust back by express and when he started
home he had a leather sack made on purpose not quite so
wide as a 50 lb flour sack but as long and he had it plum full
of little sacks of gold dust when he started home   she said
he was almost afraid but the gold mines there are not very
extensive   I think they say 8 miles square cover the whole
mines that will pay to work at all.   a great many think its
powder river mines will pay pretty well   Wm thinks there
is a great deal of good mining country about burnt river
powder river and all along there   I will now give you the
prices of provision here.   we had a plenty to have lasted us a
year but we sold a good deal of it when we concluded not to
go to Salmon river   there was a great many out of groceries
on the road   at Grand round city flour is 15 dollars per
hundred   bacon 30 cts per lb. beef 8 to 12 onions 20 cts per
lb potatoes 10 coffee 50 sugar 40 tea 80 cts to $1.00 per lb
turnips 5 cts per lb   We all on the road our company had
good luck as to sickness until we came on to snake
river   here a good many took the diarea and Harrison
Logans buried their youngest child.   and in about a week
Terry Tuttles and Mr. Tittuses their youngest, one died in
the night the other the next morning were buried side by
side   I have not wrote half what I want to but I shall have to
quit for this time   remember us all to Serepta and Carlosse
children   I should like to know if the boys have got home
from the Peak   I have neither heard a word from home nor
David and Mary since we were at Ft Larimie   give my best
respects to Uncle Edwin and aunt Paulina and family and all

the rest of our relatives there   it is of no use to name them
all for I should be glad to see or hear from any of them   I
want you to write as soon as you get this   write a long
letter   Farewell
                    Nancy C Glenn to Wm and Mary A Beckwith
                                brothers and sisters one and all
PS direct your letters to Ft Wallah Wallah or Grand Round
Valley

Letters from the Oregon Trail, 1862-1863
§ Louisa Cook

INTRODUCTION

It was in the summer of 1962 that two Oregon women, former students, Mrs. Stella Burke, of McMinnville, and Mrs. Lois Hoggard, of Carlton, brought to the editor of this set of books a bundle of aged letters. What they amounted to were letters in diary form written by Mrs. Hoggard's ancestor, Mrs. Louisa Cook, and written while she was traversing the Oregon Trail in 1862-1863. Mrs. Hoggard had discovered the letters while examining the contents of her grandmother's trunk. The two women had made typewritten copies of the yellowed sheets, including a copy for me. At that time the publication of such records of American history was not even a dream as yet. However, the discovery of the Cook letters became a motivator for the eventual project of *Covered Wagon Women.*

The writer of the letters was Louisa (pronounced Lo-EYE-sa) Cook of Cook's Corners, Huron County, Ohio. Her birthplace was New York State. As a girl she had moved with her family to Ohio. We do not have her birth date, but Mrs. Hoggard said Louisa had been born in 1833. Her parents were Elisha and Eunice Fuller Cook.

There were born to the Cooks two more daughters, Emma and Sarah.

It may seem strange, but Louisa Cook had a daughter, a little girl named Mary, who appears on many of the pages of the letters. Why did Louisa use her maiden name? The story is that she was married to a German man, Gottlieb Johlin, by whom she had given birth to daughter, Mary. The tradition is that the wedding

took place in 1850 or 1851. There is no record of Mary's age at the
time of the journey, but a good guess would be six or seven years.
Johlin deserted mother and daughter. We had so many more
questions to ask her, but Mrs. Lois Thankful Hoggard died on
August 19, 1966.

Although Louisa Cook planned to go to Oregon proper, she
stopped off at Fort Walla Walla from January to June 1863. She
and Mary lived with Lt. Col. Reuben F. Maury and his wife and
taught the children of the officers of First Oregon Cavalry for one
school year. She taught in the Idaho mining communities from
1864 to late in 1865.

In an undated letter, written probably near the end of 1864,
Louisa told of her prospect for marrying a young man named
D.M. Walters, "a thoroughgoing Christian," who was also
superintendent of the Sunday school at one of the Placerville
churches. They were married about Christmas 1864.

The marriage led to oft-expressed happiness for Louisa, but
she was not to live long. It was about Christmas 1865, that she
took seriously ill and died in her new husband's arms. He wrote to
the family back east telling them of her death, but not listing the
date on which it had occurred.

Mr. Walters worked out a way for little Mary to go back to her
grandparents with friends who were returning to the east. There
are several letters in the Cook collection from him discussing this
journey. Thus ends the story of Louisa (Cook) Walters.

There needs to be a word about Mr. and Mrs. Hiram Smith.
He was the guide and "captain" of the wagon train with which
Louisa and Mary traveled west. He seems to have been a most
dynamic man in Louisa's eyes. We have not been able to sort out
the several Hiram Smiths in Oregon. In fact, it is difficult to sort
out Smiths of any pioneer venture.

There also needs to be a word about the oft-mentioned
"omnibus." An omnibus in those days was a vehicle that was
longer than a typical stagecoach, seating ten or twelve passengers.
According to Seymour Dunbar, in his *History of Travel in America*,
Volume III (Indianapolis, 1915), p. 1017, "The American
omnibus was a modification of the previous stage-coach, and first

THE AMERICAN OMNIBUS

vehicle used in connection with the periodic transportation of city populations. Adopted by many large towns during the period between 1835 and 1855." There is no indication in Louisa Cook's letters of what happened to the omnibus.

After the death of Mrs. Hoggard, the family sold Louisa Cook's letters to a prominent New York manuscript dealer. They are now in the Beinecke Rare Book and Manuscript Library of Yale University. We are grateful for that library's permission to publish the six letters in that collection that have to do with the overland journey.

It was while browsing through Andrea Hinding's *Women's History Sources*, I (N.Y., 1979), Item 1432, p. 866, that we learned of another collection of Louisa Cook letters in the Toledo-Lucas County Public Library, Toledo, Ohio. Most of them have to do with Louisa's Walla Walla and southern Idaho years, but one of the letters in this collection was written "On the plains near Boise River," on October 12, 1862, and is included below as Letter V with appreciation and permission of that library.

LETTER I

On the plains of Nebraska 230 miles from
Leavenworth City   June 11th/62

My Dear Mother & sisters

Though far far from home not many hour[s] pass that I do not think of you & as I have a few leisure moments I will occupy them in writing to you & as usual will refer to my journal   I wrote to you and Emma[1] from Leavenworth City[2] just before we left there which was the morning of the 3rd of June. The first night that we camped at Leavenworth two of our mules strayed away and we were hindered for some time by that event though two men were out constantly in search of them they were gone for over a week.

June 3rd.   The mules which strayed away a week ago were brought in having been found 70 miles from here on the Kansas river. After an early breakfast we broke camp & came out about 13 miles from Leavenworth where we camped near a creek for the night. Our train consists of an omnibus drawn by 4 mules   a coach & 4   2 baggage wagons drawn by 4 each & 1 wagon drawn by 2 mules   & 3 men & one woman (Mrs. Smith) who ride in the saddle. Our road is hard & smooth but is over a constant succession of hills.

June 4th.   Drove about 15 miles & camped on a side hill. Was obliged to get our water for cooking and the teams from a well only 60 ft deep.

June 5th.   Left camp at an early hour. Traveled 17 miles & camped out on white water creek near an excellent spring. Went out & gathered some strawberries for tea   the finest ones I ever saw. Made our bed on the ground & slept in the open air for the first time.

---

[1] Emma Crane, wife of Amos Crane.

[2] For a discussion of the "Leavenworth Road" see Merrill Mattes *Great Platte Road* (Lincoln, 1969), pp. 149ff.

June 6th.   Rose at ½ past three. Got breakfast & started out very early. The country to day is a rolling prairie & with a few exceptions entirely destitute of timber. Traveled about 22 miles & camped away from wood or water of which however we had a supply on hand.

June 7th.   Our supply of water fell rather short this morning & we had to put our dishes away without washing. About 10 we passed through the village of Seneca [Kansas].   2 small stores a blacksmith shop shoe shop 1 tavern & a few houses constitute the town. The great scarcity of timber must be a great obstacle in the way of a rapid settlement in this part of the country.[3] At 11 we stopped on the bank of a creek where we rested about 3 hours. Gathered a cup of strawberries to eat with our lunch. A family on their way to Fort Kerney [Kearney][4] with their oxen & cows were camped near us & the woman kindly gave us a good supply of milk   the first I had tasted in a long time. Traveled about 24 miles & camped on the open prairie.

June 8th.   To day is sabbath day but at an early hour we were on our way as usual & with the exception that the ladies have laid by their knitting & sewing &c there is nothing to remind one that it is Gods day. About noon passed through Marysville [Kansas] crossed the Big Blue river & about ½ mile up the river found a beautiful camping ground & in less time than it takes me to write it the mules were unharnessed hobbled & eagerly feeding on the rank prairie grass which is so abundant on the plains. Some of the party were bathing in the river some reclining under the shade of the trees & others

---

[3]For a discussion of these obstacles to settlement see Walter Prescott Webb, *The Great Plains* (Boston, 1931), *passim*.

[4]Here she adds another variation to the spelling of the name of this significant stopping place on the overland trail. The fort was named for General Stephen Watts Kearny, but the name was changed with usage to Kearney. Lilian L. Fitspatrick, *Nebraska Place Names* (Lincoln, 1960), p. 25.

who thought the whole of the sabbath might as well be put in were washing fishing & hunting for berries or game.

June 9th.   The country to day is as usual only still more so one vast ocean of land. About once in from 10 to 20 miles we will cross a creek or small river. These are invariably lined with bushes & forest trees but with the exceptions of these there is not a bush shrub or tree to be seen. The country is not as level as one might suppose but very ridgy. Some times there will [be] 25 or 30 ridges one after the other so that no sooner are you down one hill than you commence to rise up another. Our road is smooth as a house floor & as wide as a street in a city for the last day or two. It is getting to be quite dusty nor can we expect any change for the better on that score. Carried our wood & water 4 miles & camped for the night on the open prairie after traveling about 25 miles.

June 10.   After 8 miles traveling this morning we came to plenty of water. Occasionally we pass by a house built of poles or small logs & covered with earth or turf. Sometimes there will be a three rail fence round a patch of ground but generally where you find a patch of plowed ground it is all open. About 1 oclock we crossed & camped on the Little Sandy. The water is very clear & sandy & most of us improved the opportunity & had a general wash up. We made 25 miles to day.

June 11th.   Crossed the Big Sandy in the forenoon & rode at a pretty good rate till about 2 P. M. We passed several companies some with horses but most with 4 to 6 yoke of oxen on the wagon. After making some 26 miles camped on the Little Blue. Had some Buffalo meat for supper which Mrs. Smith had purchased on the road. We have a guard out every night & to night an extra one was put out on account of guerillas but we were not disturbed. I was up from ½ past 11 till one to see the eclipse which was a total one.

June 12th.   Was on the road at an early hour & passed 5 or 6 emigrant trains who had not got started yet. Saw a great many Antelopes to day on the hills but our boys could not get near enough to get a shot at one. Traveled 30 miles to day & camped on the little Blue.

June 13th.   Left camp at 6. Traveled 9 miles & camped on the little Blue for the boys to have a Buffalo hunt as they have been almost crazy since we arrived in the Buffalo country. But I must close now for we are just nearing an office. I must close. Good bye.

LETTER II

        June 20th   On the plains 90 miles from Kearny.
Dear Mother & sisters
    At my last letter I left off very abruptly as [we] came to an office & I will begin my journal where I left off there.

June 13th.   Left camp at 6 & traveled 9 miles when we laid by on the Little Blue to give the boys an opportunity to hunt Buffalo as they have been almost wild with excitement since they came into the Buffalo country. About 10 A.M. they started off with a good supply of powder shot & ball & great anticipations but poor fellows their feathers looked sadly drooping as they came straggling into camp near night fall foot sore & weary & having secured among them all one small Antelope. There are thousands of Buffaloes in this part of the country but it is said they herd near the Antelopes upon which they depend for warning of danger & as there is nothing to screen the hunter from their sight it is next to impossible to get near them unless he is well mounted.   4 California travelers who have camped near us for a few nights were out also on their horses & 2 of them shot at Buffaloes but as they were about 15 miles from camp they saved only the choicest parts & left the rest on the ground.

June 14th.   At ½ past 3 our camp was astir & as soon as our
breakfast of potatoes buffalo meat bread & coffee was
dispatched & dishes washed & stowed away we were again on
the road. Traveled 18 miles & camped on a side hill at the
foot of which was a small pond of water & 3 or 4 elm trees in
the shade of which we set our tables & had our tea about 4
oclock. About dusk the wind which had been blowing hard
all day increased to a perfect gale & preparations were made
for what is called a Platte river storm which by the way is an
event not to be trifled with. The wagons & carriages were
drawn up side by side chained together & the outside ones
staked down. The stoves camp kettles frying pans camp
stools & every thing moveable was made as secure as they
could have been on board of ship in a storm at sea. However
the gale passed away without rain and though the wind blew
furiously till about 10 it subsided then without doing any
damage.

June 15th.   Sabbath day finds us on our way at ½ past 5 as
usual with prospects of a pleasanter time than we have had
the last 2 days which were so intolerably hot. We meet or pass
the stage daily which runs on the Leavenworth-San Francisco
route. The stage stations are from 15 to 25 miles apart. We
passed by the beginning of one to day   a tent with a half
finished pole house close by. One of our horsemen rode up to
ask for fresh water & was told that all the wood & water they
had was brought 10 miles. Some of the houses are made of
boards some of poles & then again of sods laid up like brick
work. We saw several herds of Buffaloes & Antelopes at a
distance to day also 2 tame Elks feeding near the road. Our
Cal. friends brought in an Antelope to day which they gave to
us reserving only a hind quarter for their own use. After
traveling 27 miles we came to the Platte river a little off from
which we camped for the night. I had almost forgotten to say
that which threatened us last night came to day about noon a

most terrific thunder storm coming nearer & nearer till the flash & report were instantaneous almost blinding & deafening our senses. However it passed over in a short time and we were again on our way well pleased with the change in the air by the lightning & the dusty roads by the rain

June 16th.   Started at ½ past 5 & the first mile of our road being a sort of marsh formed by the overflowing of the Platte was quite difficult for our teams to get through but after that the road was smooth & fine as ever. At 10 A.M. we came to Fort Kearney composed of barracks garrison house & government stables. A short distance further on & we came to Kearney City a place of 12 families   as many groceries and grogshops & a cobblers & blacksmith shops. All the houses here were made of turf cut out 4 inches thick & 1 to 1½ feet long & laid up the same as brick work. For floors the ground is covered with canvas or carpets & the walls are whitewashed or lined with coarse cloth & on the whole looking very cool & tidy. This style of Architecture is adoby or Doby. An Orderly Sergeant in the regular service was training round on his horse near our carriage & upon our praising his horse (which was certainly a fine one) he begged to know if we would accept a little wine & without waiting for a reply scampered off returning in a few moments with a bottle of the best imported wine which of course we accepted with many thanks. The men here seemed to be of a rough cast & we were told by a gentleman who had been waiting here 2 weeks to join our co[mpany] that drinking gambling cursing & fighting was the order of the day in Kearney. Made 18 miles & camped on the Platte. After supper went with one of our men to fish. Caught 2 and he caught 6 which made a good meal for the next morning.

June 17th   Our road to day has seemed to be perfectly level although it is said to be a gradual ascent for 300 miles. The

river is much higher than common & the current very rapid
so that it will be impossible for us to cross at the usual fording
place. Rode 30 miles & camped on Plum Creek where we
have plenty of water but no wood but a few little sticks that
we picked up on the road & Buffalo chips (you may guess
what they are) which we can gather up any where on the
Prairie.

June 18.   Passed 3 or 4 solitary Doby houses & saw herds of
Antelopes at a distance several times. The last house we
passed was a private dwelling post office & store all in one.
The building was built of hewn logs & contained 2 rooms. In
front of one was a small yard filled with flower roots in
bloom   rose bushes lilacs flowering currants & although
suffering from the drowth looking the most like civilization
of anything I have seen in a long time.   2 young Antelopes
lay in the corner of the yard with their long ears erect and
their bright saucy eyes looking around at all there was to be
seen. For 3 or 4 days we have seen no attempt at farming not
so much as a garden & the country has a very barren
appearance. The few people along the road depending upon
what they can make out of the emigrants. Potatoes are 1½
dollar per bushel corn the same sugar 20 to 25 cts. per pound
salt 8 cts flour 6 cts &c so to night we had Indian pancakes
bean soup cold boiled bacon hard bread apple sauce tea &
those who wished it had mush and milk. Our Co[mpany] is
divided into 6 messes. The men all help to harness &
unharness the mules & get wood & water & the women all
help about the cooking. In my mess is George Robinson &
Mr. Kennedy from St. Louis & Miss McClung of
Findley   Mary & myself. George sees to the wood & water
business & Maggie & myself take turns about one doing the
cooking & the other washing dishes. We have 3 stoves
among us but I prefer a fire on the ground. G. digs a little
short trench in the ground just wide enough to let the frying

pans & camp kettles rest on the edge & we can cook capitally
with this.

June 19th   Jogged along to day after the same old fashion
over the smooth level road with nothing to be seen but an
occasional Doby house & the frequent emigrant trains which
now fail to attract hardly a passing glance as they all bear the
same monotonous appearance. About noon we came to a
camp of Sioux (pro Sooz). The women & children came out
of their tents to wonder and admire our omnibus the first of
the kind probably they had ever seen. We looked in one of
their tents a dirty smoky filthy place filled with dried Buffalo
skins, & various other articles. The women wore a blanket
fastened round the neck & waist their arms & legs
bare   beads round their necks & hanging from their
ears   brass rings round their wrists & fingers   & their faces
& at the parting of their hair painted with sort of red paint.
Some of the children were in a perfectly nude state. Others
had a short cloth tied round their waist & 2 or three of the
boys had on a pair of old pants. Drove 31 miles & camped
near some bluffs.

June 20th.   Passed 2 ranches (all the houses whether fenced
in or not are called ranches) to day and 1 Indian village. Our
outfit which is said by every one to be the best that has ever
crossed the plains attracts a great deal of attention &
especially among the Indians. We traveled 21 miles to day &
camped on the open prairie about 3 miles from the forks of
the Platte about noon.

June 21st.   Started at 6 oclock & traveled 8 miles to a
fording place on the Platte. Here Mr. Smith equipped
himself & mounting the pony went about two thirds of the
way across where he dismounted & walked back going in
some places to his shoulders. He decided that it would not be
safe to cross here on account of the quick sand although it
would have saved us 55 miles travel & a peice [sic] of bad road.

In a short time again we were on our way & for 3 miles our road was a very hard one over hills & gullies of sand but after that we came into the valleys again where our road was again level & smooth. Traveled 34 miles & camped on the Platte at another fording place which we shall try to morrow. A train of 6 wagons came in just after we did with 5 yoke of oxen attached to each wagon. They started from near Omaha City about 150 miles back & had large fat oxen but their drivers like nearly all the drivers I have seen on the road are a cruel brutal set of men lashing their beasts who covered with welts would shrink from their approach & manifest the greatest fear but there was no mercy for them. Although there is plenty of grass & water for teams on the road we have passed by the dead carcasses of an ox on an average of once a mile from Leavenworth to this camp just literally drove to death. But enough of this unpleasant subject.

June 22nd.   Have just found that there is an office here where I can leave my letter & so I will close it up & sent it on. Mr. Smith is out trying the ford so I do not know if we are to cross or not. I will try to write you again in a week or so. I do not have time to write to any one but you & if any of the friends wish to hear from me they can do so through you. If you go over to the Debolt neighborhood give my love to the friends there & if you like you can let them read my letters. At Salt Lake I will try to write to Uncle John. I would give much to hear one word from Home. I might have had letters all along the road as well as not. All the rest have had letters but me but I hope at Salt Lake I shall find I am not forgotten. I hope you will save my letters as I have written a great deal that I have not in my journal & when I come back I should like to have them to refer to or look over but I must close.   Good bye.

Your affectionate daughter   Louisa Cook.

LETTER III

Jewsburg [Julesburg, Colorado] June 24th/62
Dear Mother & Sisters

I sent a letter some 2 or 3 days ago to you but I am much afraid you will never get [it] as I sent it to an office by an emigrant a perfect stranger & on the plains one does not know who they can trust. I will drop you a few lines here at Jewsburg where we intend to cross the Platte although I have not collected much to make a letter interesting yet I think even a short letter will be welcome from one so far away. I will resume my journal where I left off & if you do not get my last you must imagine the deficiency or I can supply it at another time.

June 22nd.   At ½ past 7 we broke camp & drove down to the river bank where Mr. S. was prospecting as to the chance of fording the Platte river. After riding swimming & walking in the water about 2 hours he was forced to give up crossing & we came on 16 miles & camped by a Frenchmans ranch & an Indian lodge. The squaws & children came round our tents & where we were cooking watching every motion nor could we drive them away by any signs or motions. Some were covered & looked rather clean while others were entirely naked. Just imagine 27 of us on our camp ground near the river bank 3 large covered baggage wagons & 2 carriages ranged in a row at a sufficient distance apart to admit of our tables in their shade   3 of the messes cooking by as many stoves & camp fires. Our suppers are soon ready & our tables which are converted out of our provision boxes are set & 27 of the hungriest folks you ever see are soon set too.   some on camp stools & more on the ground ready to fall to at the meal of warm pancakes bacon applesauce & tea with a hearty relish & to complete the picture some ½ dozen little greasy naked or ½ dressed Indians hanging ready to devour you

with their eyes & your victuals with their mouths & you have
a faint idea of how we looked the night of the 22nd.

June 23rd.   Rose at 4   dispatched breakfast   the mules
were brought in & preparations were made for getting our
wagons on the other side which the Frenchman had kindly
agreed to do with his five yoke of oxen for the moderate sum
of $20 dollars (By the way mules are the most timid animals
about going in the water you most ever saw & at the same
time being rather obstinate at times it will not do to risk
going across with anything but oxen as getting set in the
middle of a river ½ a mile wide would not be so pleasant).
Before the Franchman with his oxen got into camp one of
our Findley [Ohio] friends thought he would try it & waded
in till he got into water to his armpits when they concluded
that was rather too deep & so we started on. Passed several
ranches & 2 Indian lodges. Our road to day has been equal to
any turnpike a hard gravelly road & wide enough for 4 teams
abreast. Rode 22 miles & camped on the Platte.

June 24th.   At daybreak our camp was astir & by 6 we were
on the road. Our road to day has been a very hard one on
account of the sand. The passengers have been obliged to
walk a good deal through the sand banks & we passed a good
many teams who were the next thing to fast with five or six
yoke of oxen to a wagon. You would be astonished to see the
amount of emigration that is going west. A gentleman who
came in to night from Denver City 5 days on the road 190
miles says he counted 756 wagons on the way all going west.
Besides this a great many ford the river here so we intend to
do saving some 175 miles of extra travel by the same means. A
person can hardly realize that they are traveling on the plains
as emigration teams are to be seen almost any time & three or
four times a day we pass a ranch stage station grocery or
blacksmith shop. The town of Jewsburgh is made up of 6

dwelling houses a stage station & 2 blacksmith shops. Made
14 miles to day & camped about 10 oclock A. M.

June 25th.   This morning I was out of the omnibus by ½
past 3. Got breakfast & my messmate Miss McClung[5] is
washing dishes & I will finish my letter & drop into the office
here which is on this side of the river. Mary is out as usual
scouring round as far outside of the camp as she dares to go
bringing more flowers fancy stones & other treasures than
would load a mule at every camp. She is well & gets along
with all the company nicely. We have a young man along who
speaks German & she has taken a particular fancy to him.
My health has been good all the time except a bad cold &
cough. I was like to have that old pain in my side again but I
steeped up about half of the Spignut roots[6] that I brought &
it cured my cough in about 3 days. I am real glad I brought
them & only wish I had more. We have got now where we do
not have any dews & in a few days will be beyond storms or
rains. We have been highly favored about storms for though
every night there has been apparently heavy storms around
us we have only had a little taste of them. Last night there
was a heavy black cloud in the west lightning & distant
thunder but we had nothing of it but a heavy wind. Mary & I
with 3 others sleep in the omnibus. The seats are on the sides
& we have boards which we lay across & a cushion & our
blankets make a real comfortable place to lie on. Mrs. Skader
[Shaden?] at the corners[7] gave me a pillow which comes real
acceptable here. Our Kerney friend has been quite sick on
the road with a bowel complaint. He stopped at one of the
groceries to get some medicine but was told there was no call
for such things & the man said he was the first sick man he

---

[5]There were numerous McClungs crossing the plains to Oregon during the 1862
migration. We have not been able to identify this single woman.

[6]Spikenard.

[7]By "the corners" she means Cook's Corners, Ohio. This crossroads lay about half
way between North Fairfield and Monroeville, in Huron County.

had seen since he lived here. This is a very healthy climate   I
have no doubt but our company with the exception of 2 or 3
myself among the number have been more or less affected
with a diarrhea caused I suppose by drinking so much water
& change of diet. We shall hardly know how to act when we
get into civilized society again. When we get into a house we
shall be looking round for a blanket or sachel to sit down
upon & call for our tin plates & cups to eat & drink from. (I
was broke off here by breaking up of camp & not being able to
leave my letter will resume my journal). About 7 we were
down to the bank where some 25 or 30 wagons were waiting
to cross the river   nearly all families moving to Oregon
Washington Territory or Cal. A Government train lay here
& Mr. S engaged them to help him cross the river which was
about a third of a mile wide with their ox teams & large
wagons which had a water tight box. The wagons & carriages
were hitched together in 2 trains & with 10 yoke of oxen to
each of the three loads we crossed the river the mules having
been swum over before. Our wagon boxes had been raised
about ½ their width so that the water did not run in & we got
safely across. We were about 2 hours getting ready &
crossing   our bill for helping being 30 dollars. Came out
about 5 miles & camped on a creek.

June 26th.   Started from camp at ½ past 5 & traveled 30
miles. About noon we passed a stage station the only thing
life like we have seen to day. A thunder storm last night
cleared the air which was very oppressive but to day is very
refreshing. Camped on Pole creek.

June 27th.   Started at 6 A. M. Traveled 4 miles when we
came to the stage station & what has been very rare for a few
days a good well of water. Our road here led up on to a ridge
some 26 miles in length quite hilly & destitute of creeks
springs & 2 attempts to dig wells having proved a failure

although one had been dug to the depth of a hundred ft. Drove 31 miles & camped on Muddy springs within sight of the Black Hills & close to a stage station. In the evening Platt took his fiddle & our co went over to stage station & danced cotillions till 10 oclock.

June 28th.   Although we retired late last evening we were up so soon after 3 & by 5 we were on the road which proved to be a hard one on account of the sand. About 6 or 7 we came in sight of Court house rock a vast pile of sandstone & soapstone some 400 ft above the level & deriving its name from the shape of the top which is like the dome of a court house. The rock seemed to be a short distance from us but when we had driven 4 hours at the rate of 4 miles an hour we had just arrived opposite it & though it seemed to be just over yonder Mr. S. told us it was distant about 6 miles. About 9 we came in sight of one of the greatest natural curiosities I ever saw Chimney rock. We traveled 4 or 5 hours after it seemed very near us & when we camped it still seemed to be about a quarter of a mile ahead of us. Some of our party thought they would give it a closer inspection & as they went off I noticed a sly laugh on Mr. Smiths phiz which was fully explained when they came back having walked some 10 miles. The main body of the pile is the shape of a mound about 300 ft high & from the center of this a round spire or chimney rises or formerly rose to the height of 400 ft but it has crumbled away till now it is but 150 ft making the top of the spire about 450 ft from the level. A ridge of bluffs run about 6 miles from & parallel with the river between which is our road but the bluffs which I have mentioned stand out distant from the ridge. Drive 21 miles & camped on the Platte.

June 29th.   At a very early hour we were on our way & soon after passing chimney rock we came in sight of another what

shall I call it, vast pile of rock & sandstone & which at a
distance resembled closely the first sight of the penitentiary
at Jefferson City [Missouri] but as we came nearer looked
exactly like some of old castle as I have seen them pictured
out before now. If I were only a word painter I would try to
give you a description of it but Nature has blessed me with
no such gift & so I can give you no idea of it but only tell you
that it was grand splendid & magnificent. It seemed to cover
hundreds of acres rising up in some places abruptly in others
with a gradual slope to the height of 5 or 600 ft   in some
places covered with grass & flowers in others perfectly bare
or with a few scattering pines or firs irregular shaped &
divided into 2 distinct parts between which lay our road.
From one side rose a lofty bastion or tower perfectly
round   from other places were chimneys & spires & it
needed but little fancy to convert the whole into the ruins of
some old castle. Although we came in plain sight of it by 6 we
did no[t] reach it till about 2 in the afternoon. Drove 37 miles
& camped on the Platt.

June 30th.   At 6 we were on the road which to day has been
a very good one quite level. Traveled 14 miles & camped at
11 on Horse Shoe Creek near a stage station. The boys
borrowed a seine & caught a fine lot of fish while the girls
having borrowed a couple of tubs had a general good time
cleaning up. About 6 a shower came up but did not last long,
& by 8 the camp was all quiet. Are within 35 miles of
Laramie.

July 1st.   Started about 8 this morning & traveled 26 miles.
The first part of the road was quite sandy & hilly but the last
12 miles was quite level lying close to the river on one side &
steep rocky bluffs upon the other in some places so near as to
just admit of but one team passing over the road. Camped on
a creek a branch of the Platte at 3 in the afternoon 9 miles

from Laramie which place we will pass through to morrow. All the co are looking for letters from home there but poor Louisa. At Laramie we are 525 miles from Salt Lake City. We have had a very warm day to day as warm as any first of July day I ever experienced in Ohio. I am sitting in the mouth of Mr. Smiths tents with a board on my knee on which I am writing. Mr. S says tell your mother that we had some of the best fish for supper that was ever eat & that her girl gets along with the journey over the plains much better than he expected she would. So much for him. We have just come in sight of Laramie where I am to leave my letter. Mr. Smith says give my love to your mother. I can hardly write when the carriage is going as you will see. When I write next I will tell you about a war dance I saw to day. O how I wish I was going to get a letter to day as the rest expect to. My love to all the friends. I do not write to any one but you.

Good bye   Mrs. Louisa Cook

LETTER IV

July 15

1 days drive from the summit of the Rocky mountains
My Dear Mother & Sisters

A very hard days drive yesterday has so fatigued our teams that we must lay by to recruit today & I embrace the opportunity to write beginning where I left off with my journal.

July 2nd.   Left camp at 6 & passed through a variety of scenery at times level & again hilly with high rocky bluffs rising up to a great height. About 10 we came to an Indian village numbering some 300. Near the center of the encampment a sort of flag was raised & round this was a circle of warriors dancing or rather hopping round & round to the tumming of a drum & tinkling of a little bell & their own monotonous war song. They were decked off in all their finery & occasionally as some of them got tired they would drop out & others would take their places. On inquiry at a ranch near by found that these were Sioux who had just returned from a fight with the Pawnees bringing home 4 scalps & were now celebrating the victory. We saw several Indian graves near by being a sort of box some of them painted & decked with feathers & raised to the height of 12 or 15 ft on poles. About noon we came to Fort Laramie where some 600 troops are stationed. There were some very neat looking houses here built of Adoby & painted over the residence of the officers. We were told that there were but 2 white women in the place. Made 16 miles & camped on the Platte.

July 4th.   No thundering of cannon rattling to & fro of carriages filled with pleasure seekers or attractive displays announced to us that to day is the anniversary of our national independence & yet not unfit is it that quiet & stillness should reign when we realize at what fearful cost our Government is struggling to maintain those rights which our ancestors have handed down to their posterity. Later than usual our camp was astir this morning for at the request of the gentlemanly keeper of the station near where we camped Mr. S had promised that we should lay by till noon & give the boys an opportunity to fish. Accordingly about noon a coach & four came rolling up from the station & taking on our passengers were soon out of sight & returned about 11 with a good supply of splendid fish. By 12 we were on our way over the roughest road we have found yet. We are among the Black hills & it has been some down & a good deal up all the afternoon. Twice they were obliged to fasten ropes to the omnibus & keep it from tipping over on the sidling hills but we got to camp safe & sound after traveling 14 miles.

July 5.   Broke camp at ½ past 6 & resumed our journey
over 26 miles of as rugged road as one could wish to see.
Laramie peak is still in view & all around are high rocky hills
bluffs & peaks covered with cedars or pines or else with rocks
pebbles & hard heads. At noon we laid by on a creek with a
red sandy bottom & bordered with forest trees. Rested an
hour or two & went on till 3 when we camped near Chiles
Ranch.[8]

July 6th.   Rose at 5 & dispatched breakfast washed dishes
& wandered around camp till 8 when we resumed our
journey. Found the road very hilly & rocky the rocks being
of a bright red color. Passed a ranch on the banks of a creek &
at 3 camped on Box wood Creek[9] having traveled 18 miles.

July 7th   Started at 6. Passed through the creek & over a
very rough road until about 10 when we came down again
into the Platte bottoms where the road was more level.
Through all our journey we have found many flowers that
remind us of home. Among these are the larkspur which
grew in great perfection June pinks Morning star snowdrop
flowering currant &c &c. Hear many reports about Indians
& some of the ladies are very much frightened. Musketoes
have troubled us for several nights.

July 8th.   Was on the road by 6. At 10 came to the Platte
bridge.[10] Laid by an hour or so when the teams were again
hitched up & we crossed over paying a toll of 5 dollars a

---

[8]The only reasonable explanation for this reference is that she heard the words,
"Chiles Branch" wrong. There was an alternate trail that began in the vicinity of Fort
Laramie called the "Fur Trappers' Road" or "Chiles Route." It was in 1850 that the
overland trail oldtimer, Joseph B. Chiles, guided by an old friend, Joseph Reddeford
(Joe) Walker, a mountain man, turned off the main trail to follow a different route on the
north bank of the Platte. Helen S. Giffen, *Trail-Blazing Pioneer: Colonel Joseph Bellinger
Chiles* (San Francisco, 1969), pp. 35-47. See also Gregory M. Franzwa, *Maps of the
Oregon Trail* (Gerald, MO, 1982), pp. 108-121.

[9]This was probably Box Elder Station on the east side of Box Elder Creek. Aubrey
L. Haines, *Historic Sites Along the Oregon Trail* (Gerald, MO, 1981), pp. 170-71).

wagon & 50 cts for horsemen. After crossing we struck into
the tide of emigration from Omaha City. Saw our Cal friends
for the first time in a good while. Drove 28 miles & camped
on the Red Butes near the Platte.

July 9th.   At the first ranch we came to our horsemen staid
behind & borrowed a seine to fish but after making 5 hauls &
catching 2 fish came on & overtook us about 12. Met a
mountaineer from whom Mr. S bought a part of an Antelope.
Drive 22 miles & camped by one of the best springs I ever
saw where the water bubbled up between the rocks at the foot
of a hill.

July 10.   Was up before sunrise but did not get on the road
till 7. We found the road quite sandy. About 12 we reached
Sweet Water Bridge[11] where a party of the Ohio 6th cavalry
are stationed. Crossed the bridge and passed Independence
rock a large body of solid rock or layers of rock some 300 ft
high & a mile in circumference.   5 miles after we came to
the Devils Gate the most wonderful sight I ever saw. To the
right of the road was a vast pile of rocks & 4 or 5 of us left the
carriage to ascend to the top. About the center of this vast
pile we came to the Gate which is a cleft or Gap looking to us
as we looked down as though the mountains had parted in
the center & each quarter settled back leaving a chasm
apparently a thousand ft deep at the bottom of which the
sweet water river run[s] bubbling along as clear as a crystal. I
ascended to the highest peak & looked over & it seemed as

[10] As yet there were no military persons stationed at Platte Bridge. Soon after Louisa
Cook's mention of the bridge and its overland station, however, the locale became the
center of activity of a single unit of the 2nd Battalion, 6th Ohio Volunteer Cavalry. It
was a "one-company post." The main reason for its station there was to protect the
overland telegraph. Robert A. Murray, "Trading Posts, Forts and Bridges of the
Casper Area — Unraveling the Tangle on the Upper Platte," *Annals of Wyoming*
(Spring 1975), VII, pp. 22-23.

[11] Sweetwater Station was also occupied by the Ohio cavalry unit during the Civil War.
Haines, *op. cit.*, p. 196.

though I could never catch my breath it was so awfully grand. This rock as well as Independence rock was covered with the names of travelers. Near by was the grave of a man who becamp dizzy at this Gap and fell over killing him instantly. Drove 26 miles & camped on a little creek of the purest of water but very poor grass for our teams.

July 11.   Our campgrounds was so bare that to day we went but 7 miles & laid by for the day.   6 of the boys went out to hunt in the bluffs or mountains which appear to be a mile off but are really 7. We are now on very elevated ground but there are hills or ridges that rise to a great height. The boys found snow 5 or 6 ft deep & had a game of snow ball. They saw some game but the emigration has thinned & frightened them so much that they could not get near them.

July 12.   To day we have passed bluff & rocky ranges & several emigrant trains drawn by oxen. Snow is visible at the highest point. Met a party of soldiers who were leaving this road which is being changed to another route. Traveled 25 miles & camped on Sweet Water.

July 13th.   Sabbath day finds us on our road & perhaps not one half of the co will once think that this is Sunday to day. We have found the road very hard on account of sand & have been obliged to walk a good deal. About noon we found a grave near the road. On a board at the head we were informed that John Scott had been killed by Youngs who was traveling with him & that he was buried here by emigrants July 6th. Further down the board we were told that Youngs had been overtaken by Emigrants tried & shot & 2 miles further on we found his grave. Drove 25 miles & camped.

July 14th.   To day we passed the graves of 2 white men who were killed by the Indians about a week ago. They had fallen behind the train when the Indians attacked & murdered them taking their teams & whatever of value they had in their wagons. We are appraoching the summit of the Rocky range & have had several long hills to climb to day traveled 35 miles & camped near some bluffs.

July 15th.   Our teams were so much jaded by yesterdays drive that we lay by to day to recruit. Spent the day in washing cooking &c. A train of 16 wagons drawn by mules & horses passed by bound for Washington Territory.   1 of the wagons was covered with a large flag looking very conspic-uous with its red white & blue stars & stripes.

July 16th.   By six we found ourselves traveling over one of the best roads I ever saw smooth gravely & hard as a pavement & very level. At noon we came opposite the snow or wind river mountain which we have traveled in sight of 3 or 4 days. It has the appearance of an irregular shaped mound & the snow which crowns the top looked like a bright silver cloud against the blue sky. About 3 we came to the summit of the Rocky Mountains or what is called the South Pass where the Sweet Water river runs to the east & the Pacific Springs run to the west. Soon after we passed a snow bank about ½ mile off the road apparently but little higher than our heads. The nights for 2 or 3 of the past days have been very cold & this morning I ate my breakfast shivering with my shawl wrapped close round me. When I combed my hair there was so much electricity about it that I could scarcely get it done up. For the last 200 or 300 miles the soil in places is strongly impregnated with alkali or saleratus so as to be white with it in spots. The grass is much greener in these places & is very bad for teams. I will send you a little in this letter. We find some fine stones which I would like to send you specimens of cornelian & Agates &c.

July 17th.   Started about 7 & traveled 18 miles over an excellent road with but few hills & very little sand. The country is said to be almost level here for 80 miles on the summit of the mountains. Snow is visible all the time.

July 18. At an early hour we were on our way passing 2 camps one of 25 & 1 of 18 wagons all drawn by cattle ½ of which are cows. All the trains we pass nearly have cows yoked in to the wagons. A long line of mountains are visible covered with snow lying to the north of where we passed through. Crossed the Big and Little Sandy before noon & after traveling 28 miles we camped on the Big Timbers creek at 3 P. M.

July 19. Started at 7 & passed a long train bound for the west. All the trains we come to we pass & never see them again. Even our Cal friends who have bid us good by 4 or 5 times because they were going ahead have concluded to travel behind us. 1 of their co has joined us Charles Williams by name. There are no trees in view scarcely any grass & it is quite difficult to find feed for our teams. The whole country is covered with an herb resembling wormwood in appearance & smell but called wild sage. It grows about 2 ft high in bunches as large as a ½ bushel & the stalks about as large as a bean pole die down every year making very good fuel & indeed is all we have had to burn a good part of the time since we left the land of Buffalo Chips. About 11 we came to Green River which we were obliged to cross in an old tub of a thing dignified by the name of ferry boat.[12] A rope was attached to each bank which were about 40 rods apart. To this the boat was attached by 2 ropes or pulleys & being drawn up to a sort of staging not far from the bank the men waded out to it & pulled on the wagons by ropes taking over 1 wagon & 2 or 3 mules at a time. We were 1½ hours crossing paying a ferriage of 30 dollars. All the streams of water are much higher this spring than they were ever known before & when Mr. S went through here before he drove through them all without any trouble. Drove 19 miles & camped at 2 P. M.

---

[12]This is an apt description of Lombard Ferry. Haines says this was the most important of many crossing places in the vicinity. *Op. cit.*, p. 250.

July 20th.   Ate our breakfast of Johnny cake bacon &
coffee just as the sun was coming up & were soon on our way
again. About 10 we came to Hams Fork which being much
higher than usual was very difficult to cross & the soil being a
sort of quick sand only heightened the difficulty. The wagon
beds were raised so that the water should not run into them
& they crossed over one by one. The omnibus was too heavily
loaded & 2 of the ladies & myself rode over on mules drawing
our clothes & feet up under us to keep from getting wet.
After we got across one of the wagons & the hind team went
down in the quicksand clear to the wagon box & the other
teams had to move as fast as they could till we got up on
higher ground. Drove 13 miles when we came to an excellent
spot of grass on the banks of a creek where we camped for the
night.

July 21st.   At an early hour we were on our road which we
found rather hilly. About noon we came to Black Fork a
branch of the Green river but it was so high that we were
obliged to go 10 miles out of our way to cross. We have 3 or 4
cases of mountain fever Mrs. Smith among the rest. The
patients are very sick for 2 or 3 days but Mr. S soon breaks it
up with Blue Mass[13] & quinine. Drove 31 miles & camped
near Fort Bridger.

July 22nd.   I expect we shall have a chance to put in letters
here so I will close & seal this up. We are within 100 miles of
Salt Lake & I look forward anxiously for letters from *home*.
My health is good & so is Mary. I have lost that sallow sickly
look that I had at home and am only black now. Remember
me to the friends & let Uncles folks & any who wish read my
letters. I will send this to Emma & she can send it on to
Mother. If we stay long at Salt Lake I will write you from
there & let you know my ideas of Mormonism.   Good Bye
Your affectionate daughter & sister
Louisa

---

[13]A preparation in pill form containing finely divided mercury.

LETTER V

On the plains near Boise river Oct 12[14]

Dear Sister Emma

I wrote a letter to Mother last night & will put in a few words to you   In the first place this is one of the greatest old trips that was ever heard of & we had the full sight of the *Elephant* you may be sure[15]   Only think of not sleeping in a bed for 6 or 7 months not eating at a table drinking out of tin cups eating on tin plates spread on the ground   no letters from home   no news about the war or the country   wandering for weeks among the mountains   teams nearly worn out   provisions nearly gone & then talk about seeing the elephant   well we are with the soldiers now & as we are all right now & look forward to getting through sometime this fall   you would laugh to see us come into camp about 3 every afternoon tired hungry & of course cross   ragged shoes every article of clothing trimed with fringe (all the style here) hoopless spiritless & disposed would we give way to our feelings to be disatisfied with every thing   but after supper what a change   some 6 or 8 camp fires burn brightly round the corell & round these a cheerful group of men & women seated on a box inverted pail or true Indian style squatted on the ground laughing over the exploits of the day & cracking jokes at one anothers expense   truly with all that is disagreeable there is much that is enticing about this wild

---

[14]This letter is among the collection of Louisa Cook letters in the Toledo-Lucas Public Library, Toledo, Ohio. All others are in the Yale collection.

[15]"Seeing the Elephant" was an expression for having lived through the total experience of the overland journey. Professor John Walton Caughey of the University of California defined the phrase as "going through a trying and unpleasant experience and getting the best of it, or at least as coming out alive." J. Rea, "Seeing the Elephant," *Western Folklore*, XXVIII, No. 1 (Jan. 1969), pp. 21-26. See also Peter Tamony, "To See the Elephant," *Pacific Historian*, XX (Winter 1968), pp. 23-29. Merrill J. Mattes has an entire chapter in his classic book, *The Great Platte River Road* (Lincoln, Nebr., 1969), on "Elephants of the Platte," pp. 61-102.

gipsy life   I suppose you have enjoyed yourselves at home
as usual this summer grumbling if your biscuits werent light
enough your coffee sweetened too much or not enough
potatoes are done sweet cake heavy apples too sour & so on
never thinking how glad your sister Louisa has been to get a
dry piece of bread & a tin cup of coffee thinking it was
sumptuous fare if there was only enough of it   well I dare
say I relish my meals much better than you do but if ever I
get into civilized society again wont I know how to enjoy
it   I have been much disappointed in what I have seen of
the Indians   I thought when I got away from the white
mans settlements where they could roam at will & live
uncontaminated by society that we should see some of those
noble qualities that have been attributed to them by so many
writers but O dear what a contrast   filthy degraded deceitful
& treacherous they seem to me to be but a little above the
brute creation   They often visit us in camp to beg or
steal   no difference which   sometimes a blanket around
them or perhaps an old shirt or vest or coat seldom but 1
single garment   There have been a good many emigrants
killed along the route by Indians but we have been very
watchful never being without from one to four guards but
one night since we left Leavenworth & then we lost 2
oxen   we know that we are watched all the time but they do
not like to attack a good sized train & we stick close
together   Indeed we do not realize that there is any danger
only when we hear of others being killed or loosing stock   we
often pass graves where some poor emigrant has died or lost a
wife or child   A week ago we passed three little graves & on
coming up to the soldiers last night the parents of 1 of the
children the father very sick & I fear unlikely to recover
His disease like most others is Mountain Fever   There are
no children but Mary in Mr Smith's train but in the
waggons accompanying him there are some 24   well I can

think of nothing else & will close   write often & do not wait to get an answer or if you do not hear from me for a long time you must not think I am dead or married (might as well be one or the other) but keep writing   Direct to Portland Oregon.

Your affectionate sister
Mrs. L. C. Cook

LETTER VI

Walla Walla Jan 11/63[16]

Dear Mother

Nearly a month has elapsed since I wrote to you & indeed I guess over   but every hour brings along its work with it & I seldom find leisure for writing or but little for reading. We are having beautiful weather for the time of year hardly any cold or wet weather. A very little snow fell one night but was off by noon. My health is excellent. Have had a slight cold but not such colds as I used to have at home. The most that I miss here is the news as they happen along every day. All we get here are from four to five weeks old & then of doubtful authority. Everything we do hear however puts such a discouraging aspect on our side of affairs that it makes me sick almost to read it. How much I would like to hear from home & all my friends as they are now. I have found but very few acquaintances here. People do not visit here as they do at home. It is more as it is in a city. One hardly knows their next door neighbor. As far as I can learn there is quite a sympathy for secessionism not only here but throughout the whole coast. Lieut Col Maury[17] with whom I am staying is a graduate of West Point a Unionist & a gentleman but the Col of the regiment who lives next door is believed to be

---

[16]At this point the journal across the plains is missing. The story is resumed three months later.

secretly a strong secessionist. So is Gen Alvord[18] & many of
the officers who are high in rank. I think however a majority
of the soldiers are loyal union men as well as the mass of the
people. A meeting was held in town a few days ago to
discontenance the passing of the greenbacks but finally broke
up without accomplishing anything. Every thing is very
dear here. If you want a pen holder or a brass thimble you
have to pay a quarter for it. I got me a pair of shoes for myself
& Mary the other day for which I paid 6 dollars 4 for mine &
2 for Ms. They were the third pair I have got for her since I
got here. She has had several presents which have come very
good & this morning she was out to play & found a gold
dollar. With what she has had given to her she has three
dollars & a quarter of her own. I am sorry I could not have
brought a supply of things to last till I go to Cal as I expect
things are more reasonable there than here. We have no
Sabbath here at the fort. I have not been to church since the
4th of May the last Sabbath that I was at the corners. I dont
know whether I wrote to you that Mr Surles & Mr Atherton
called on me or not. They have gone to Auburn [Baker Co.,
Oregon] about 100 miles from here. I have not heard from
Mr Smith since I left them only that they got through safe to

---

[17]Lt. Col. Reuben F. Maury was a veteran of the Mexican War, who had crossed over
to Oregon in 1852. He joined the First Oregon Cavalry and served throughout the Civil
War, both at Fort Walla Walla and in Indian campaigns in western Oregon and
Washington. He was a West Point graduate. He died in Jackson County, Oregon, in his
85th year. *Quarterly, Oreg. Hist. Soc.*, VIII (March 1907), pp. 77, 328.

[18]General Benjamin Alvord (Aug. 18, 1813-Oct. 16, 1884) was a prominent military
leader in Oregon during the Civil War. He was a West Point graduate who had fought
in the Mexican War. When the Civil War broke out he was in Oregon as Chief
Paymaster and was placed in command of the Department of Oregon. He raised troops
to form the First Oregon Cavalry. Most of the action seen by Alvord was against the
Indians of eastern Washington and Oregon. From 1872 he was Paymaster General of the
U.S. Army. Howard McKinley Corning, *Dictionary of Oregon History* (Portland,
1956), pp. 6-7. Thomas M. Spaulding, in his article on Alvord in the *Dictioary of
American Biography*, describes him thus: "A kindly, unassuming, studious man, his
interests were scholarly, and his abilities of a sort little appreciated in an army whose
duties lay chiefly on the frontier." (N.Y., 1928), pp. 235-36.

Portland. I suppose we passed through a good deal of danger from the Indians without knowing any thing about it. A good many emigrants have been murdered on the Snake river route as well as on other routes farther south. I have seen very few here as they are not allowed to come on to the reservation. New Years night was celebrated here by a grand Military ball got up by the soldiers. I did not go over but was told that it was a nice affair. The room was large allowing eight set to dance at once with cannon field pieces & other weapons of war arranged around the room interspersed with evergreens & the national colors arranged in a most tasteful manner. There is a great scarcity of girls here say perhaps one to every 100 men. In town they say there is not ½ a doz unmarried ladies to be found. I have no particular arrangements for the summer yet but think perhaps I shall go on to California. I have written to Uncle Robert but have no answer yet. I wish you would send me a Toledo paper once in a while especially when they mention anything about the third Cavalry. Write to me as often as you can & if [I] leave here before they get here I can have them forwarded. M says tell Grandma she hung up her stockings & got them full of candy & nuts a doll a pin cushion & a little flatiron with a goose on it & a little stand to set it on & that she washes her dolls clothes all the time so as to iron them with the little flatiron. If I was sure you would get this I would send Sarah a dollar to have her likeness taken to send me. They only cost 2 dollars on patent leather here.

Goodbye   Louisa

Trip for the Colorado Mines, 1862

§ Ellen Tootle

INTRODUCTION

Grandmother was a very interesting person and her grand-
children were devoted to her. They talked about her continually
so that she became real to me even though I was too small to
remember her. When she died Grandfather came to live with us
and he died in 1908. He was around six feet tall and she was very
tiny — little hands and feet. She spoke French fluently and was a
voracious reader especially of poetry and the classics. She was a
kind person and did a great deal of charity work.

The above words were written in a letter to the editor by Ellen
T. Lacey of St. Joseph, Missouri. Miss Lacey is a granddaughter
of the Tootles and has been most helpful in supplying information
about her grandparents.

Ellen Duffield Tootle's birthplace was Hagerstown, Maryland.
Hagerstown is just a few miles south of the Mason-Dixon line in a
part of Maryland that experienced seriously divided loyalties
during the Civil War. She had been born on November 27, 1832,
the daughter of Mr. and Mrs. William Duffield Bell. He was a
prominent newspaperman. Her mother, Ellen Bell, was well
educated and had been active as a school teacher for a number of
years.

On Thursday, June 5, 1862, Ellen Tootle wrote in the overland
journal published here, "Seven weeks from the time we were
married." Her wedding date had been on April 17, 1862, in her
Maryland home town. She had met the groom, Thomas Eggleston
Tootle while on a visit to relatives in St. Joseph, Missouri.
Thomas Tootle (b. April 4, 1820, Marion, Ohio) was a prosperous

banker and businessman in St. Joseph. He ran a well-known dry
goods store. The purpose of the delayed honeymoon journey was
to scout out the possibility of expanding the business to Denver,
Colorado. During the following years the dry goods business was
expanded to Denver and to Helena, Montana, in addition to
several stores in Iowa and Nebraska.

Over the years of their married life there were several children
born to the couple: Mary Armstrong, b. Aug. 9, 1863, who
married Judge William Knowles James; Ellen Bell, b. Feb. 10,
1865, who married Graham Gordon Lacey, and Thomas Tootle
who died in infancy. The Tootles were Methodists. they lived out
their lives in St. Joseph. Ellen died in April 1904, and Thomas in
1909.

One feature of their journal was the speed of travel. They
started from Plattsmouth, Nebraska, on June 4, 1862, and reached
Denver, Colorado, on June 21, 17 days later. They visited towns
and mines along the face of the Rockies for a number of days, then
they turned their backs on Denver on July 14 for the return
journey. They arrived back at Plattsmouth 17 days later on July
31. The reason for the rapidity of their journey was that their
wagon was drawn by high quality Missouri mules, which traveled
twice as fast as oxen.

The only person who accompanied them on their journey was a
mule-skinner named Warren. We don't learn his surname.
According to family members he was a free black man. We know
nothing more about him.

Ellen Tootle's diary was published in the *Museum Graphic* by
the St. Joseph Museum, Vol. XIII, No. 2 (Spring 1961). It is
here published with their permission and with that of Miss Helen
T. Lacey, the descendant, quoted above.

We have also found most useful Sheridan A. Logan's definitive
book, *Old Saint Jo*, published in 1979. Mr. Logan has been
personally helpful as well.

Ellen Tootle is very explicit in her descriptions of the mines
and towns in the gold region of Colorado. As further descriptions
of them, the reader will find helpful the following publications:

Muriel S. Wolle, *Stampede to Timberline, The Ghost Towns and Mining Camps of Colorado* (Boulder, 1950); Harry Hansen, ed., *Colorado, A Guide to the Highest State* (New York, 1970), revised edn., and, of course, that indispensible publication of the Colorado Historical Society, *Colorado Magazine.*

THE DIARY

Started from St. Joe, May 27th, 1862, on the "West Wind" at 10 o'clock p. m.

May 29. A storm last night compelled the boat to lay by 4 or 5 hours, so that we did not arrive at Plattsmouth, Nebraska, until 1 o'clock. Were awakened in the night by the rain coming on us and found the berth quite wet in spots and some of our clothes on upper berth completely saturated with water. Though it stopped raining in the morning, it continued cloudy and just before we arrived at Plattsmouth, came down torrents. We had to climb the hill in wind and rain, our feet slipping back every step we took. Staid with Mr. Hanna, Mr. Tootle's partner. Were received cordially by himself and wife, (both Kentuckians) and treated with the greatest kindness.

Plattsmouth is situated on the bluffs. It is much larger than it appeared from any one point. There is but one place from which the whole town is visable. Like all new towns the houses are of board with one or two exceptions which are brick. The location of the place and country around are beautiful. It is one of the principal points from which the emigration and freighting for Colorado, California and those countries start from. It will, after awhile, be the chief route as there are no obstacles on that route which the other roads possess, no rivers to ford and road very fine. That western trade is even now immense and what supports the place.

Eggs, potatoes, and butter are very cheap. A farmer went to the store and offered 10 bushels of potatoes for a pair of shoes for his wife, priced $2.50, and haul them to town (10 miles.) In the fall they will not dig them for that price, but in the spring, will sell them for whatever they can get. Nebraska, Iowa, and north Missouri, the farmers raise a great deal of sorgum [sorghum] (Chinese Sugar Cain) and manufacture not only their own molasses, but for sale too. Some farmers, the poorer ones never have sugar in the house during the year, but make their preserves, pies and sweeten their coffee with sorgum. Some of it is as clear as honey.

May 30. The presbyterians had a "reception" as they termed it for the purpose of assisting in raising funds to build a church. They were entertained by Charades and for refreshments, cake and ice cream. Charges — 10 cts. admittance, 10 cts. for a large saucer of ice creem and slice of cake. It rained and there was such a small attendance that the Charades were postponed though the ice cream was all sold. Friday, the evening appointed, though it rained again, it did not interfere. The Charades were well enacted for persons of no practice, indeed some sustained their parts very well and with a good deal of vivacity. It was quite amusing.

May 31st. Saturday. Went to Sidney. It is in Iowa, southeast of Plattsmouth on the opposite side of the river, but not on it. It was a cloudy day and rained several times, notwithstanding which we had a pleasant ride. The scenery is very beautiful, timber, bluffs, and rolling prairie, nothing monotinous. We passed through 3 quite pretty little towns, Pacific City, Tabor, and Glenwood. Mr. Tootle drove his mules for the first time and though they are very fine ones, he had to be whipping and hollering at them all the time like all mules. Sidney like Plattsmouth, is a small town. Contains about 500 inhabitants. It is situated on high prairie and the houses not so scattered. It looks larger. The houses are nearly

all white, gives it a neat appearance. We staid with Mr.
Tootle's uncle. He is living in a large house and large
rooms. A luxury one appreciates in this new country.
Everything had such a home like appearance and the cooking
so like home and everyone so kind, I would have liked to
have remained longer.

Wednesday, June 4th.   Did not get back to Plattsmouth
until late Monday evening. Mr. Tootle could not get through
with his business and preparations in time to start before this
morning. Did not get off until 10 o'clock. Had to make 35
miles to arrive at a camping place which we reached about 8
o'clock P. M. Were not as comfortable today as we expect to
be, things were just put in every way. The inside of the wagon
is filled nearly to the top with boxes, trunks, comfortables,
blankets, guns, a matress, all the etc. of camp life. As we were
so late starting, did not stop for dinner, but ate a rhubarb pie
Mr. Hanna gave us. It was very soft and rather difficult to
dispose of having no plates to hold it, no knife to cut or fork
to eat with. We took our first lesson in the use of fingers as a
substitute. By the time we got into camp, the mules and pony
picketed for the night, our ham and crackers eaten and the
wagon cleared so as to spread the bed, it was 11 o'clock.

June 5th, Thursday.   Seven weeks from the time we were
married. At the very hour, we were seated on the prairie
eating breakfast. As it was only our 2nd meal, we did not
aspire to anything but cold ham and crackers. Mr. Tootle
says I cannot do anything but talk, so would not trust me to
make the coffee. Boasted very much of his experience. He
decided to make it himself, but came to ask me how much
coffee to take, for information, I know, but he insisted, only
out of respect. The coffee pot holds over 1 qt. I told him the
quantity of coffee to 1 qt. He took that, filled the coffee pot
with water then set it near, but not on the fire. I noticed it did
not boil, but said nothing. When they drank it, they both

looked rather solemn and only took one or two sips. I
thought it was time to have an opinion upon it. As Mr.
Tootle would not volunteer one, I inquired how the coffee
tasted. He acknowledged it was flat and weak, but insisted I
did not give him proper directions. He consented to let me
try it at supper time. Stopped for dinner where we heard
there was water, but it was so muddy, even the mules would
not drink. Had ham, dried beef, crackers, pickle and syrup
for dinner with brandy today. The brandy and whiskey we
brought for medicinal purposes, but indulged in a little as we
had just started on our journey. The first day, the cork came
out of the whiskey bottle and spilled more than half, to Mr.
Tootle's great disappointment. Indeed I don't believe he has
recovered from it yet. Camped at a beautiful place in the
evening. A stream wound round the foot of the hill and the
sides of the hill were covered with large trees. Got into camp
at 5 o'clock. Mr. Tootle shot three snipes today. Warren
cleaned them for breakfast. I was all impatience to try my
skill in making coffee. I watched it anxiously until it was
boiling and waited with the greatest solicitude and I must
acknowledge some misgiving, for them to taste it. Oh, but I
was rejoiced and relieved when they pronounced it very
good. Warmed some dried beef in butter. As it was my first
attempt at cooking, felt a little nervous as to the result.
However, everything was cooked very well. Washed dishes
in hot water. The first time we had enough and time to warm
it. Think we can live quite cleanly. The wagon was arranged
more comfortable today, things stored away under the seat in
the lower part of the wagon between the mattress and bottom.
It did not take but a little time to prepare for bed. Retired at
10 o'clock. Warren wakened us this morning at 3 o'clock. As
it was 11 when we retired last night, had rather a short

allowance of sleep. I protested against being wakened so
early, so we got up at 5 this morning, but find it will be
necessary to rise at 4 o'clock, rather more early than agreeable.
12 wagons were camped near us. Two parties, one going to
Denver, the other to Washington Territory. Passed wagons
today from Denver to St. Joe, ladened with hides. Went 30
miles today.

May [June] 6th, Friday.   Warren awakened us a little after
3 again. Cooked the snipes with Mr. Tootle's assistance.
They were delicious. Had soaked crackers for breakfast. My
first appempt and I did not soak them enough. Still they
were very good and a little change. Dropped the stock of one
of the guns. Warren had to ride back after it which detained
us ½ hour. Took dinner as yesterday on the open prairie. No
water excepting for the mules. Mr. Tootle brought with him
a preparation of lemon (as he thought) but it proved to be
tartaric acid and sugar, he had been cheated. It was refreshing,
though rather a poor substitute for lemonade. Camped at 6½
o'clock. Washed our persons for the first time. There was a
house partly built which we went into for the purpose, just a
few yards from our wagon. Felt so comfortable afterwards.
We undress at night though it is not customary on such
trips. Took sheets with us and spread our bed as we do in the
mornings at home. A family lives in an adobe house where we
camped. They call it adobe, but it is only sod, square pieces ½
yd. square piled upon one another with the grass side down.
The outside wall is the thickness of two pieces of sod, or 1 yd.
The inside walls only one piece. The chimney and roof is of
sod too. It is quite picturesque. Came in sight of the Platte at
5½ o'clock. The scenery was very fine, the country became
more rolling, along the Platte. Hills covered with timber and
a creek tributary to it. Passed 3 or 4 camps of ox wagons,

consisting of from two or three wagons to a dozen. Met a
number of wagons returning from Pikes Peak. Retired at 11
o'clock. When we camp, Mr. Tootle and Warren first
unharness the mules and pony then picket them. After that
build a fire and put the water on to boil. Then either Mr.
Tootle or myself make the coffee and get supper together.
While they feed and picket pony and the mules for the night,
I prepare the bed and wash the dishes. For breakfast we go
through the same routine. We have cold dinners.

June 7th, Saturday.   Mr. Tootle put on his traveling suit
for the first time. It consists of a flannel shirt, one is blue with
a blue and white plaid bosom, cuffs and collar. The other is
scarlet flannel with a sulfureous[1] striped with white for a
bosom, cuffs and collar. Pants pepper salt cloth. Cold days or
mornings and evenings he wears a coat.

My traveling suit is a cotton material brown plaid minus
hoopes, dark stockings, brown cambric skirt, brown hat
trimmed with brown ribbon and blue veil covering head and
face leaving a hole through which I could see and breath. For
a change I have a blue calico bonnet with a beaux at least ½
yd. long.

Today we came into Platte River bottom and found the
dust very disagreeable, but only for a little while. The road
through the Platte bottom is sand from 2 inches to over 1 ft.
deep. The mornings and evenings are cool indeed sometimes
cold, but through the middle of the day, it is very warm. Saw
3 antelopes at a distance. Flowers like sweet-peas and fox
gloves, another that resembles cow-slip exactly excepting the
clusters are larger. None of the green leaves resemble the
garden flowers. Nearly all the prairie flowers are fragrant.
There is quite a variety of colors and shades chiefly blue,
pink, red, purple, and yellow.

June 9th, Monday.   We have not seen any snipe since the

[1]Greenish-yellow color.

2nd day but great numbers of doves, generally in pairs, but frequently in flocks. There are blackbirds too and occasionally we see a lark and some brown birds. I don't know their names. The Platte is now very high and muddy. When it is low, it is clear. The bottom is sand. There is no timber in the Platte valley, all the wood is obtained from the islands in the river. Nearly all the ranches are adobe. Warren talks in his sleep. Last night he said, "Mr. Tootle, I have a black silk lash on my whip 18 yds. long, must I drive until I use it up?"

There was a strong wind when I rode pony this morning. As I had nothing out of my trunk, had to don a black sacque coat — of Mr. Tootle's.

The travel is much greater than the first few days. The roads from Omaha, St. Joe and Atchison come into the road just before and after we pass Fort Kearney. Every few miles we meet trains, some emigants, but generally freight trains. Drove 41 miles Saturday, as we did not intend traveling on Sunday, but the place we camped was a mile or more from a house, no wood, no timber, and no water, but at the ranch. We were told that 5 miles over was a ranch where we could buy wood and find water, and 10 miles a ranch with timber and water. When we reached the 1st ranch, found no wood, no good camping place and no water but the river, so we went to the 10 mile place. The timber was on two miles so we camped in the plains. For 10 cts. bought 5 sticks of wood about 3 ft. long, 3 or 4 inches in diameter. We had dinner and supper together as we did not get into camp before 10 o'clock. Had boiled potatoes and fried flitch.[2] Both new dishes, so we enjoyed them very much. By the by I lost a bet on the last. Mr. Tootle bet me a new dress I would eat fat meat before I was half way to Denver. I entirely forgot it, and ate 3 pieces of fried flitch, when he very triumphantly

[2]Cured and salted side of bacon.

reminded me of it. As we had not been able to wash for two days, both got on pony, (I rode behind Mr. Tootle) and went to the Platte to bathe. The river was so muddy, we were afraid to go in it for fear of holes or quick sand, so we had to content ourselves with a sponge bath. It was a lovely evening, the scenery so fine, nothing could surpass it. The sky was a bright rose color, the Platte flowing beneath it reflecting its rosiat tints and studded with islands of all sizes from 1 yd to 1 or 2 miles long, some covered with high grass and all have trees, some evergreen. That was all the timber in sight. Behind us the prairie was stretched out for miles bounded by the bluffs. The Platte though from 1 to 1½ miles wide is nowhere more than 1 to 4 ft deep. It had more islands than any river in the world. We counted 7 just in front of us in a few hundred yards. In other places I counted 40 or 50 in a small distance. They contributed very much to the beauty of the river.

When we got back to the wagon, we lunched on canned peaches, then retired. Peaches were never more relished. We rose early this morning about 3 o'clock. I ride every morning and evening on pony. The trains we pass are for Pike's Peak, California, and Washington Territory, mostly ox trains, some mules occasionally a horse train. There are ranches every 5, 10, 12, 15, sometimes 20 miles. Every ranch is a sort of house of entertainment, has a bar room, and little store attached to it. There are with few exceptions, wells at them and the only places good water can be obtained, so the trains always camp near them and stop to water at least. At every ranch from 2 or 3 to 6 or 8 trains were camped, some trains consist of 2 or 3, some of 10 or 12 wagons. Yesterday did not seem much like Sunday. Read a few chapters in the Bible, the only way I could observe it.

June 10th, Tuesday.   Warren wakened us this morning 15

minutes of three, telling us it was going to rain. To our great
joy it rained but a few moments. Met a stage from St. Joe just
where the road comes into the main road. Met it at the first
town on the road after leaving Plattsmouth called Nebraska
[City] and consists of the stage office, which is of boards, one
other board house, 1 log, 2 adobe, one of the last is a sort of
bank "Stock of Exchange" is the sign. The woman that kept
the stage office house was quite genteel in her manners. Mr.
Tootle asked her if I could have a glass of milk. She brought
each of us a plate with a glass of milk and two slices of fruit
cake (molasses cake with raisins in it) very nice and I enjoyed
it extremely. A man came in from Pike's Peak. He had 4
apples in his hand, gave one to the woman, one to her sister,
one to a widow and handing the other to Mr. Tootle said he
never liked to slight a lady and asked if I would not take it. I
was most glad to get anything that looked like fresh fruit.
The house the stage stopped at or "Station" as they are
termed, had 4 or 5 large rooms. The land lady told me it was
not completed, that they had to ship everything either from
the Missouri, 200 miles, or Denver, 400 miles. That the
timber all came from Denver. They could get it much finer
and cheaper and transportation was less. Arrived at Fort
Kearney 2 o'clock P. M. Found a letter from Eddie. Never
was a letter more welcomed. Camped in the square of Kearney
City, 2 miles from the Fort. Mr. Tootle bought 2 loaves of
bread. Never enjoyed anything more in my life.

June 11th. Wednesday.   It had every appearance of a storm
last night, so we camped in front of an old adobe house. It
was uninhabited. It did not rain, but was such a dirty spot
that we concluded next morning to ride until 8 or 10 o'clock.
Then take breakfast. There were two ranches a few yds from
us and the men seemed to be intoxicated so Mr. Tootle did
not like to retire until they went into their houses and it

became quiet. It was 12 o'clock before he came to bed.
Warren called us at 2. I could not get to sleep again. At 4 we
started. Warren commenced hitching at 3. At 9 we camped
for breakfast. Mr. Tootle bought a quart of new milk for my
breakfast. My but I did enjoy it. We will take a lunch as we
ride along and not stop until evening. We prefer this
arrangement as we have the coolest part of the morning to
travel in, have worked up an appetite for breakfast and I can
sleep as long as I wish. There are dead mules, occasionally a
horse and great numbers of oxen lying along the road. It is
caused chiefly by the alkali which is in the soil and
impregnates the water. Persons that are ignorant of it let their
cattle drink at the pools of water. The wells are so little
impregnated as not to be injurious. Many cattle die from
fatigue. The sand is deep and the hills long, it is very hard on
them. Until today the water has been good. I would not
drink it, but Mr. Tootle and Warren did and it made them
sick. Wood sells 5 cts. a stick, 3 ft. long and 4 inches in
diameter. Corn sold at Plattsmouth 25 cts. per bushel. 30
miles from there, Mr. Tootle paid $1.00. Here it sells for
$2.40. Saw two ducks in the road yesterday, but they would
not let Mr. Tootle get near enough to shoot them.

June 12, Thursday.   The ranch we camped at last night was
a greater distance than we had been told. Then we had to
drive 1 mile farther for grass so that it was 10 o'clock before
we got into camp and 12 before we retired. It was so warm
and I had slept so much during the day that I could not get to
sleep. There was a young antelope at a ranch. We watered
and an Indian man and boy drove up. While we were at
breakfast, a filthy, dirty squaw and papoose came up.
Fortunately we were done. The Papoose had a little dirty
yellow flannel, (something between a sacque and shirt) on,
nothing else and it hardly came to its waist. It ran about

where it pleased. The squaw had drawers and skirt with a buffalo robe wrapped around her. Skirt, drawers and robe were all the color of dirt. We had sardines for breakfast. Mr. Tootle remarked "Indians will eat all the grease they can get." Gave her the box with the oil and some pieces of sardines. Then offered her the fat from the fried flitch. She held out her hand for it. He motioned her to hold the box and poured it in. She then began dipping the crackers we had given her in it and drinking it with great gusto. It made me sick. Came upon a wigwam consisting of 6 or 7 lodges. They are made of a dozen or more poles 12 or 15 ft. long, 5 or 6 inches in diameter at the bottom, tapering up. The larger end is put in the ground, and the small ends all together stick out of the hole at the top. The hole is at the top in one side for the smoke to escape and triangular, each side ½ or ¾ yds. long. There is another similar hole at the bottom for ingress and egress. The lodges are made of buffalo skins sewed together and there is a piece the size of the holes hanging to one side so they can close them up when they wish. They look picturesque in pictures, but to see them dispels the romance. The Indians are all filthy looking creatures. The ones we meet now are Sioux. They are uncivilized. Some few are dressed in citizens clothes, nearly wrapped in blankets or robes. Some boys even 10 or 14 years old with nothing but a dirt colored shirt to their waist.

June 13, Friday.   Passed Cotton Wood Springs at 5 o'clock A. M. Came upon another Indian camp, they are at every ranch we pass now. We seemed to have come into mosquito region last night and this morning. They swarmed the wagon. We could scarcely eat supper for them.

June 14, Saturday.   Last night camped at a station. Mr. Tootle got a pitcher of delightful buttermilk. The house was very clean and neat, of log, the door, walls and ceiling

covered with coffee sacques. That is the case with all the
houses when they make any pretensions to comfort. There
was no timber in isght all day yesterday and this morning
until we passed "O'Fallons Bluffs", then we saw bushes and
occasionally a tree on an island. We have been travelling
since Thursday on the bluffs. The road is very rough up and
down hill so that we travel about 3 miles an hour. Since we
passed O'Fallons Bluff, we are travelling through the
bottom. Yesterday passed the place where the river forks. We
travelled along the South Fork of the Platte. The scenery this
morning was unsurpassed. To the left were level plains spread
out for miles, bounded by bluffs. To the right were the bluffs,
lonely broken, rugged, with a gap through which we could see
the South Fork of the Platte bordered on both sides by prairie
so level that they look like the meadows of Maryland. Beyond
them the bluffs of the farther side of the South Fork of the
Platte, and in the distance the bluffs of the North Fork at a
short distance have the appearance of ranges of mountains in
the distance. Pony was so nearly well that I resumed my
riding yesterday evening.

degraded race. Mr. Tootle bought the ham of an antelope
from them. It took him more than ½ hour to wash it clean.
We fried some in butter for dinner. It was so tender and nice,
so delicate and pleasantly flavoured, much nicer, I think,
than venison. After washing it, it destroyed Mr. Tootle's
appetite, he never could relish it. We occasionally see the
graves of some Indian chief or braves or their wives. 4 or 6
poles 6 or 8 ft. long are put erect in the ground, the shape of
an oblong square. The upper end is generally forked. Then
other are laid across them on the tops, to support the corpse
which is wrapped in a blanket with a piece of buffalo robe or
vermillion colored cloth spread over them. Northwest of
Denver is a stream called Vermillion creek where they get a

vermillion clay they color with. There are camps of Indians at almost every ranch. We meet numbers travelling, some walk, some ride on ponys. It is chiefly the men who ride. they carry their tents on ponys. They tie the poles in two bunches, one on one side the other on the other side of the pony, put the tent, (folded up) on his back near the upper end of the poles. The large ends of the poles are exact side of the pony's head, the small ends drag on the ground. Sometimes they have their baggage or papoose tied between the poles just below the horses tail. They are tied to both sides of the poles and hold them together. Until 2 o'clock today the wind blew terrifically. Blew the dishes off the table (boxes) capsized the table, almost blew me over.

June 16th, Monday.   Came to Julesburg or Overland City about 4 o'clock. It is the most important point on the road. All the crossing of the Platte for California, Utah, Oregon, and Washington on this road is done here excepting a very little at the "old California Crossing" about 25 miles below. The city consists of 2 stables, 1 blacksmith shop, wagon shop, one station, all the property of the stage company. A hunting dog followed us today from a ranch. The Indian dogs are nearly all half wolf. Saw a prairie dog yesterday at a station. Some men caught it away from its hole and run it down. It was about the size of a Gray Squirrel and looked much like one of a yellowish gray color. Its ears are so small as scarcely to be perceptible. Its head is perhaps more like a rabbit. They are more of the nature of a ground squirrel than any other animal and what is called their bark is nothing like the bark of a dog more like the noise a squirrel makes, indeed I thought at first it proceeded from a bird, and frequently mistook it for the noise of the creaking of the wagon wheels. They are so quick in their motions that it is almost impossible to shoot them. Mr. Tootle fired at several, but they dropped in their holes before the shot could reach them. At least he did not think he hit them, but he could not tell. The prairie for hundreds of miles is covered with their holes. The soil is so sandy beyond Fort Kearney they do not attempt to cultivate it. They told me at a station that they heard of some one trying to raise potatoes. The islands can be cultivated and sometimes are. I find I cannot sleep after they commence preparing to start, so I get up at 3 o'clock with Mr. Tootle and ride from 4 or 4½ to about 7, then take a siesta when I return to the wagon. It is so pleasant riding early in the morning. We only take 2 meals now. We found we lost too much time having breakfast before we started, the heat of the day would come on by the time we were through. By rising at 3 o'clock, starting at 4, we can travel 12, 15 or 20 miles before breakfast, stop for it at 8, 9, or 10 o'clock, we do not require but two meals, then lay by 12 or 1 o'clock, the mules are resting during the warm part of the day, and fresh for the afternoon. Yesterday had to ride 15 miles to a station. The place we camped Saturday night was so disagreeable that we could only find time to read a few chapters in the Bible. Had to brown coffee, our coffee had given out and did not know how soon we could find a ranch clean enough or if the proprietors would permit it.

June 17, Tuesday.   Yesterday evening the cactus commenced for miles and miles. Almost all the way to Denver the prairie is covered with the Prickly-Pear Cactus. The flower is generally straw color pale or deep. Sometimes it is crimson. There are a few other cactuses all grow low. Excepting the prickly pear, all are round. The flowers of them are pink and very pretty. Mr. Tootle killed one of the large rabbits this morning. It was immense for a rabbit. They are very light grey on their backs, white underneath. Their ears are very long. The sand which was black has become yellow. There are nettles of a beautiful straw color. Pony deliberately laid down with me this morning. The sand was very deep and he got tired. We will be through the deep sand in a few days. The Platte is so high that in several places it has overflowed the road. Came into Colorado Territory only yesterday near the "old California Crossing". Saw more dead oxen than usual yesterday and today. The Sandhills are very hard for them to pull up and there is a great deal of alkali in the soil here. Mr. Tootle found two beautiful pink cactus. He planted them at a station so we could get them when we returned.

June 18th Wednesday.   Two antelope crossed the road about ¼ of a mile ahead of us and disappeared over the bluff. This is not the season for buffalo and this road is two much travelled to see many. They told us at a station that the Indians had driven them to the Arkansas to prevent the whites from shooting them. In coming up the sand hills today about every 100 yds passed a dead or dying oxen. The hills are very long and sand 1 ft. deep. Met a number of trains returning from Denver without freight. Two or three wagons are fastened together. All the oxen that are not required for use are driven along. It is done for economy, not half the hands are necessary. One man can drive three or four wagons and one of the loose oxen. They sell wood now for 10 cts. per lb.

June 19th, Thursday.   We see but few birds now. Oh, Occasionally doves, and a large bird with long neck and legs. Mr. Tootle thinks it is kingfisher. Denver is about 600 miles west of St. Joe. If I remember correctly about the computation of time, here (500 Miles west) would be nearly ½ hour behind St. Joe time, but strange to say, they are ahead of St. Joe. They are very fast people. 300 miles from St. Joe, they

were 30 minutes before St. Joe time. 400 miles, 35 minutes.
By the watches here the sun rises at 5, sets at 8 o'clock.[3] See
great numbers of prairie dogs. Came in sight of the Rocky
mountains today about 12 o'clock. Mr. Tootle saw them two
hours before he pointed them out to me. 115 miles from the
mountains and 100 from Denver. They present the appearance of white painted clouds, excepting they are more decided
than clouds and their outlines more distinct. Pictures of the
Alps are correct representations of them. Have seen mirages
frequently, but today saw finer ones than ever before. The
representation of water was perfect of a large lake with rushes
growing in it and timber on the border and in places where
the timber opened, the water ran through as perfectly as in a
natural lake. The clouds were reflected in it as in real water. I
believe the greatest curiosity we have witnessed since we left
home was two whirlwinds today. The large one was at such a
distance we could not have as fine a view of it. The other was
only a few yds. from us. Its connection with the ground was
almost severed. It looked like a little cloud of dust for 6 or 8
ft, then for 50 or 60 or more it formed a distinct tube or pipe,
a perfect sand spout from 9 to 12 inches in diameter. We
could see the sand draw up on the inside and descend upon
the outside. It was a perfect and distinct hollow tube. After
awhile the wind curved it and it gradually dissipated, but not
until at least 15 minutes after we first saw it. What seemed
strange was that there was so little wind as scarcely to be
perceptible.

June 20th Friday.   Came to Bijou Creek [Colorado] this

---

[3]Before what we know as "standard time," people went by "sun time." they set their
time pieces at noon as they traveled westward. If there was a town clock, it was set every
day at noon. It was in 1873 that Dr. C.F. Dowd, principal of Temple Grover Seminary
for Young Ladies, Saratoga Springs, N.Y., proposed the idea of "standard time," i.e.,
four time zones across the United States. It was adopted by the railroads on Nov. 18,
1883.

morning and found the first timber for 8 days. Saw a number of antelope today, and hundreds of prairie dogs. Their houses on the outside are like large ant hills from 1½ to 3 ft in diameter, made of gravel they throw up out of the ground.

Nothing could be more grand than the mountains today. Only their tops are covered with snow, down half the distance visible today. A greater extent of range came in sight than yesterday. Were in a storm today the most severe part passed by us.

June 21st, Saturday.   Arrived at Denver about 8 o'clock P. M. It is real luxury to live in a room and sleep in a bed again. Cheyennes and Arrapahoes came into town yesterday with the trophies they had taken in battle with the Utes. The Utes are the mountain Indians, the others are plains Indians. The Indians of the mountains are always on terms of deadly hostility with the Indians of the plains. The party that came into town had some trophies from the war, scalps, a few prisoners aned some ponys. They had war dances all night and during Sunday, but left Sunday evening. I regretted so much we could not witness the dance. Attended the Episcopal church in the morning. Bishop Talbot,[4] the Episcopal Bishop of the northwest preached. He is a native of Virginia. At night we went to the Methodist. The Catholic is the only other church. The Episcopalians have no church, but use a room. Denver is situated on the Platte about 18 miles from the base of the mountains. It is but 5 years old.

---

[4]The Right Rev. Joseph Cruickshank Talbot of the Protestant Episcopal Church was consecrated Bishop of the Northwest in 1859. His giant diocese was composed of Nebraska, Colorado, the Dakotas, Utah, Montana, and eastern Idaho. He liked to call himself "Bishop of All Out Doors." He was also to look in on conditions in New Mexico and Arizona. "Joseph Cruikshank Talbot," *Appleton's Cyclopedia of American Biography* (New York, 1889) VI, pp. 21-22; Myra Ellen Jenkins, "New Mexico — 1863," *Historical Magazine of the Protestant Episcopal Church*, XXXII, No. 1 (March 1963), pp. 221-23.

June 25th Wednesday.   Gov.[5] took a company of Artillery
and followed the Indians that were in town because they stole
horses and furniture from the whites. They are a part of a
tribe that would not sign a treaty with the U. S. Government.
They promised him to leave the territory in a few days.
Started at 9 o'clock for the mountains. As we approach, the
first range looks like immense sand bluffs covered with short
grass or pine trees of immense size. From the time we leave
Denver until we get to the mountains, the road descended.
When we get into the mountains we ascended ridge after
ridge and descended but little. There is a long, long hill and
so steep in going down one feels that they are never coming
to the bottom or rather you think all the time you are coming
to the foot but it is only the base of one of the long hills that
compose the very very long one. Just after we entered the
mountains we came upon Golden City. It is almost deserted.
A very small town about 2 miles from Golden Gate. When
we arrived at the Gate, I thought it was the terminus of the
road. Nothing but mountains rising up in every direction.
The road after passing through the gate turns off at a right
angle around the base of one of the ridges of mountains and
continues at the base, the mountains rising at each side of it.
There are the most beautiful wild flowers richer in color and
larger than the ones on the plains. A flower like our blue
cultivated columbine, but 3 or 4 times as large, Larkspur and
several flowers the same as our wild flowers. We saw one field
of quite fine wheat and quite a number of gardens. The toll
gate man had a magpie. It was the shape of a crow. Its head
and neck black, its wings and tail blue. The first gold found
was in Cherry Creek which runs through Denver. There was
so little, it did not pay for working. My sacque dropped out

---

[5]Governor John Evans of Colorado Territory had been appointed by President
Abraham Lincoln. Marshall Sprague, *Colorado, A Bicentennial History* (New York,
1976), pp. 36ff.

of the wagon coming down the very long hill. It quite distressed me. Because it belonged to my travelling suit and it will be spoiled. There are two hotels on this road very well kept. We thought we could get to Central City and would not stop, but the mules were so jaded that we stopped at a little log cabin. Everything looked clean.

June 26th, Thursday.   The log cabin we stopped at had two rooms and the garret or loft was divided by a partition into two rooms, that to my joy and surprise we had a room to ourselves. We could only stand upright in the middle. There is so much competition on this road that they are obliged to have good fare. For supper we had worked biscuit, boiled ham, fried potatoes, a large dish of green peas (the first we have seen this season) and eggs. Peaches and elegant rich cream. Tea and milk. For breakfast, we had the same. We enjoyed the peaches and cream though an outre dish for breakfast. They cannot raise vegetables on the mountain. There is too much frost. All those tender vegetables are raised in the valleys of the mountains. Radishes, turnips, and those hardy vegetables only, are raised on the mountains. Wagons pass every day from Denver to Central City and over the frequented mountain roads, very frequently with fresh meat and vegetables raised in the valleys, and canned fruits and vegetables. A great quantity of the latter are used. The only way in which I was conscious of the rarity of the air was by becoming fatigued when walking a very short distance. It is extremely hot here in summer in the middle of the day and frost every night. They gave us a feather bed to sleep upon, but it contained so few feathers we could feel every slat in the bed. But everything was so much better than the appearance outside led us to expect that we were delighted. Came down a hill 3 miles long, but not so steep as the one yesterday. Arrived at Central City about 9 o'clock A. M. the livery stables here is on the lower floor of the hotel. Our room

was immediately over it. The Verandah and Metropolitan
are the fashionable hotels of the place, both kept by the same
man. Our room was in the Metropolitan, very rude and
indifferent accommodations. The whole Gregory diggins[6] is
a very rough looking place. They are continuations of little
towns each bearing different names. When a man discovers a
lead, he builds near it and as others come to work it, they
build up along it, thus forming a town. The most central and
important is Central City. So we stopped there. As we entered
the city we met wagons loaded with quartz and others with
sand, going to the mills. The first and largest mills are the
Black-Hawk. There are no locks on the doors out here,
nothing but a latch. Visited the mines this afternoon. Went
upon golden hill. The Gregory mines, the richest here in the
mountains, as is the custom, have adopted the name of the
discoverer. He is from Georgia. He would work a lead until
the presence of gold became certain, then sell it. In that way
he made his fortune. First visited Mr. Martin & Leir's mill.
Mr. Leir visited the mines with us, but gave us some very fine
collect all fine ones and you can only obtain them from them.
Of course there are different qualities of gold and different
qualities of quartz. The purest gold found in the quartz is of a
bronze color. The finest quartz, I mean the quality, that
yields most abundantly and the finest quality of gold is a
prussian blue. The gold is found in veins of quartz, very light
and porrus, lying on the surface. The rock at each side of the
lead or vein of gold quartz is white or light greyish quartz,
called wall rock. (They term everything quartz out here).
The veins of gold in this part of the mountain are confined to

---

[6]Two fine references to the Colorado Gold Rush, its miners and mining camps, are
Phyllis Flanders Dorset, *The New Eldorado: The Story of Colorado's Gold and Silver
Rushes* (New York, 1970), and Muriel S. Wolle, *Stampede to Timberline: The Ghost
Towns and Mining Camps of Colorado* (Boulder, 1950).

a belt about ½ mile wide and makes its first appearance at the
base of a hill east of Central City and runs west about 3 miles.
Out of that belt, little or no gold is found. In it, if you take up
a pan full of dust in the street or anywhere, it will contain at
least 3 or 5 cts. worth. The richest part of the Gregory mines
is called the "patch" and is about ¼ mile square. The whole
of it is covered with holes, piles of sand and quartz, sluices
and every spot of it worked. Here I saw the cradle or rocker
in use. It is used in sluice mining. It is set under the trough.
As it rocks, the water runs off the sides and the weight of the
gold sinks it to the bottom. It is the shape of an old fashioned
child's cradle, wider and the sides more sloping. Has a sheet
iron bottom with larger holes through which the gold falls to
a second bottom. The sluice or gulch mining is done by a
continuation of troughs, the lower end resting on the trough
below it. That is what gives them the inclination. The
troughs are about 1 yd long, have strips across the bottom to
arrest the gold, or two bottoms, the upper one with holes.
The water running such a distance the weight of the gold
deposits of course with sand which is washed from it, in pans
generally, sometimes cradles. They clean the troughs every
Saturday, generally, and take out the sand and gold, wash the
sand away. The gold found in this way is called gulch gold, It
is the purist. The nuggets are all found in this way. Surface
gold or that found on the surface has less foreign matter than
quartz gold. Quartz gold is that found in the quartz rock.
That found 200 ft down is called lead gold. In the sluice
mines here, the richest is found in yellow earth. Here they
dig down the banks. Down at Terryall, Pikes Peak, it is done
by a hydraulic machine, the pipes play with water upon the
banks, just as fire engine pipes play upon a building and wash
it down. The quartz rock and sand is hauled to a mill,
shoveled into a trough over which iron pounders of different

weight, (in the mills we visited, they weighed 800 lbs.) 10 or
12 pounders. They are so arranged that the falling of one,
raises the adjoining one and visa versa, so that half the
number are raised at one time. They fit into a die of metal
upon which they crush the quartz into very fine powder.
Water runs through the trough all the time, carrying the
quartz after it is pounded, upon plates spread with mercury
with which the gold forms an amalgamate and the quartz
dust runs off. As 1/10 of the gold (or rather quartz powder
containing 1/10 of the gold) runs off in the water before it
leaves the mill, just as it runs out of the trough, it runs over
two rows of plates 1½ or 2 yds long or ¾ or 1 yd wide, covered
with mercury. Once a week, generally Saturday, the plates
outside the trough are cleaned and put into a cradle, the
mercury evaporated by heat and thus the gold obtains a
comparative purity. The pounded quartz after all the gold
that can be taken from it is extracted. It is called tailings and
contains about $40 to the cord this imperfect mode of
extracting does not enable them to get. When a miner
discovers gold his right is paramount to all other claims. If he
discovers it under a house he digs thus undermines the house
and lets it tumble over or else tears it down previous to
commencing work. All that is necessary is to give the
occupant notice of an hour or two to leave. I saw a number of
houses tumbled over. The discoverer of a claim has a right to
300 sq. ft. Any one else to only 50 sq. ft. All their expenses
is the recorder's fee of 60 cts. In working mines when they
get too deep to pitch out the earth and rock, it is drawn out in
buckets by a windlass, but when it gets too low, it is done by
horses. Ropes are attached to the buckets and run over
pulleys around a large wooden drum which has a shaft to
which a horse is attached to turn it. They are introducing
steam engines as a substitute. The lands of gold here runs

east and west and what is singular all the leads point to a
certain knob in the mountain. The sluice mining pays about
an average of $8 a day to a man, that is, a man finds that
much gold in a day. Quality averages from $7 to $15 per day.
The Black Hawk mills do a more extensive business than
any other mills, average $3200 per week, but only about ⅓ is
clear. The other mills average but $200 per week. Mr. Leir
said their expenses were $100 per day. They pay $1.50 a
sqare inch for 24 hours. It is brought from the Snow Range,
12 miles. As it enters the mills it runs through a square box
which has the grades to measure it. Silver and copper are
both found in the quartz that contain gold, but iron, chiefly
in the form of pyrite. In the leads of very fine gold here, opal
is found. It is a milky white with the colors of the rainbow. In
the George Gulch, rubies are found in abundance. Wages
vary from $1.00 to $15.00 per day and even more. To bore
through 1 ft. of rock costs from $15 to $40. At Pikes Peak,
there are other mines discovered since these, yet have not
proved so rich. Got back to Denver 6 o'clock this evening.
The Black Hawk mills payed out $3200 before they cleared
one ct.

Monday, June 30th.   Started this morning for Pikes Peak
via Colorado City. The scenery is finer than any we have
witnessed since leaving home. The different ridges of the
mountains and hills are of every shape. Numbers of them
have the appearance of having the tops cut off and are
perfectly level, some for two or more miles in extent and are
cultivated. Some have rocks on the top. One large conical
hill, seemed to have the apex cut off and an immense rock, 65
ft. high set down upon it. The roads are splendid, as smooth
as a floor and superior to any gravel walks in private parks.
They are all gravel hard smooth and level, the finest in the
world. We have not got into the mountains, but seem to be

between some outside ridges and spires of the mountain. The flowers since we have got into the mountains are much richer colors and more numerous. They are of bright scarlet, crimson, purple, and blue of different shades and yellow and a few white.

July 1st, Tuesday. The roads are more hilly though just as smooth, still gravel. Came today upon the head waters of the Arkansas. They are Monument Creek and La Fontain Quebouil[7] or fountain of the boiling waters. Monument Stream empties into La Fontain Quebouil. It derives its name from the white monuments on its banks. They are composed of quartz held together by a cement of lime and sand, seems to have been washed into the shape they now are, which is every variety, pyramids, spires, columns, square monuments, some of the columns decrease in size towards the top, others increase in size towards the top. They are generally in groups and at a little distance have the appearance of a cemetary. Several of the columns had a large, flat, square slab of limestone on top like the cap on a pillar. They were 3 to 6 inches thick and extending beyond the column about 6 or 8 inches on all sides. The monuments are from 3 or 4 ft. in height to 40 or 50 ft., in height. Some at a distance resemble cabins so much that we wondered at persons building on such high mountains, such inaccesible places. Others were perfect representations of pieces of architecture. At a distance, we could not get near them, they seemed to have pillars, cornicing, entablature and all the parts of architecture.

July 2nd, Wednesday.   Arrived at Colorado City. It is the capital of the territory. It has about 50 houses, but not more

---

[7]Here she comes pretty close to the name given to Fountain Creek, which early French explorers had dubbed *La Fontaine Qui Bouille* (The Spring that Boils), so called because of bubbling springs at its head. It is now Fountain, El Paso Co. "Place Names in Colorado," *Colorado Magazine*, XVIII, No. 1 (Jan. 1941), p. 33.

than a dozen have the appearance of being inhabited. The inhabitants of the city and southern part of the territory wish to retain the seat of the government there, but the citizens of Denver want it removed there, and I expect will eventually accomplish their object as they have more influence. Pikes Peak is 1½ or 2 miles from Colorado City and is 12,000 ft. to 12,500 ft. high above the level of the sea. The ascent is both difficult and dangerous and the air so rare and cold that some who have ascended have had their health permanently injured. One man died immediately or within a few days after having ascended it. In the valley it is very healthy. A citizen who has resided their 2 or 3 yrs. said she knew of no sickness or not one death from disease during that time. Several persons that had come there in delicate health had recovered. The springs in which the fontain rises are soda. They are not hot, but are called boiling because that escape of the gas causes the water to bubble up as if it were boiling. The taste of soda is very perceptible. They possess also a strong acid taste. With tartaric acid and sugar, they told us it made good soda water. We had no tartaric acid but took some vinegar off of pickles. It effervessed and would have been quite palatable, but as Mr. Tootle remarked "it was too pickly" Very nice soda biscuit can be made with the water. There are 3 soda springs and one chalybeate.[8] Some pretended to detect the taste of iron, but all of the springs tasted alike to me excepting the smallest one was the strongest. Where ever a hole is dug near it fills with water and bubbles up just as the springs. The bottom of the springs are white from the deposit of soda. The Indians and Spaniards and all the inhabitants from New Mexico and Colorado Territory who are sick resort to it for their health. It is said to accomplish some wonderful ones, cured inflamatory diseases. I was told a

---

[8] Iron salts.

woman who had been confined to her bed for years with
rhumatism was entirely cured in a few weeks. They certainly
are a great and very interesting curiosity. Another place of
interest was the Garden of the Gods. It is an opening
between two ridges of the mountains and entirely surrounded
by them, containing numbers of red, pink, white and lead
colored rocks of immense size, indeed all sizes from a few ft.
to 300 & 400 ft. high and as many in bredth. Others are
columns and of every shape. The red ones are old red
sandstone and a concrete sandstone. The bluish white and
lead color limestone and the lead white gypsum. The entrance
is not wider than 16 or 18, between rock from 200 to 400 ft.
high. At one side is a pure white one of gypsum and beside it
a greyish white limestone. The other side of the entrance is a
red one. Some resemble the ruins of castles and the pink and
white beside the red ones bring out the different colors so
distinctly that the effect is much more beautiful and
imposing. After you enter is an immense old red sandstone
one 3 or 400 ft high and as broad. A few ft. in front is a pink
one about half the size, in a line north is another immense
one light-greyish limestone with veins of pink and red; a few
yards from it another the same size, red sandstone; and in
front of it a gypsum one of lead white color and so they are,
over the whole garden; small ones interspaced between the
large ones. It is most aptly named, just such a place as one
would suppose the Gods might once have inhabited, but now
in ruins. The most beautiful flowers in it too. In one of the
red sandstone rocks there is a cave. The stratum of old red
sandstone must be at least two miles wide extending north
and south, sometimes upheaved in long ridges just like a wall
along the ridges of the mountain 10 or 12 ft. high, other
times in isolated rocks or in clusters. One of the party killed a
rattlesnake at the mouth of the cave. We returned to the

hotel, took dinner, and left for Denver by the same route we had come there. We had intended taking the road that led through South Park, visiting the Buckskin Tan, Tarryall, and Idahoe mines and returning by Clear Creek, the scenery being represented as very fine. On account of our time being limited, we were compelled to abandon it and return by the road we came. When we got to Colorado [City] one of our mules was so much fatigued as to alarm us and Mr. Tootle feared travelling through the mountains might unfit them for the journey home as soon as he was compelled to take it. It was with great regret we turned around. Another circumstance that had considerable weight in deciding us was the number and kind of flies. They were so large and had annoyed the mules so very much causing them to bleed a great deal. A Mexican that came down the mountain, the road we had intended taking, said they were much worse up there and had nearly killed his pony, the blood was dripping from all over it.

Left Colorado 3 o'clock P. M., Thursday, 3rd of July. Stopped at a house where an old acquaintance of Mr. Tootle lived and staid all night. In the morning his daughter went with us to the top of the highest mountain in that neighborhood. We could look down upon the others and over the prairie as far as the eye could see. It was grand. Many of the mountains were level on top. As we came down, we gathered some beautiful specimens of quartz and other stones. I never enjoyed anything so much in my life. Over the whole side of the hill, around all the trees for yards were laying these beautiful stones, crystals as clear as glass, pure white, yellow, red, green, brown, black, all colors and all sizes, polished smooth as glass and bright by friction. They looked more like french candies than anything I could compare them to. I gathered first my dress skirt full, then my under skirts, so heavy I was loaded under the weight. Mr. Tootle gathered great many too, but he was satisfied with fewer, or rather he knew we could not carry all the stones on the mountains home, so we selected the most singular looking and threw the others away. It almost made the tears come to have to leave them behind. Started after dinner and travelled to within 20 miles of Denver. So passed the 4th of July. More real pleasure than any 4th ever brought to me before. Yesterday evening saw a porcupine. It was very large. In running, curved its body up and down like a measuring worm. It ran so fast, Mr. Tootle could not get his gun in time to shoot it.

Saturday, July 5th.   The man at whose ranch we stopped took us to where there were two petrified trees. The trunk where it broke off from the root was lying just where it was broken. The whole tree was not petrified, but just 3 or 4 yds of it in different places, yet just in the line it fell. The ground was covered with pieces of wood you could not tell were petrifacations until you took them in your hand. The second tree was more beautifully petrified, where there was more pitch in it. It was petrified harder, of richer colors and parts of it where there was a good deal of pitch was crystalized. The tree was broken off about a yd from the ground, there was the old trunk and the fallen tree laying for 2 or 3 yds with the splinter sticking up and broken just as a live tree. Both were fine. We brought a number of specimens away. Mr. Tootle sent in an old chunk which must have weighed 60 or 70 pounds which you could not distinguish from an old chunk of wood, but by the weight and touching it. Reached Denver Saturday evening perfectly delighted with our trip. The grass in the mountains is a peculiar kind containing so much nutriment that it is not necessary to feed the cattle even in winter when the snow is on the ground. They get at it through the snow. The soil is sandy so the snow does not lay long. In the mountains the climate is very mild in winter excepting on the elevated parts. Persons generally locate between the ridges in the gulches. The country is very healthy and but little disease. The air is so rare even at Denver people feel sleepy all the time and in place of rising in the morning refreshed feel languid. I was told by some persons that in the period of 3 or 4 years, ones become seriously debilitated and others contradicted it. In the Rocky Mountains besides gold are silver and lead mines. In the South Park, salt is made from the salt lakes. The mountain ranges are 250 miles. When emigration first commenced here and before roads were made, they went over the tops of the mountains, up one side and down the other. Frequently it was so steep they would have to cut down the largest trees they could find and chain them to the wheels of their wagons to hold them back. I was told all the houses of Golden City (which is at the base on the Plains) was built of these trees. Men were at the foot of the mountains ready to seize them directly they were loosened from the wagons, would hew them into logs, then sell them. Learned a new and appropriate name for Yankeys. A servant of all departments at Colorado city, a wild, harum-scarum, kind-hearted girl, they called Texas because she came from there, though born in Mississippi, said "I would die for a Southerner, but would not give a cent for a *Pinch back Yankey*".

July 14.   Reluctantly and after a most delightful visit turned our backs on Denver and the Rocky Mountains. The wind blew terribly for several hours so that neither veil or goggles protected us from the dust. Indeed, Mr. Tootle could not see to drive, but had to turn off of the road and stand still for 10 minutes at a time. It was short fortunately. They told us at the first station they seldom had such severe storms. Here

they said it hailed and the hails were the size of a hen's egg.
Cut to pieces everything in the garden. It was very cold
during and after the storm.

July 15.   Camped at Bijou station.[9] They were going to tear
it down the next day. All the women had left. The men
offered us the use of the kitchen so we cooked supper there.

July 16, Wednesday.   Camped at Bijou Creek. Passed the
Junction at 4 o'clock. Camped at a ranch 6 miles beyond in
Alkali Bottom. Winged ants collected in swarms on the top,
front and back of the wagon just like bees when they swarm.
Mr. Tootle forgot to bring the meat he bought in Denver, so
we had or could not buy any fresh meat. We got very tired of
salt meat. We depended upon buying butter and potatoes
along the road, and did not succeed in purchasing any meat.

July 17.   Breakfasted at Beaver Creek Station. Have been
annoyed by gnats. They sting severely though not larger
than the point of a pin. At first I mistook them for a speck of
black sand. A storm came up and we stopped at the American
Ranch Station[10] until it was over. Got our supper there.

Saturday, July 19th.   Mr. Tootle shot a wild duck. We are
going to have it for dinner tomorrow. Last night came into
mosquito region. They were in the thickest swarms I ever
saw. Flocks of black birds follow the horses and cattle, settle
on the backs, fly around them to catch the mosquitos and
flys.

Monday, July 21st.   Camped Saturday night on the river.
Had no drinking water, so Sunday had drive to a ranch 6

[9]Bijou Station, CO., was one of the best known stopping places on the Overland Stage
Line. Ben Holladay had just taken it over in late 1861. Bijou was 20 miles frm the next
station to the east, Beaver Creek, the longest distance apart of any of the stations. Frank
A. Root and William E. Connolley, *The Overland Stage to California* (Topeka, KA.,
1901) pp. 70, 102, and *passim*.
[10]American Ranch Station in Colorado was also known as Kelly's Station. *Ibid.*, pp.
102, 222.

miles ahead. Did not start until 6 o'clock as we had so short a distance to travel. We had no light bread, no butter, or milk, nothing to fry the duck in. When we got to the ranch, no one lived there, but a man, and we could get nothing but water, and that was no good. They told us the next ranch was 8 miles, so we concluded to drive there. There we could not even get water, so had to drive 5 miles farther to the Animal Springs. It was one o'clock when we got there. Cooked our duck and enjoyed our dinner. Tried to make soup of the legs and wings but failed. Though I watched it closely, the water boiled away and the duck burnt. Breakfasted at Gills Station.[11] No one lives there but a Frenchman. His house was so clean and neat that we cooked our breakfast there and ate it in the room.

Thursday July 24.   Camped near a ranch. A rain storm came up. The first we were in. We went into the house to make milk soup just as it commenced to rain. Went back to the wagon before 9 o'clock and it was still raining and dark as Egypt. I had just that evening spread clean sheets on the bed. When I stepped over the seat my foot went into a puddle of water. I put the other down. It went into another puddle. Every place I put my hand was either wet or in water. The matches were so damp they would not light. Mr Tootle and Warren had gone to feed and fix the mules for the night. It seemed an age before they came back. The fleas were devouring me, so all I could do was to stand or sit in the puddles of water and catch and murder fleas until they came back. I felt savage enough to murder anything even myself. When Mr. Tootle came back and lighted the lamp, we found everything wet, excepting his blanket shawl. Not a very pleasant prospect for the night, however, we got things

---

[11]Here she probably means Gilman's Station in Nebraska, another important stage stop, *Ibid*. See especially the fold-in map at the end of Root and Connelley's book.

arranged more comfortably than I had any expectation,
thanks to Mr. Tootle's ingenuity. We turned the wet side of
the matress down, spread some soiled clothes for a sheet (we
had but 2 pairs of sheets, one was soiled and I had put it to
the side of the wagon to keep out the air, the others were on
the bed when the rain commenced). We used Mr. Tootle's
shawl for a cover.

July 25, Friday,   Had a storm in the middle of the night. It
thundered and lightninged terribly, rained very hard. Mr.
Tootle arranged the wagon so we did not get wet. Arrived at
Fort Kearney a little after 3 P. M. Bought some meat, tough
and not nice. Took supper at the last house on the stage road.

July 26, Saturday.   Saw a fine field of corn about 20 miles
east of Kearney. The man said it was put in with the plough
and had not been touched since. A little Frenchman had a
bed of melons the other [side?] of Kearney, they looked
flourishing, but he said they required a great deal of attention.
He had to water them every day. The soil beyond Fort
Kearney they do not attempt to cultivate excepting upon the
islands of the Platte which are more fertile. Along the sand
hills wild cherries grow on bushes from 1 ft to 1½ ft. high.
They are the size of our common sour cherry, but taste
exactly like our wild cherry. They have plumbs that grow in
the same way, some on bushes as high as 5 or 6 ft. both red
and yellow. At Colorado City, they have a blue plumb that
grows like these cherries.

July 28 Monday.   It is intensely hot today, warmer than
yesterday which was the first day we experienced any
inconvenience from the heat. The mosquitos swarm around
us at night and the fleas almost devour me. Last night, Mr.
Tootle made a fire in the frying pan and smoked the
mosquitos out of the wagon and me too. I did not know
which was more disagreeable. Yesterday, swarms of winged

ants settled upon our wagon. There must have been millions. they were smaller than the ones that visited us before. Rode 25 miles yesterday. We thought it 10 or 12 miles to the next station and concluded it would not be more unprofitable riding a short distance than loll around and sleep when we got tired reading. To ride awhile would be a little variety and rest us, but the station was twice the distance we were told.

July 29, Tuesday.   Travelled 50 miles yesterday from 4 o'clock in the morning until 10 at night, stopping only 2½ hours for breakfast. We took our supper in the wagon as we rode along.

July 30, Wednesday.   Arrived at Salt Creek, 3½. Our first camping place as we went out. Salt Creek rises in salt lakes. Within the last year a quantity of salt has been made from the water of the lakes. Last Sunday, Mr. Tootle resolved not to chew anymore. He had been breaking off gradually for the last 3 or 4 months. For a few days he felt nervous and badly, but now feels better (Insert: June 14, 1863, has been smoking ever since he returned).

Thursday, July 31st   Mr. Tootle smoked one pipe yesterday, another today, the first since we have been married. Arrived at Plattsmouth about 4 P. M.

Monday, Aug 4th.   Left Plattsmouth for Sidney [Iowa]. Had to cross the Missouri in a row boat. Felt a little nervous.

Returned to St. Joe from our visit to Pikes Peak Monday, August 11th, 1862.

Journal of a Mormon Woman, 1863
§ Mary Elizabeth Lightner

INTRODUCTION

The journal published here is a strange mixture of a day-by-day diary and a running commentary, much like the "Commentaries" of Keturah Belknap in our first volume. It is mostly in the past tense such as "we slept on our baggage," and "The captain has built a breastwork of sacks of grain." However a number of references are written in the present tense such as "One of our passengers has just saved a man from drowning," and, writing about Florence, Nebraska, "This is the gathering place for those who intend crossing the plains. . ."

A careful analysis of the text of the entire document, especially her usage of both the present and past tenses, shows us that her reminiscences were written, as were the diary sections, while on the journey.

Mary Elizabeth Rollins was born on April 9, 1818, in Lima, New York. Her rich life of 95 years ended with her death on December 17, 1913, in Minersville, Beaver County, Utah. She was married to Adam Lightner on August 11, 1838, in Liberty, Clay County, Missouri.

Mary took a keen interest in a new religious movement that was taking place in that area: Mormonism. She was baptized into the faith of the Church of Jesus Christ of Latter-day Saints in October 1830. Her husband never joined her in that religion throughout their long life together. He died on August 19, 1905.

Mary was sealed to the founder of Mormonism, Joseph Smith, in a "consecrated marriage" in February 1842. Adam Lightner seems not to have objected.

The Lightners lived through the Mormon tribulations both before and after the death of Joseph Smith on June 27, 1844. His death caused a scattering of members of the faith. The Lightners were among them. Adam Lightner was a carpenter and plied his trade, so the family traveled up and down the Mississippi valley, settling in different communities where building was going on. He also worked occasionally in general stores. They lived for a time in such places as Nauvoo, Illinois; Far West, Missouri; Hudson and Willow River, Wisconsin; and finally in Stillwater, Minnesota. Through the years ten children were born to them. Three of them died in early childhood. The following lived to maturity: Caroline Kezia, b. Oct. 18, 1840, Missouri; George Algernon, b. Mar. 23, 1842, Illinois; Florentine, b. Mar. 23, 1844, Illinois; John Horace, b. Feb. 19, 1847, Illinois; Elizabeth, b. Apr. 3, 1849, Wisconsin; Algernon Sidney, b. Mar. 23, 1853, Minnesota; Charles, b. Mar. 17, 1857, Wisconsin.

It was while they were at the gathering place, Florence, Nebraska, that Mary Elizabeth's brother-in-law showed up to help them on their journey. She writes, "On the 20th of June my sister's husband, Edwin Bingham, arrived to take us to the valley." Edwin Bingham had become a citizen of Beaver, Beaver County, Utah. The federal census taker visited their home during the summer of 1860 and listed Edwin Bingham, 28-years-old, a farmer, and his wife, Phoebe J., age 23. There were three children at that time: Edwin F., age 4; Bernand A., age 3 (male); and Phoebe C., age 1. There was another person, much beloved by Mary Lightner: that being her mother, Keziah Keturah Van Benthuysen, who was evidently living with the Binghams. The census taker listed this lady as age 64. He just gave up on the long name and shortened it to Kezia Berk.

When the party reached Beaver County, Utah, Mary's brother, James Henry Rollins (called Henry by his family) came out to meet them. He and his wife, Evalina, were living in Minersville, Utah, a busy little lead mining town surrounded by good agricultural land. Henry and Evalina had traveled to Utah in 1848. In 1849 he had joined the gold rush to California, traveling first south out of Salt Lake City, then west to San Bernardino, where he helped to establish that city as a Mormon bastion. He did not stay in California long, but returned to Utah to settle in Minersville. He served as Bishop of Minersville from 1860-1869.

Henry dictated a "Recollection" of the California journey in 1898. It is in the Utah State Historical Society. It was published in 1954 in *Journals of the Forty-Niners, Salt Lake to Los Angeles* by the Arthur H. Clark Company, volume II, pp. 261-68, of the *Far West and the Rockies Series*, edited by LeRoy R. and Ann W. Hafen.

We have chosen the version of Mary Elizabeth Lightner's journal published in the *Utah Genealogical and Historical Magazine*, XVII (Salt Lake City, 1926). There are other versions, typewritten and printed, but, after careful study, we feel that this one is authentic.

PERSONS NAMED BY MARY ELIZABETH LIGHTNER

Br. Martin was probably Jesse B. Martin, whose diary is to be found in the Huntington Library, San Marino, California.

John Riggs Murdock was an energetic overlander, who was known to all as "Captain Murdock" for he was so active in guiding newcomers over the plains to Utah. He made eleven round trips and brought more emigrants overland than any other leader. Andrew Jenson, ed., *Latter-Day Saint Biographical Encyclopedia*, I (Salt Lake City, 1901), p. 305.

Ziba Peterson was one of those under whose preaching Mary Lightner had become a Mormon. He had been sent by Joseph Smith to take the new message to the "Lamanites," i.e. the American Indians. In this he failed and so was disciplined by the church. H.H. Bancroft, *History of Utah* (San Francisco, 1890), p. 75.

Br. Stork is so-far unidentified.

Brigham Young, Jr., was the son of the Mormon leader and Mary Ann Angell, born December 18, 1836, in Kirtland, Ohio. He would become a member of the Council of Twelve Apostles in 1868 and president in 1890. Jensen, *op. cit.*, pp. 121-26.

SOURCES

Principal sources for Mary Elizabeth Lightner and her family are as follows:

Hubert Howe Bancroft, *History of Utah* (San Francisco, 1890).

Davis Bitton, *Guide to Mormon Diaries and Autobiographies* (Provo, Utah, 1977), pp. 212-13.

Kate B. Carter, "Mary Elizabeth Rollins Lightner," in *Our Pioneer Heritage*, Vol. V (Salt Lake City, 1962), pp. 305-25.

LeRoy R. and Ann W. Hafen, *Journals of Forty-Niners Salt Lake to Los Angeles*, in *Far West and the Rockies Series Historical Series*, Vol. II (Glendale, CA, 1954), pp. 261-68.

Andrew Jensen, ed., *Latter-Day Saints Biographical Encyclopedia*, (Salt Lake City, 1901).

Merrill J. Mattes, *Platte River Narratives* (Urbana, IL, 1988), p. 582.

Third Generation Records, microfilm, South Salem, Oregon, Stake Library, L.D.S. Church.

Utah Genealogical and Historical Magazine, XVII (July 1926), pp. 193-205; XVII (Oct. 1926), pp. 250-60.

Richard S. Van Wagoner, *Mormon Polygamy, a History* (Salt Lake City, 1986).

THE JOURNAL

On May 25, 1863, we embarked on board the steamer "Canada" for St. Louis, and took up our quarters on the lower deck.[1] All was neat and clean and we slept on our baggage. On the 26th we commenced taking on wheat, until the boat was heavily freighted. We had no chance to cook. Charles and Adam were very sick with the measles, and no chance to make them comfortable. We came to Rock Island Bridge,[2] which is a dangerous place for boats to go through. At the draw of the R.R. Bridge, a number of vessels lay ruined nearby. Many of our passengers were badly frightened, for we attempted the passage five times before we succeeded in getting through. On the 28th, seventeen horses

---

[1] The starting point of their journey was Stillwater, Minnesota.

[2] Rock Island, Illinois, lies opposite Davenport, Iowa. The island is the largest on the Mississippi. The famous railroad bridge had been built in 1855.

were taken on the lower deck, which made the atmosphere very impure. In the evening, five or six soldiers came aboard with foul company. Brute beasts in the form of men fill the place, and the scene is almost intolerable. On the 29th, we are lying at Montrose [Iowa] unloading grain. Nauvoo[3] lies on the opposite side of the river and looks deserted enough. One corner of that once beautiful temple, alone remained, a monument of former beauty and grandeur. It was raining hard or I should have crossed the river to see it. But as I looked at it from this point, and thought of what it once was, blossoming forth in beauty, with a population of seventeen thousand inhabitants, I felt to mourn over its present desolation. I thought, "Can it be that I shall see the place no more? Where once the Prophet stood and moved the hearts of the people to worship God according to the new and everlasting covenant, which had been revealed through him to the people in this generation, and where he gave himself a martyr for the cause he taught." One of our passengers has just saved a man from drowning, he was sinking for the third time, when rescued. My oldest boy, John, was quite sick, and throat very sore; the other children better, but cross. On a Saturday we arrived in St. Louis; it was raining hard. We went aboard the steamer, "Fanny Ogden," for St. Joseph. We were to have a stove to cook by, laid in a supply of provisions, and fancied we should be half way comfortable, but it proved the reverse. We were transferred to the upper deck until the storing of Government supplies was completed, then five hundred mules and horses were taken aboard; consequently we had to remain on the upper deck all the way from St. Louis to Omaha — wind and rain for company; nothing but

[3]This was the Mormon Zion, which they had built in 1839 after they were expelled from Missouri. It stood on the east bank of the Mississippi in Illinois. It was at one time, 1845, the largest city in Illinois (population 20,000). After the death of Joseph Smith in 1844 the Mormons abandoned it to fire and demolition.

bread and dried beef to eat, as the deck hands had stolen our vegetables. A soldier was put on board for home, who had lost his leg in battle; another very sick. We sat near a long box for two or three days, that contained a corpse. Our progress was slow, half the time on sand bars.

We met a steamer coming down, saying the rebels were gathering in great numbers and would fire on us. We had a cannon and soldiers on board for our protection; for myself I felt no fear. The captain has built a breast work of sacks of grain and tobacco boxes. All hands prepared for action. June 3rd all was excitement, and a sharp lookout was kept, looking for the enemy every moment. At Lexington [Missouri] the town was almost destroyed by cannon. Houses, partly demolished; it was here my husband's brother, a Unionist, was killed. We passed a gloomy night, some on trunks doubled up any way to get a few moment's rest; but strange to relate, not a shot was fired at us, although in a rebel community. We passed Liberty landing and Independence; things remain about as they were twenty years ago. We stopped at Kansas City; plenty of Mexicans were there, loading teams for Mexico. On June 6th, we arrived at St. Joseph, all tolerably well, considering that we had not had a chance to change our clothes or undress since leaving Minnesota. We found the river banks lined with Sioux Indians, who were being removed from Minnesota by the Government, for their massacre of the whites.

June 7th, we laid all day at this place; in the evening the Indians had a pow wow dance. We then boarded the "Emilie" for Omaha — some saints came aboard at the same time, bound for Utah. I felt to rejoice, for I had not seen the face of a member of the Church for over 18 years. Monday we landed at Omaha in a heavy rain storm; rode to Florence, six miles, without a cover from the rain, and stopped at a cabin, wet through. We had no fire and no chance to make one, so laid down in damp bed clothes; next night had the cholera and was sick three or four days, and my babe had bowel complaint very bad. Thursday some immigrants arrived with the small pox. Two are dead and ten more sick. One of the number spent the evening with us; we shook hands with them; they said nothing about the disease; the next day they were sent to the hills, where tents were provided for them. On Saturday seven hundred persons from England arrived here enroute for Salt Lake. This is the gathering place for those who intend crossing the plains. Today, saints from Africa and Denmark arrived here. Their tents were scattered over the hills, and when the camp fires were lit up at night the scene was beautiful to behold. It makes me think how the children of Israel must have looked in the days of Moses, when journeying in the wilderness; also to see some hundred mules in an enclosure, all sleek and fat — looks like prosperity indeed. The train of five hundred teams from Salt Lake are hourly looked for. Three deaths occurred in the Danish camp, and some three or four weddings. June 15th, the children have picked three dollars worth of wild strawberries, that helped us considerable. On the 20th my sister's husband, Edwin Bingham arrived to take us out to the valley. We were glad to see him. Sunday fixed all day for a march in the morning. We started; Monday night we camped out, and such a night — thunder, lightning and wind, but we slept, or rather stayed in our wagons, did not get very wet, but felt rather stiff — we cooked our breakfast, milked our cow, dried our things, and were ready for another day's tramp. One company of 50 or 60 wagons is ahead of us, and a good many behind us. It is quite amusing to see a corral formed and the cattle driven into the center of the corral of wagons to keep them safe. Each man unyoking his own, all

done in the best order. We had a good man for captain of our
company. I don't think we could have got a better one. We
have meetings every evening. July 3rd, passed a very hot
day, up with the dawn, cook breakfast with buffalo manure
for fuel — do up our work and travel sixteen miles, hard
wind most of the time. Tired out when camped for the night.
One wagon upset in a mud hole, no one hurt.

July 4th.   All well. Caught up with the company ahead,
John R. Murdock, captain; had a dance in the evening.
Traveled well the next day, saw a variety of beautiful flowers.

10th.   Nothing of interest has occurred, the weather very
hot. Had another dance, we are on a large prairie, saw a
buffalo herd, and passed through a dog village. Cunning
little fellows, dodging in and out of their burrows. Nothing
of moment has occurred for four or five days. The prairie is
one vast desert as far as game is concerned, except now and
then a rabbit or sage hen. One of the brethren killed an
antelope and gave me a nice piece. Friday camped at Pawnee
Springs, the water boils up from a great depth, there are four
of them, but I am told that a few weeks ago, there were but
two. The flowers are very pretty and of all colors.

18th.   All well, warm when the sun is out, but chilly under
a cloud.

22nd.   Had a thunder shower, no sickness as yet.

23rd.   One man sick — at noon, a babe belonging to some
of the saints from Australia, died very suddenly. We have
had a hard time today, traveling through sand hills, had to
double teams.

24th.   Mr. Lightner quite unwell.

25th.   Very hot; traveled through a great deal of sand, saw
plenty of prickly pear, it does very well to look at, but not
good to handle or walk over. Three Indians came into camp,

driving two yoke of oxen, which our captain traded for, as they belonged to the company ahead of us and will be given to their owners. One of our wagons broke down, which delayed us three hours.

27th. He is better, but babe very sick with canker and bowel complaint.

28th. Morning quite foggy, passed some natural curiosities, one called the court house, from its resemblance to that edifice, also a large rock formed like a church steeple and called the chimney. This part of the country is the most barren and desolate that I ever saw. Nothing to relieve the eye but sky and sand and hills, expected to see some buffalo but am disappointed.

29th. Passed a small government train from the fort, often meet a few persons passing along in this dreary place, as though they were in the States.

30th. Passed a trading post, three tents and a few trees, which did my eyes good, after seeing so much sand and barren soil.

31st. It has blown sand dust, enough to choke one, all day. Passed two deserted stations, and four graves of immigrants.

August 1st. Among the hills and rocks most of the day, and dust an inch thick. Saw the telegraph station; it consists of two log houses, outbuildings and a good well of water which was worth a great deal to us. Nothing but hills and sage-brush to be seen. No grass save in patches along the river. Camped in dust as if in the middle of the street in the States. Baked a shortcake, fried some bacon and had tea for supper after dark. Tired almost to death — lost the children's pet rabbit today.

2nd. A train of government wagons and soldiers passed us to settle some difficulty with the Indians and gold seekers. Our train stopped this afternoon to fix wagons and do our

washing, the young folks danced and played until twelve at
night — we always have prayers in the evening.

3rd.   Saw some returned Californians, who spoke well of
the Mormons in the Valley. We lost one of our cows from
drinking alkali water. Saw six more dead.

4th.   Lost an ox. More sick from the cause. A child fell out
of a wagon and the wheels passed over both limbs, but was
not much hurt. Passed sixteen dead cattle, from the other
train. This is a heavy loss.

8th.   Came to the telegraph station, quite a little place. Saw
a large freight train, had coffee, bread, and thickened milk
for dinner. We fixed up and passed through the aforsaid
train; all well.

10th.   Come to another station, crossed the Platte River
Bridge, which is a good structure. Camped on a large hill,
more dead cattle. The prospects look gloomy enough.
Elizabeth crazy all night with the tooth ache — been so for
two days.

11th.   The eleventh of August, the anniversary of our
marriage — twenty-five years of joys and sorrow have passed
over my head since then. Years never to be forgotten. Came
to what is termed the "Devil's Back Bone." It consists of a
long range of rocks, and looks as though they were thrown
up from beneath, and pointing up like ice in a jamb. It is a
singular sight. A company of gold seekers camped near us.
Our company lost more cattle. Came to a saleratus lake,
which looked like ice in the distance. We cut out a great
quantity of it to take with us, as the captain said there was
none in the valley.

13th.   Passed another station, also "Devil's Gate," which
consists of two mountains of rock so near together that a
wagon can pass between them. The walls on each side are

perpendicular, rather sloping on the other side, and so high that a man on the top looks like a small boy.

15th.   Had breakfast of bacon, fried cakes and coffee, traveled on a good road for miles, then stopped — cooked dinner. wind blowing gale of sand all over us. I think we will get the proverbial peck of dust before we get through — our cow sick, no milk for two or three days. Some sage hens and rabbits were killed today. We have had fresh meat but once since leaving the Mississippi River.

16th.   Sand and gravel all day, feel sick and cross; for if there is a bad place in camp, we are sure to get it. Antelope was killed today.

17th.   Saw mountains covered with snow in the distance; up and down hills all day; heavy wind; camped in a good place for a wonder, writing by fire light. Danes are at prayers by themselves — our folks the same. While I, poor sinner, am baking bread. In fact, I don't much like our preacher. He strokes his beard to much, and speaks too low.

18th.   Saw a lot of antelope; two were killed. The captain gave me a nice piece. Saw a camp of immigrants close by, another not far off. Camped on a hill for dinner. The hill was covered with small black rocks. It is a beautiful day, ice formed in our buckets as thick as a knife blade. More game was killed today, but little or no sickness has befallen us so far, the captain says we are greatly blessed to what some of the companies were. I hope we will continue to be, until our journey ends. We have been in sight of snow for two or three days. It looks cool for the month of August. We are on the highest land on this side of the Mississippi. Here, on the eastern side of the mountains the rivers flow toward the Atlantic, and on the western side, to the Pacific. The scenery is grand. A bear was killed weighing near four hundred pounds, and was divided among our company of sixty

persons. I could not stomach it. I don't believe they were
made for man's food. We are now in Utah, but I don't see
much change in the face of the land for the better; but I can't
see much, as I have been quite sick for six or seven days.
Crossed Green River Sunday evening, it is a beautiful stream
of water, and plenty of trees on its banks. Two trains are close
behind us, which makes us hurry to keep the front place, for
the roads are so dusty we can hardly see our front teams.
Stopped at a station where our men were required to take the
oath of allegiance to the United States government, our
wagons were searched for powder, etc. I have not much to say
for the past week, as I have been very sick all the time, was
administered to by Brothers Stork and Martin — and was
helped immediately. We saw a stage pass twice yesterday, and
more travel today — which makes it look more like being in
the land of the living. Snow all around in the mountains,
only think of it; snow near, and yet almost smothered with
dust. A stage passed with two of our missionaries, one was
Brigham Young, Jr. Arrived at Fort Bridger, a nice place,
good and substantial building. It looks comfortable. The days
warm the nights cold. Last evening we bought some onions
and potatoes, which were quite a treat. They did us good, as
we were getting the canker bad, from so long a diet of salt
pork, but I trust our journey is nearly over. The earth at this
place is of a reddish color, and the mountains look somewhat
greener than they have for some time.

31st. Passed through some mountains in a round about
way, they look solemn in their grandeur; rising one above
another, and their verdure of many colored hues and rocks of
various shades looked beautiful to me; if I had the materials
and time I should paint some of them. One of the curiosities
of this place is a spring of tar. The people get it for their
wagons. The weather cold but pleasant. Passed a mail station,

also a field of grain. It looked nice, but I should not like to
live there. There were some singular looking rocks, very
large, they appeared like huge blocks of clay, sprinkled full of
pebbles, and inclined to be red color. The earth in many
places looked like burnt brick — near is a large cave in the
rock, it has a singular appearance. It is called the cascade.[4]
Some fruit was brought in at famine prices — apples eleven
cents apiece.

September 1st. Passed through Echo Canyon. The scenery
is beautiful to behold, such rocks I never saw. Saw a few
houses and potato patches, also a mail station which looks
comfortable. I think from the appearance of things, Uncle
Samuel feeds his men and animals pretty well. I feel weak
today, from not having proper food (we have been on short
rations for seven or eight days) and breathing in so much
alkali dust. Camped near the town of Weber. Came over a
narrow road on the side of a mountain. It looked dangerous.
Came to W. Kimball's Ranch, he is rich in cattle and sheep.

September 3rd. Rained last night for the first time since we
left the Platte River. I hope it has laid the dust. I think it is
the fourth rain we have had on our journey so far.

14th. Camped at a station in dust enough to smother one.

15th. Arrived in Salt Lake City on Emigration Square.
All well — went through some of the streets; there were
some beautiful houses, orchards, and shade trees.

17th. Started south to Beaver County. My brother, Henry
Rollins, whom I had not seen for twenty years, with his wife
Eveline, met us, and conveyed us in his mule team south.
Stopped at an old friend's in Springville, had a nice time —

_____

[4]We have been unable to locate this cave. It is not mentioned in the sources on caves
in the Great Salt Lake region. See Ellen Hundley, "From Utah to Texas in 1856," in
Vol. VII of this series, p. 136, fn. 1, for a discussion of caves of the Salt Lake region.

heard from a good many old friend's. Had plenty of fruit to
eat. We traveled through a fine country. Saw some boiling
springs, and some large cold springs, so deep no bottom has
been discovered, and they are full of fish. We arrived in
Minersville September 20th, 1863, and found my dear
mother and sister Phebe, all well and glad to see us. We were
thankful to find a home and friends, after an arduous journey
of one thousand miles in an ox team — besides our trip on
steamer from Stillwater, Minnesota, to St. Louis, then up
the Missouri to Omaha.

A Letter from the Oregon Trail, 1863
§ Elizabeth Elliott

INTRODUCTION

"Poignant" is a word which would characterize many documents appearing in this series. This is especially true of this letter. It was sent to us by Mrs. Elizabeth Kay-Pitts of Medford, Oregon, who had seen a notice of our project in the Medford *Mail-Tribune.* We are grateful to her for the use of the letter and for her furnishing information about the Elliott family.

Traveling with a large company of 1863 overlanders from Marshall County, Iowa, the Elliott family planned to settle in Benton County, Oregon. They began their journey with three little children: Maria, age 7, and twin boys, Dayton and Fremont, age 3. The poignancy of her letter lies in her reporting of the deaths of children along the way, including one of her own, Fremont.

Henry Elliott and Elizabeth were both Ohioans, having been born and married in that state. Elizabeth, born May 18, 1836, in her letter refers to herself as "Libbie." They moved from Ohio to Indiana just after their marriage, and their first child, Maria (pronounced Mar-EYE-a) was born in Indiana in 1856. They then moved to Marshall County, Iowa, where in 1860 there were born twin boys, Dayton and Fremont.

Henry was a diligent farmer, and the rich farming land of the far-away Willamette Valley in Oregon was like a magnet drawing them even farther west. They were spurred on by correspondence from Henry's brother, William H., who had settled in Benton County, Oregon, with his wife and three children. The mother of this family was another Elizabeth Elliott. The two wives with the same name, living in Benton County, adds difficulty in searching out their records. Henry and Elizabeth lived near Monroe.

Elizabeth Elliott lived a long rich life. The date of her death was July 26, 1927. The following obituary appeared in the Corvallis, Oregon, *Gazette-Times* on July 28:

> Body brought to Benton County — A dispatch from Salem says Mrs. Elizabeth Elliott, 91, who had lived in Oregon 45 [*sic*, actually 64] years, died instantly Tuesday night at the home of her daughter, Mrs. Kay, of Salem, when she tripped over a porch rug and fell headlong to the sidewalk, five feet below the porch. She received a fractured skull and deep lacerations. . . . The aged woman was well known as one of the leaders in the fight for educational progress in the Willamette Valley. Mrs. Elliott will be buried in Monroe. She is survived by two daughters, Mrs. W.H. Kay of Salem and Mrs. Edgar Grimm of Nome, Alaska.

Families who traveled in the same wagon train as the Elliotts from Marshall County, Iowa, were mentioned by Elizabeth. They were the Logsdons and the Howells. She misspells both names.

The U.S. Census of 1870 lists two families of Logsdons and one of Howells. These people were all Benton County neighbors, named in the census as follows:

Charles Logsdon, age 34, and his wife, Margaret, age 29, both born in Illinois. Two children, Mary, 3, and Margaret, 1, were born in Oregon. Charles Logsdon was a farmer.

Thomas B. Logsdon, age 40, and his wife, Mary O., 27, both born in Illinois, and one child, Leona, one year old. Thomas was also a farmer.

George Howell, age 47, and his wife, Margaret J., 43, were both born in Ohio. Their children, all born in Iowa, were William A., a school teacher, age 21; Mary, 15; George P., 13; Rachel, 10; and Jesse, 5. This, too, was a farm family.

THE LETTER

Camped at noon on little Sandy
June the 12th   1863

Dear neglected Parents   through a multitude of
troubles and cares I have neglected answering your kind
letter which we received at Ft Laramie   I will in the first
place tell you about the sickness we have had in our
company   there has been 44 cases of measles in the company
from Marshall Co [Iowa] and our own family   I mean,
there was 3 deaths in about 3 weeks, Mr Howal lost a babe
about 8 months old   it died a few miles the other side of
Laramie so they got a very nice coffin for it   Mr Logestons
babe was the next   he was about 2 years old,   the next was
Mr Logestons boy about 5 years old,   they were not in
reach of any place to get a coffin therefore they buried them
in boxes,   the mother of the 2 children will be confined in a
few weeks, any one would think so much trouble would kill
her but she bears it well,   I will now tell you about our own
family,   Fremont & Dayton took the measles about the
same time, but they did well, as we supposed but just as they
were getting over them, they took the whooping cough,   the
diseases both work on the lungs you know and their lungs
were naturally rather weak so they have had a dreadful
time,   we thought several days ago we would have to leave
his body on the plains, but they are both now a little
better,   if they do not take cold I think they will get
along,   just as they were getting over the measles Maria
took them   she was pretty sick for several days,   before she
got real stout I took them   I was confined to the wagon
several days, and before I got so I could cook or do anything
Henry was on a mountain viewing the Devils gate and when
he went to come down he jumped from one rock to another

and sprained his ankle so you can see we have had a terrible
time

July 2nd

My Dear Parents   since I commensed this letter our
family circle has lost one of its members   Freemont is no
longer a sufferer on this earth,   he died Sabbath afternoon
June 21st. we had a Physition at Ft Bridger   he pronounced his worst disease dropsy,   he had been terribly
bloated for 2 weeks,   the doctor gave medicine for him but
it did not seem to do him any good,   his disease was of such
a nature that he could not lay down to sleep for over 2
weeks   he set up day and night,   well he suffered along
until 3 or 4 days after we left the Ft,   Sunday afternoon
about 2 oclock he was taken with fits   he had 7 or 8 very
hard ones   about 4 he died in a fit   he was sensable to the
last minit   when he took the fit he died in he tried to
straiten his little fingers and said oh dear ouch,   while one
hard fit was on his dear little eyes and mouth jerked as
though it would kill him   he looked at me and reached his
dear arms out to me and said *Oh Libbie.* he was so
sensible,   Oh dear I never shall forget that pleading look, it
seemed as though it would break my heart   I could not ease
his pain, but he is gone   his suffering is over.   we laid him
at the foot of a mountain by a splendid spring, we was not
where we could get a coffin so some of our company took 2
cracker boxes nailed them together lined it with bleached
muslin so it looked very well,   I had had his red stockings
his shoes his linen coat and pants put on him and his light hat
in his hands   Oh he was such a pretty corpse,   he looked
very natural   Some of our co said they never saw such a
pretty corpse   Oh how I wanted his likeness taken and sent
it to you   he did look so sweet with his summer suit on and
his hat in his hands,   little did his Aunt Maryann or his

Aunt Sarah think when they made his coat and pants they
were making his burying clothes   little did any of us think
of the like or how different we would off talked and acted,
but I suppose he is better off but it is so hard to part him and
Dayton   but the day he died we thought they would be
buried in one grave for Dayton was taken worse the same
time Fremont was and some thought D would die first,   well
we watched over him all night while Fremont lay a corpse
expecting every moment to breathe his last until about day
he began to get better   he has been gaining very slow since
untill last night he was taken worse,   we was up pretty near
all night with him and today he is very sick,   if we save him
it will be with the utmost care   he has become so very weak
and poor I dont know as I ever saw as poor a child,   we have
had so much sickness and trouble on the road I have fell
away very fast,   I was weighed while at Ft Bridger and I
had fell away 21½ lbs, and I have such heart rending trouble
since I presume I have fell away a good deal more,

William Howels lost his youngest the 20 of June a little
girl about Fredies age,   she was buried the 21 and Fremont
the 23rd   they lay side by side,   it was a great satisfaction
that we did not have to leave him alone

there has been 5 Children died out of our co since we
started   Fremont talked a week or so before he died   so
much about going to Grandmas to get some bread and
milk,   poor little sufferer he did get so tired jolting along in
the wagon   Dayton talks so much about him   Oh how we
all miss him   he was so lively, allways saying something
cunning   how dreary our wagon looks without him   tell
his little cousin he used to have so much pleasure and
sometimes some difficulty with he had not forgotten
them   he often talked about them and their plays   it seems
to me now that I can never get reconsiled to his death   it is a

loss that cannot be made up   I would like to write something
about the natural curiosites we have seen on the road but my
mind is not settled enough now   maybe before we get a
chance to send it I will write more   after we left Ft Bridger
we took the old Oregon road   Fremont was buried 60 miles
from Bridger on this road   we have had no trouble with the
Indians since we started but there has been trains attacked
this season   we have saw a great many graves of persons
killed by the Indians last season,   I have not lost one hour
sleep on account of fear from them since I left home,   we are
now in a train of 34 wagons   we are now 800 miles from
Benton Co Oregon

 We are now on the fery boat crossing Snake River
 you must write to Oregon

     Libbie   Father   Mother

"Travels and Incidents," 1864

ʃ Harriet A. Loughary

INTRODUCTION

One of the treasures relating to the woman's suffrage movement of the late 1800s is a collection of the papers of Harriet (Hattie) Loughary in the Oregon State Library in Salem. Mrs. Loughary was a co-worker of Abigail Scott Duniway. The papers are made up of essays and clippings written by and about Harriet Loughary, who wrote a column for Mrs. Duniway's paper, the *New Northwest*. The library has opened up the collection for use of this editor. There are also hand-written copies of her speeches made to women's groups, churches, the general public, and even to the legislature in Salem and to its committees. She was thought of as a brilliant speaker and nicknamed "the Patrick Henry of the new dispensation." Among the collection is a diary written while crossing the plains in 1864. It relates the day to day experiences of a well-educated, thoughtful woman who, even with six children to watch out for, found time to get down on paper details of the journey.

One feature of this diary that commands our attention is that it is written on the printed letterhead of the clerk of the McMinnville Public Schools, District 40. Also printed at the top is the short line: "McMinnville, Oregon, 189__." What this says to us is that this rendition of the diary was written by her sometime after 1890. There is no question that the diary was written by Harriet Loughary. We presume that in her late years she carefully copied her 1864 diary page by page and line by line, with some revisions. She added a "Preface" and a closing essay about what Oregon meant to her.

If the diary had been copied by someone else, not the original writer, we would not have published it in this collection. However, as it is clearly her own revision in her own handwriting, we see no reason not to include it.

Harriet A. Buxton was born in Virginia on November 27, 1827. She was married on June 1, 1848, in Burlington, Iowa, to William J. Loughary, who had been born in Jacksonville, Illinois, August 28, 1834. He was a teacher in the Burlington schools.

The Loughary family seems to have settled first in Polk County, Oregon, near its northern boundary with Yamhill County. They soon moved to Salem in Marion County to get a better education for their children at Willamette University. They are listed in the census of 1870 as living in Marion County.

In 1878 they did settle once more, this time on a farm south of Amity in Yamhill County. That is where they lived out their lives.

They were looking forward to their sixtieth wedding anniversary on June 1, 1908, when Harriet died of stroke on November 5th, 1907. The funeral was held in the First Baptist Church of McMinnville on November 8th. William lived on until January 16, 1911.

Before they left Iowa, Harriet Loughary had given birth to eight children. Two of them had died in infancy. Those who crossed the plains in 1864 were as follows:

Lowell, age 13 in 1864. He lived to become a well-known lawyer and a prominent citizen of Albuquerque, N.M. In his late years he was a judge.

Laura Louise, age 12, became the wife of a medical doctor, John J. Nicklin of Amity, Oregon.

Martha, age 10, grew up to become the wife of Harvey Henderson.

Harriet, age 6, married William Campbell of Portland.

John B., age 3, became a doctor in Seattle, Washington.

Susan, age 1, became Mrs. E.W. Wallace of Salem.

There would be one more child born to the Lougharys: William, who was listed as one-year-old in the 1870 census.

ON THE SPELLING AND PRONUNCIATION OF THE FAMILY
NAME: Harriet Loughary's name is spelled "Laughary" in some
of the records of her life. She consistantly used the "Loughary"
spelling. Others of the same name spelled it Lowary or Lowry and
so it was pronounced (rhymes with dowry). It is even debatable
whether it should be Harriet or Harriett. The family seems to
have spelled it both ways.

Sources for the life of Harriet A. Loughary:

Obituary, *Portland Oregonian*, Nov. 7, 1907.
Obituary, McMinnville *News Reporter*, Nov. 8, 1907.
Obituary, W.J. Loughary, McMinnville *Telephone Register*,
January 20, 1911.

We are especially indebted to Mrs. Ruth Stoller of Lafayette,
Oregon, for her help. She is a very competent historian of Yamhill
County.

THE TRAVELS

A BRIEF JOURNAL OF

The travels and incidents of an emmigrant ox train across
the plains and mountains, from Burlington Iowa,
on the Mississippi river to the Willamette Valley,
on the Columbia and the Pacific Ocean.

In the year of 1864—
By Mrs. W.J. Loughary

PREFACE

Tis said "Happy is the nation without a history; and still
happier the family without a break in the smooth current of
uneventful years."[1] Yet in spite of these visionary words the
world goes on making and repeating history. The incidents

[1]This is Harriet Loughary's version of a quote from the introduction to a work by the
18th century Italian writer, Cesare Beccaria (1736-1794), *Treatise on Crimes and
Punishments*.

of each day's travel, over the long and perilous route from the
Mississippi valley, to the great Columbia valley, as sketched
by the writer, will not be of sufficient interest to attract the
attention of the public generally, but the family and friends
of the writer may glean some facts, dates and incidents from
the journal is why it is dedicated to them.

THE DIARY

March 30th. [1864]   Made only seven miles to New
London [Iowa] where we visited a Mr. Otto and spent the
night.

31st   Left early next morning, reaching Mt Pleasant in
Henry Co. at noon. After purchasing a few needed articles
Hastened on hoping to reach a brother in Jefferson Co. but
muddy roads compelled us to stop. Here we made our first
camp. Never having any experience in camping we pitched
our tent on a hillside. This taught us a lesson not to be
forgotten that the hillside is not the place to set a tent or a
hen   The next morning some of our children had rolled out
of the tent and down the hill.

Apr. 1st   Moved out early   reached Jefferson spending
the night with friends.

Apr. 2nd   Cold and raining. Left for Fairfield   Here we
met a Mr Williams who gave us some very valuable
information relative to our journey. In the evening camped
at a small creek.

Apr. 3rd   This being the Sabbath we expected to remain in
camp until Monday, but the heavy rain had swollen the
creek so it seemed hazardous to wait, so we pressed on to
Agency City an old Indian trading town,[2] which deluged
with water making it impossible to make a camp, so we

---

[2] Agency City, now Agency, had been established as a Sac and Fox Indian agency in
1836. G.R. Ramsey, *Postmarked Iowa* (Crete, NE, 1976), p. 437.

sought shelter in an old crowded Hotel, ate our cold lunch
slept on the wet floor on our blankets   paid $4.75—

Apr 4th   Pushed on to Ottumwa on the DesMoines river
and the terminus of the Chicago, Burlington and Missouri
river Rail Road[3] being the only R Road west of the
Mississippi river. Thence on to Blakesburg to visit our
parents, where we stopped a few days.

9th   After parting with our dear ones, we started out in a
western direction toward Albia the County Seat of Munroe
[Monroe] and camped in a grove

Apr. 10th   Started in a northwesternly course through
Brennon valley, then six miles farther to Marysville and
camped at an M. E. Church

Apr 11th   Again we started on through muddy roads and a
driving rain to English river, over which was an unfinished
bridge. Here we met our first delay and danger. Our cattle
refused to go on the bridge.   one fell off, but was saved. The
oxen were unyoked, and driven over singly; and the heavy
waggons pushed over by hand. In the afternoon passed
through the beautiful town of Knoxville, a County Seat[4] with
spacious Court House, five Churches and a beautiful school
building. Two miles farther we came to White Breast river,
which presented as formidable an outlook as the one just
passed. The same process of unyokeing cattle and going over
single file, minus the cow going overboard.

12th   Cool and clear travel to day through Warren County.
Nooned, and lunched in a rail fence corner when I pencilled
a few notes while eating   Afternoon hurried on, and passed
through Pleasantville, which seemed to have been robbed

---

[3]The Chicago, Burlington, and Quincy Railroad connected at Burlington with the
Burlington and Missouri line to Ottumwa. It was a busy railroad during the Civil War.
Thomas Weber, *The Northern Railroads in the Civil War, 1861-1865* (N.Y., 1952), pp.
4, 288-9.

[4]Knoxville was the county seat of Marion Co., Iowa.

pleasantness being Quarantined with small pox but we were allowed to pass through at our own risk going six miles farther and camping at Sandyville   Here we paid 40 ct per bushel for corn for our stock. Wood very scarce, but coal plenty.[5]

13th   We now pass through the most sparcely settled portions of Western Iowa. Indianola a small town stands out alone in a large prairie where countless numbers of prairie Chickens frequent. Killed some for supper, after passing on to St Charles on a creek, where we found an abundance of wood.

14th   Snowed on us last night but we kept warm in our tents and waggons.

15th   We are now nearing the Missouri river, and the country more thickly settled   Camped at Wintersett   Here we found Rev. W. O. Eggleston an old friend and Pastor of the Baptist Church. He gave us late papers which were much welcomed   In the afternoon, traveled again through a large open prairie where the northwestern wind blew to almost a blizzard   Reached timber late at night   camped and lit a large bonfire then supper — a few more notes of travel, and to bed   Snowed on us through the night but were warm and comfortable in our wagons and tents

16th   Traveled all day over an uninhabited country reaching a small village at night and camped   Here we found grain, paying 50 cts per bushel in "Green backs" worth in exchange only 40 cts to the dollar   We met here the first emmegrants teams going to Oregon waiting for grass and rest

17th   It being the Sabbath wanted to rest but want of grain urged us on until noon, when we camped

18th   Traveled all day through a newly settled country.

---

[5]Readily accessible bituminous coal underlies some 20,000 square miles in 20 Iowa counties. *Iowa, A guide to the Hawkeye State* (N.Y., 1949), p. 8.

Paid 75 cts for frost bitten corn with our "frost bitten" money

19th   To day, we arrive at Lewis in Cass County   Here we laid in our trip supply of flour, at $2 per hundred lbs

20th   Travel all day over bad roads, and reach Beals at night twenty miles from the Missouri river

21st   Ten miles of travel brought us to Silver Creek where we expect to lay by and rest and wait for grass.

22nd   This morning Mr. Loughary goes to Council Bluffs to get mail, returns in the evening with letters from home, and news from the seat of war which was a great treat to us.

Large numbers of emmigrant waggons are centering here, and in Council Bluffs   Rendezvousing and preparing for the march   The whole country is so dotted with tents and covered waggons, as to resemble an army in quarters, some going to the newly discovered Idaho gold mines, but mostly families on the way to Oregon and California. A great many "Copper heads" from Missouri hiding away from duty rendered their state by the conscription   fearing to go farther unless in well organized trains, are here in waiting

May 2nd   We take up our line of march and go into Council Bluffs three miles from the Missouri river. This town is an old French and Indian trading station at the base of a very prominent bluff, mentioned by Lewis and Clark in their expedition across the plains in 1804. Here were about one 1,000 wagons waiting to equip and cross the river. There was only one ferry boat and it with only capacity to cross about fifty wagons a day

May 3rd   Start out before day light and got to into line for crossing the river finding fifty wagons already in line ahead of us. About noon cross and drive into Omaha Nebraska After casting one last look at our own proud Iowa State, we hasten on seven miles   Came on Prairie Creek still quite sick with Malarial fever

May 4th   Again move on over some beautiful country, newly settled   some good improvements and young or-orchards planted   At night reach Elkhorn river, about twenty miles from Omaha, and remain several days   Here were a large number of wagons waiting for grass, better roads and a larger number of wagons to form a train or company. Here is the reservation of the Pawnee tribe of Indians which were quite harmless, and friendly, but they were an annoyance because of their constant begging and pilfering

May 8th   Still in camp, being drenched by a three days constant rain, and still sick. It became noised through the camp that I had the smallpox, which caused a general stampede among the campers, all of them pulling out and leaving us alone   The Indians also shared in the panic, leaving also, which we greatly enjoyed as no more guarding our property was necessary.

May 9th   To day weather better, roads better, and grass better. Move camp, and reach Fremont, a small Nebraska village, yet owing to its location and surrounding, is destined to have a future. We bought corn at this place for 90 cts per bush   Reach the Platte river at sundown, just in time to go into camp to face a fearfull "Platte storm"

May 10th   Still storming with strong westerly winds compelling us to move behind a steep bluff for protection Afternoon — the storm having spent itself, we moved on up the river to North Bend. We met here H. Coad and Co.[6] one of our fellow townsmen who had started in our advance   The Platte river is a very uneven stream in width, depth and general course, Quicksand banks which pile up sand in one

---

[6]There were a number of Coads who settled in Oregon. We have not been able to identify this one.

place, leaving bare sand islands in others causing the water to be always muddy   not a rock, or pebble, for six hundred miles up.

May 11th   On the march again. Are now in the great Platte plains proper which is one vast scope of level country on both sides of the river varying from two, to ten miles in width. No organized companies yet   the road is white with moving trains going in a "go as you please" style, there being no danger of Indian hostilities yet. We see here telegraph poles, the line from California to Salt Lake then to Fort Kearney, on the east side of the river. Stations at only the above places west of the Missouri River at Omaha, there being a stage line and post office   here we got news of Gen Grants recent great closing up victories, having heard no news since leaving Omaha.

13th   Reach Columbus to day. A small village on the Loop [Loup] Fork of the Platte   Bought corn for $1.25 per bush, and $4.00 per bush for meal to feed our horses   We had some difficulty in crossing the river which was overflowed, with bridge partly submerged with water and driftwood, but these obstacles left us no choice. We must cross. So one by one the teams plunged in Sometime on the bridge, and at other fording with drivers wading waist deep   at times holding to the oxens horns, but with much slashing, splashing, yelling and pluck, we finally all got over, paid the ferryman $1.25 per wagon with our 40 ct greenbacks. We found some sticks, rocks and bark   made a fire and dried our wet garments   cook our supper and went to sleep. We now travel fifteen to twenty miles a day

14th   No difficulties have confronted us to day. The weather all that could be desired   Some pretty wild flowers are found, but we miss the sweet songs of birds. The river here is quite wide and shallow all over studded with little green islands of willow and creeping vines

15th Sunday   Having a much needed rest but was only from travel   Some of our party washing, cooking, hunting, fishing, sleeping. After dinner read my bible and thought of home which we were daily leaving behind   We are now camping every night at places fixed by our guide books, where wood, water and the best grazing are available. At this place was a solitary grave, on a rough board at its head was cut the letters J. F. D. Some one had buried the loved one while camping there   It was not expected of a large train to stop during the day to bury their dead this being the reason that we so often find graves at camps.

May 16   Again move out. Owing to such a sameness in the country, roads, travel, to day was quite a monotonous and uneventfull one. There were no more Indians, to attract our attention. The Pawnee tribe had been left behind, and the more noted Sioues we had not reached

May 17   To day, came up to some traders ranches where we bought a small supply of grain for our horses and mules paying $1.50 per bus.

May 18   Weather growing warmer. Country more rolling and bluffs or table lands visible. Make a hard drive and reach Grand Island in the Platte and go into camp. Scarcity of grass compelled us to ford all the cattle and horses across the channell, about two feet deep to the island where grass and wood were plentiful. This Island is twelve miles wide and about forty long. We found in camp here, the New brothers our neighbors also L. P. Reed, Willhouse [Hillhouse?] Glandden and Carpenter, from Burlington Iowa, bound for the Idaho gold mines.

May 19   To day passed a village of prarie dogs   The separate little inclined hole in the ground, where each little animal makes his home and as thick over the ground as peas in a pod, is why, it is called a village. Hundreds of little heads were peeping out of the holes, but they are so quick in their movements that an expert marksman can scarcely kill one. Snakes also numerous in these sandy knowls, but quite harmless. Yet some of our boys who were accustomed to kill copperheads took pleasure in killing them.

May 20th   At noon, arrive at Fort Kearney, on the south side of the river. As mentioned before a large number of emmigrants were here waiting to organize to get mail & two men were sent over for our mail. They soon returned with the news. Col Wood,[7] in command of the U. S. Soldiers at the Fort had just been informed by a messenger, that eight men in an emmigrant train had been murdered the previous night at cottonwood Springs some twenty miles ahead of us. As there had been no apprehensions of things up to the time, a real live panic throughout camp was the result. After much consultation by the older and wiser heads, the final decision was that all wagons in camp were to immediately move out in a body, to the next camping ground ten miles distant, and there organize & make all possible arrangements made for an attack by Indians. We were now nearing the Siouxs, which we knew were the most treacherous of all tribes.

May 21   In camp at Grand Island again   The cattle were crossed to the Island again and strong guard. While the horses and mules were tethered, or staked near camp; waggons formed a corrall, with tents and families inside the enclosure, with more guards stationed. The night of anxiety

---

[7]Merrill J. Mattes says that this was Major John S. Wood of the Seventh Iowa Volunteer Cavalry who had been detached to command Fort Kearny. Wood would rather hunt buffalo than Indians. He did so with the help of a pack of greyhounds that had been left at the fort in 1854 by an eccentric English soldier of fortune, Sir George Gore. *The Great Platte River Road* (Lincoln, 1969), p. 230. Capt. Eugene F. Ware, *The Indian War of 1864*, Clyde Walton, ed. (N.Y., 1960).

and watching came and went but no Indians. Indians always
seem to know if they are being watched, and rarely molest a
well protected train.

22   This morning all the men in camp were filed up into
line when Dr. Farwell[8] of Burlington Iowa was chosen as
captain of our company, and C McAllister assistant   certain
rules and regulations as is always necessary regulating guards
&c were made and signed   Our train consisted of thirty
three wagons, ninety one men, besides women and children.
After forming in the regular line of march, as ordered by the
Capt. we moved out well equipped for any emergency.
Nooned at Elm Springs   Heavy thundering at this time
indicated a much dreaded Platte hail storm which is often as
disastrous in stampeeding cattle as Indians. In the afternoon
the storm threatenings had so increased that to reach camp
seemed impossible   Therefore Capt Farwell ordered a halt
— form a corrall, and secure the cattle inside if possible.
Every man and woman and child was working yelling
screaming unyoking oxen, unhooking horses, driving stakes,
pounding oxen over the head to subdue them, digging holes
in the ground to bury wagon wheels. Meanwhile down came
the hail followed by blinding sheets of rain lightning, sharp
peals of thunder, drenching both man and beast,   added to
all, darkness closed down upon us fireless tentless and
supperless. Yet the guards must go on in their order cold, wet
and hungry, while all others crouched in or under wagons
and waited, like Paul for day.   This is only a faint
description of a Platte Storm.

May 23d   Storm being over we start out easy. At 11 oclock
reach a camp with plenty of wood water and grass where we
lay over to dry up our soaked beds, tents and clothing, and

---

[8]Here she mis-spells the name of W.J. Farley. She corrects it in her entry for May 23,
below. Dr. Farley settled in Dayton, Oregon and lived out his life there. Olof Larsell,
The Doctor in Oregon (Portland, 1927), p. 227.

mending ox bows, ropes, and tents, the results of the previous
storm and at night closed up with a dance on a sand bed.
Owing to some dissatisfaction our company divided   The
gold seekers wanted to travel faster than the families, leaving
fourteen wagons with Capt Farley with us   We are now
passing beautiful rolling prairie lands covered with sage
brush and different varieties of cacti. Also lovely wild flowers,
resembling and in beauty and fragrance, equaling our
cultivated roses, lilies, pinks & peonies. Some of our men
went to day hunting for buffaloe and antelope but saw none.
While the bleached bones of the buffaloe are strewn all along
the road, not an animal seen. The needless and wanten
slaughter of these once numerous animals, has almost caused
them to be extinct   To day we follow the telegraph line on
the north side. It is now running parallel with the California,
Salt Lake, and Missouri river stage road. Occasionally we
get a glimpse of an emmigrant train on the south side, but the
largest amount take the north side
May 24th   To day we layed by, while arrangements were
made to send one of our men home, he having been sick for a
long time. They decided to get him over the river, onto the
stage line to be picked up by the next stage   The river now
is much narrower and of course deeper, and must be ferried,
so a good wagon box was plugged up with rags and bits of old
rope — two men with paddles, one paddling the other
wading and swimming alternately, got him over. While
waiting the Capt advised the men to get long poles (wood
plenty here) and lash them with log chains to the axle trees of
their wagons directly under the beds, to be used for wood
since guides said there would be no more timber for the next
two hundred miles. Willow bush and buffalo chips only for
fuel
May 25th   Weather fine and road good. Travelled eighteen

miles and camp again at "The Platte"   We heard here
another report of Indian troubles at Pawnee Springs, eighteen
miles in advance. A small mule train with several hundred
head of mules, and horses, were in camp while two men and a
boy were guarding the stock while grazing. A short distance
away two Indians, one with a gun, the other with a bow and
arrow, rode up to them, making the usual signs of friendship,
the men returning the friendly signs. Then suddenly drew
their arms, shot and killed one man and wounding the other,
and quick as a flash galloped away leaving the boy shooting at
them   As soon as it became dark a horde of them came back,
stampeded and captured the entire herd of stock valued at
$2,000

It's much faster and pleasanter to travel in small trains
especially with herds of livestock but men take desperate
chances in doing so

May 26th   The news of the trouble last night had created
much fear and anxiety in camp but go we must Indians
storms sickness or any other excuse, and we must camp at
Pawnee Springs at night.   there was no alternative for that
either. As we came in sight of the place, everybody was
looking and listening for Indians, but none came, but
doubtless they were watching every move of our train while
in some hiding place. But a white man was there with
whiskey furs and other articles, claiming to be trading with
the Indians   He was strongly suspicioned as having a part
in the depradations, and put under guard   There were but
few slept in camp that night — all were on guard, and armed
to the teeth, and none were guarded and watched closer
than the lawless, renegade white man, and he knew it too.

May 27th   Left Pawnee Springs early this morning after
looking by the road side at the grave of the murdered
man   it was marked thus "J. N. Manning killed by Indians

at this place May 24, 1864, from Pike County, Missouri"
Notices of this kind were more especially to warn following
trains to be on the lookout and such is the superstition
among Indians that a grave is never molested   In the after
noon saw great alkali beds of snowy whiteness, another
apparent danger to be guarded   Cattle seem to like alkali
water which if taken in large draughts kill them. Also the
first jack rabbit was seen, but not captured   They have a
habit of running and jumping in a circuitous path that
puzzles both dogs and gunners at first

May 28th   To day, overtook a train in which was the
wounded man of the fated mule train at Pawnee Springs. He
was recovering   No Indians to be seen   Camp on the river
again. This being a beautiful May sunset, we, after the usual
camp work, sit on the river bank and pen a few notes

May 29th   Our course to day was over sandy ridges
Leaving the river for a time, and camp at a place where a
temporary well had been diged by former trains. Two other
trains were here in camp   One was that led by Mr E. Smith
of Mt Pleasant Iowa which we had been eager to overtake
Mr Smith had crossed the plains over this route a number of
times. Was quite familiar with the country the different
tribes of Indians, and their habits and haunts, and with his
family, was now enroute with a well protected train, to the
Idaho mines. Our train, small since the division was joined
to his under his leadership, which was much enjoyed by us,
now travelling through the Sioux Indian country, and
depradations being frequent both before and behind us

May 30   Our large train moved out early going over heavy
road all day. Sand from two to four inches deep. In the
afternoon we saw the first Sioux Indians, but they doubtless
had been watching us for some time. Later on we came to one
of their villages or wigwams made of buffalo skins. A more

hideous, half naked lot of men women, and children we had
not seen while herds of ponies and half fed dogs increased the
unsightly scene. Some of us prepared to pass by as quietly
and quickly as possible, but they as usual began to show signs
of friendship, which our captain said must be recognized by
us.

May 31st   The roads to day were very hard. Indians
following us at intervals all day, begging and offering skins
moccasins and beads for fishhooks ammunition and provisions. Camp early, and every preparation possible for our
safety, fearing an attack from the Indians nightly   All the
stock was kept well rounded up and guarded, while grazing.
A large firm corrall made of wagons, and every head of cattle
placed inside before dark   Horses and mules securely staked
on the outside. The whole well guarded with armed
men   We had ninety men in our train now and an equal
number of women and children   Soon after dark before
many had retired, there was a general stampede of all
stock   The cattle inside plunged and bellowed upsetting
wagons scattering the guards and were gone in an instant
while the horses on the outside were snorting and pulling on
their ropes, breaking them like pipe stems, and they too,
many of them, were gone. Capt Smith, who always was ready
for an emergency, was soon on his little yellow horse which
was always kept near by his tent at night, galluping around
camp screaming at the top of his voice "put out every light in
camp   all the women and children lie flat down immediately" and "every man on duty with his gun"   "enough
remain to guard the camp   the others go after the stock"
Then such bellowing on short notice. Some of us had never
known   The bells on fast retreating cattle, the neighing and
hallooing of horses, the yelling and swearing of men, the
crying of women and children, the Captain screaming for

quiet, then added to this a rain was approaching and very
dark which was a fitting time for an Indian attack. All this
and much more made it lively for awhile. But soon the stock
was overtaken and rounded up and broght back and well
watched for the night, every man sleeping with his gun. Our
Capt thought that an Indian had crawled near the camp in
the darkness, and frightened some of the stock effecting a
stampede, hoping to get them so far away in the darkness to
be driven of by a band of Indians in waiting near by, but feared
the pursuit of so many men.

June 1st   Notwithstanding the scare and excitement of the
previous night all were aroused at early dawn to begin the
usual preparation for another day   Our horses and cattle
sent out to feed, scattered ropes, chains ox bows, tent poles
and wagon covers &c were put to right as far as possible.
Meanwhile a hastily prepared breakfast was gotten, the
guards called in with the stock and soon we were in motion
again, with a stiff cold wind and rain confronting us. All day
long we climed sand hills, and deep sand plains, and went
into camp at 3 oclock, P M cold, wet, hungry and tired, at a
barren place where the only apology for wood was green
willow brush, and wet buffaloe chips   Think of it with a
company of men women and children in such a plight. A few
of us had some of the poles that had been lashed to our wagon
beds, for emergencies, and, feeling that the time had evidently
come, they were brought forth but like the few loaves and
fishes in the wilderness "that were among so many"   Capt
Smith ordered a spare ox yoke from one of his wagons cut up
in kindling. A man looking on said "Capt its too bad to burn
the yoke"   Yes said the Capt "but its still worse for us to
have no supper   Split it up Jim"

June 2nd   A cold rainy & cheerless morning dawns upon us
without wood, so we were ordered to remain in camp until

noon, while some hunted for game and others for a few dry sticks of willow brush to dry us off and cook our dinner, both were quite lucky   a number of jack rabbits and a still greater number of dry sticks, to cook the rabbits.

June 3d   Once more a cloudless sky. How we did enjoy the sunshine. The low range of the Rockies are visible.

June 4th   After travelling for several days over heavy roads through sand hills and plains we reach the river again and go into camp. Here we saw a newly made grave marked "Willie Shaw, killed by accident May 3d 1864"

June 5th   To day we came in sight of Court House and Chimney Rocks, but our guides tell us that they are twenty miles distant.

June 6th   The cold northwesternly winds that sweep through the distant mountain gorges, increasing in its velocity as it is driven over the vast plains of the Platte river were something we inlanders could not comprehend on a bright June morning   During the day we came up to more Indian wigwams. The Indians came out to our trains manifesting signs of peace. Of course they are always pleading for peace, when they are not committing depredations. There were a number of "Squaw men" here or more definitely speaking white men who were living with squaw wives; men who have escaped from justice in some form.   many have run away from home because of the war and have taken refuge among these hostile savages. These men are a great menace to the emmigrant trains, since it is doubtless true that they plot and plan the most of the terrible massacres committed by the Indians, while they hide among the women and children. Not many of them would escape the guns of our men if they could only get at them.[9] We got into camp at

_____
[9] Sometimes "Indian" massacres were really carried out by white men.

night on the river opposite the Chimney and Court House
rocks. They are of a soft sandstone standing out alone among
the low barren sand hills on the south side of the Platte.
Chimney rock is about one hundred and fifty feet high, large
at the base, then gradually forming a spiral shape very much
resembling the spire of a large church. The other is much
larger at the base, and is cone shaped, which gives it its name
"Court House Rock". They seemed so near us, that two of
our boys went over the river and started for the rocks, but
darkness over took [them] before they made half the distance
so returned to camp. Travellers tell us that the winter winds,
and summer storms are gradually washing them down.

June 7th   To day we past the surveyed line between
Nebraska and Idaho territories,[10] having been two months
crossing Nebraska. Camp to night in the land of gold yet the
mining district, for which some of our party are destined is
far in advance. The place is "Rawhide creek"[11] where is an
Indian Agency, Ft Laramie being not far from here. We
were annoyed very much with the Indians following us,
holding out moccasins, beads and dressed skins, to give for
provisions, ammunition, fish hooks and old clothing.

June 7th   We were told that Fort Laramie was not far
distant which knowledge made us eager to get an early start
as we all expected to get letters from home, and news from
the seat of war, but after pulling through heavy sandy roads
all day, were sent into camp at night still ten miles from the
Fort.

---

[10]Present Wyoming was part of Idaho Territory from March 3, 1863, to May 1864.
Word had not got to the travelers before this date, June 7, in Mrs. Loughary's diary.
C.J. Brosnan, *History of Idaho* (N.Y., 1948), pp. 181-3.

[11]Rawhide Creek (Goshen Co.) had been a center of fur trade activity. There is a legend
that it got its name because a man traveling west had vowed he would shoot the first
Indian he saw. This turned out to be a young woman, and he shot her. Her people
captured the man and skinned him alive, so the name "Rawhide." Mae Urbanek,
Wyoming Place Names (Missoula, MT, 1988), pp. 163-4.

June 8th   This morning all was bustle and hurry. We
wanted to get to the Fort. Our eyes were strained to see it if
possible to see some marks of civilization, and still more to
get news. At 11 oclock we arrived. As soon as possible a great
many men hastened to the fort   It also is on the other side of
the river. The stars and stripes were proudly floating over it.
At the sight of which brought forth cheer after cheer from
the throats of hundreds of lusty men, women and children,
who all know and feel what true patriotism means. A small
flag had been tucked away in our wagon, which was
immediately brought forth, fastened to a willow rod, and tied
to our wagon bow, which soon attracted the attention of the
train and then another burst of cheering rang out. At this
point some of the men returned with letters from loved ones
at home, which filled our already glad hearts with joy. The
news that filled us to overflow was the great Union victories
by Gen Grant's Army. At night we proposed a ratification
out in the wilderness. We could not have any fire works, but
by a united effort we got together enough willow and sage
brush to make a camp fire, around which all gathered to have
a good time and to give vent to our patriotism. An old
battered violin and a wheezy accordian was brought out to
give tone to the occasion. We sang with hearty good will
"The star spangled banner" "The red white and blue"
"Hang Jeff Davis in a sour apple tree" and every war song
that we knew. At the close of each such shouts of patriotism
rent the air of the quiet evening were never heard. There are
a number of rebels in our train who joined it for protection,
that did not enjoy our ratification of Union victories, but
they skulked off in silence and went to bed

June 9th   This morning one of our rebel travellers came to
our wagon where the little flag was still floating and said "I
think you orter take that thing down"   Said I "What

thing" "That flag" said he "you might get into trouble if you dont." "*You* might get into trouble if we do." This is American soil and that flag would float over us here as elsewhere" said I By this time a number of men came to the rescue and but for the timely advice of our cool Capt, there would have been rebel blood shed in the sands of the Platte and his body thrown into the river

June 10th Leaving the Fort and all other marks of civilization except the one road track we again moved on finding after starting that we had made quite a serious mistake in not crossing the river at Laramie, and recrossing again at the upper Platte Bridge, thereby missing to a great extent of the Black Hills. Owing to such fearfull roads over the Black Hills, we made a short days drive and camped at a spring. It was soon learned that one man had been killed and two others wounded by Indians two nights before. This made the place a little uninviting, but there was no choice we must stop at a good watering place. Our cool headed captain soon had all necessary arrangements for safety made, so all suppered, slept, having some faith in the saying that lightning never strikes the second time in the same place.

June 11th We begin climbing the Black Hills this morning in good earnest. all day long witness to us the most novel and picturesque scene that it had ever been our pleasure to witness, climbing around and up steep mountains and huge black projecting rocks, with here and there a scrubby pine growing in a crevice of a rock and occasionally a beautiful flower "wasting its sweetness on the desert air" Up and up we wind and turn until a high point is reached and then go down again. Such was the danger of being hurled into some dark canon on either side, or driven forward into another team that two, and often three wheels of each wagon was securely locked with strong ox chains. After reaching the level we could only rest awhile since no water or grass was there. So the poor tired animals were goaded and whiped on until night and then only a few green weeds and no wood.

June 11th   We were called up and ordered to move out before breakfast hoping to find water and grass for our hungry stock. At 8 oclock reach a camping place where grass and water was found, but the first object that met our eyes was a newly made grave by the roadside with the following notice written on a slip of paper and tacked on [a] piece of bark at the head of the grave. "Killed by Indians last night, beware"   His faithful dog which had not been captured was watching the grave and could not be induced to leave with food or coaxing. As gruesome as the place appeared we must stop long enough to get feed for our stock and breakfast for ourselves. In about two hours Capt Smith ordered the train to move. We soon came to Alder Springs where a small train was resting   There we got the particulars of the murdered man. Two men with one four mule wagon, going out to the Idaho mines loaded with provisions and mining outfit, decided to stop at that point instead of going on the Alder Springs with their train. While they were preparing supper and the mules were grazing near by a party of Indians on horseback swooped down upon them shooting one and with arrows killing and wounding the other, then driving off the mules   Thinking that both men were dead they returned later and pillaged the wagon carrying off all valuable articles $800.00 in gold and $600.00 in Greenbacks. The wounded man crawled in a hiding place until a party returned, fearing something had happened, buried the dead and carried the wounded into Alder Springs. Doubtless a white man had planned it as the Indians would not know that Greenbacks were valuable

June 12th Sunday.   A day we have not rested for a month

and must not now owing [to] the scarcity of wood and grass and fear of Indians. One more days travel we were told, would get us out of the Black hills. At night reached the Platte river once more. During the night a terrible thunder and rain and hail storm came up, almost deluging us, but we are becoming educated to almost any disaster now.

13th   Clear and cold since the hail storm. Pass "dry creek" and wind around steep and craggy points forming a complete circle

June 14th   Again we are ordered to move at the first peep of day without breakfast. We could go hungry with little effort, but our hungry and tired stock *must* not if possible. After six miles of heavy travelling, find grass and water.

June 15th   Our road to day was through a sandy barren country with a few sage and grease wood bushes growing, but where cactus is wedged in everywhere. It was with difficulty that we found enough space to spread our noon lunch. We have met swollen streams broken bridges, hail thunder Indians cold hunger and now last but not least, great plains of cactus a terror to man and beast

June 16th   Our road to day is but a repetition of yesterday until noon we reached a cotton wood grove. We rested in its shade and listened once more to the sweet songs of birds. But we must leave this beautiful oasis behind as readily as so many unpleasant scenes. The heavy roads with but little grass are plainly telling on our stock. A mule from one of our company teams dropped dead in its harness, so a general halt is ordered until another animal from the drove can be put into service. A party of guardsmen drove the whole band of stock two miles and found grass

June 17.   We are now nearing the Missouri river pass, and therefore the country is more fertile. Instead of such barren hills and sandy plains, have some cotton wood groves and green vegetation generally. In the afternoon reached lower bridge of the north Platte   The stream is swifter narrower as we approach the mountains where is its fountain head. Here is the junction of our road and the "Bannock cut off", the latter leading to the new Idaho gold mines. There was here a large number of teams in waiting for a larger company. The route is a new one, and said to be a very perilous one. It was only a blazed trail through the mountains which only the most daring gold seekers would dare take. After bidding good bye to a number of our company, which had joined the Bannock route party, we moved on up the river

June 18th   We rested until noon, and then pushed on to the upper bridge of the North Platte, yet not crossing any of them, our route all the time on the north side. Here is a Soldiers Station, also a supply store under the protection of the Garrison. Our Capt. very generously ordered a halt of sufficient time for all the company to visit the barracks, cemetery and store. Any thing along the line of civilization was a treat to us and was equally enjoyed by the pent-up men in the garrison. There was also nearby an old Indian cemetary which the more curious ones of our comapny visited. It was of a certain tribe that never bury their dead in the ground, but elevate them, with all their affects in trees or tall poles placed securely in the ground. In the afternoon, saw for the first time snow covered peaks in the distance with clouds dropped at half mast; this to persons who were born and raised in the Mississippi valley where no mountains exist was a rare sight, and yet numbers of our party never saw it.

June 19th (Sunday)   Which is only in name since we had not rested on the Sabbath for over a month. To day we bid adieu to the old Platte river. Along its banks we had travelled, rested, camped ate and slept for two months. Now to go in a northernly direction, coming to another junction of a road

known as "Bridgers cut off," another short cut to the gold
fields. At sunset reach "Willow Springs" having travelled 23
[28?] miles without water for our stock. In places of scarcity
of water we always carried water in casks and demijohns for
our selves.

June 20th   During the night a number of our mules strayed
off, which detained us until a late hour. While waiting, we
found some gooseberries on scrubby bushes growing around
the spring branch which were an unusual treat, when added
to our daily bill of fare, — bacon and beans. We pass
Prospect hill, supposed to have been prospected for gold.
Nooned at a clear creek when we saw our first Antelope. So
excited were our boys that they dropped their lunch, hungry
as they always were, and made for the Antelopes, but they
were soon out of sight. At night found the water strongly
impregnated with Alkali, but were compeled to use it.

June 21st   As a result of the Alkali, found one of our best
oxen dead, from drinking too much of this water. One of our
faithful milch cows was speedily conscripted and forced into
service. We could do without milk, but the teams must go.
The Rocky Mountains, which for days past have looked like
a heavy black storm cloud stretching along the western
horizon, have now materialized into mountains, rocks, and
snow clad peaks. Yet, with our slow pace of travel, will not be
reached for some days.

June 22nd   Camp in a low sandy basin where evaporated
Alkali looks like great snow beds, and can only wish they
were as harmless. Our stock must be kept in close watch all
the time lest they drink too much of the water. Early in the
day we reached "Sweet Water" river, called such by its water
being impregnated with Alkali giving it a sweet brackish
taste. Here we found another Soldiers station, only eighteen
men, under command of Capt Kernan [Shuman?]   A

telegraph station was also here, where we once more got in communication with civilization. Learned the late war news, — more decided Union victories, which was most cheering news to us. Saw here the wounded man, who had so narrowly escaped from the Indians near Alder Springs. Our next point was the celebrated "Independence Rock", which stands out independent and bold in a lovely little valley of the "Sweet Water." It is of solid granite, oblong at the base, its highest peak being 150 feet while it covers two acres of ground. It seems to have been thrown together in all manner of shapes, peaks, table rocks, crevices and basins where snarly evergreens seem to be growing in solid masonry. Nature has provided steps which are worn smooth by the hundreds of emmigrants that have climbed it. Hundreds of names and dates have been chiselled into the rocks, many of which are almost illegible by the rough hand of time. After two hours spent in exploring the massive rock we moved on four miles farther to Devils Gate where we were permitted by our Captain to remain until morning, and view the great work of nature The Devils Gate is formed by the rapid current of the Sweet Water, rushing through a narrow passage of solid rock 400 feet high then plunging into a basin forming numerous cascades, one half mile in length. The projecting rock at the top of the falls are so close and the passage narrow as to almost reach the opposite side by a single leap. Our first adventure was to scale the rocky summit of the gate way. We climbed up up over rough rocks and smoothe ones, some so steep and smooth that for safety we took off our shoes, finally reaching the summit we peeped over as best we could into the dark, deep abyss of dashing, foaming cataract below. Then returning we next started up the narrow path along the river bank until we reached the gate or cavern. The darkness, the dampness, and the danger of being precipitated into some chasm made it a gloomy place, then looking up 400 feet through the small passage light penetrated, we saw beautiful vines, flowers and mosses clinging to the rocks. We sat down and rested and sang "The battle cry of freedom" while our united voices echoed and re-echoed through the cavern. It was a sublime scene which made us exclaim "How wonderful are Thy works Oh Lord" and yet surround with enough darkness and danger to suggest the name of "Devil".

June 23d   After a day of sight-seeing, and a night of rest, we were in good plight to resume our journey towards the setting sun. All along our road to day, we see the carcasses of cattle and horses that have been poisoned by drinking Alkali water.

June 24th   A thunder storm gathered and threatened to swoop down upon us but we were fortunate in escaping it. Camped at night at the base of the mountains. The "Wind river" range are white with snow and of course quite cold at night and morning, but our camp life is such a busy one that we have no time to consider the weather. Since leaving the Bannock road, where our hired man left us for the gold region, my work has been greatly increased. In addition to preparing food and beds for eight in family, I am compelled to harness and drive a four horse team[12] while my husband and our thirteen year old son looked after feed and water and loose stock. My husband yoked and drove the ox team and with the aid of the small children got the wood, water and all manner of camp work. Every horse was unharnessed, and every ox unyoked at noon to give jaded animals rest, as well as food. This order must be implicitely obeyed, since to lose one animal affected the whole train as no one could be left behind. Camp at night where we for the first time found "bunch

---

[12]This shows that they were using both oxen and horses with their wagons. They had to travel at the speed of oxen, about 3 m.p.h. Horses could travel faster, probably 5 m.p.h. Merrill J. Mattes admires her grit in driving a four-horse team. *Platte River Road Narratives* (Urbana, IL, 1988), p. 581.

grass," a very rich grass very much like our timothy grass

June 25th   We start out climbing rugged hills, and then deep winding gorges along the course of the Sweet Water. At 3 o'clock we went into camp at a lone bachelors ranch and black smith shop, where many breaks and bents in our train were mended

June 26th   Sunday. Lay over to rest the teams while the men recreated by hunting fishing and repairing generally. A number of us had a miniature Sunday School in our tent, closing it by singing "Rest for the weary." During the day our quiet was disturbed by the sudden screams of the children who were playing near the river side. Our little five year old daughter Mattie fell over a steep bank into the river and but for the timely aid of her older sister who plunged in after her and the screams for help, both would have drowned

June 27th   This morning left Sweet Water going over a very rocky road bed five miles and camp at Soap Suds. Nearby is a mining camp, men prospecting for gold. We found here J. D. Jones, once a neighbor in Iowa, who asked us to stop and look over the gold mines. Our obliging Capt ordered a halt, and as few of us had ever seen gold except in coins, we were glad of the opportunity. Soon all with spades, dishpans, buckets, butcher knives, and wash pans started for the gold, but after some hours of useless toil returned without sight of gold

June 28   Raining and sleeting as we pulled up camp   At noon reach another solders station. When we leave our road and take "Landers Cutoff,"[13] going northward. Camp at

---

[13]This was a short cut surveyed and graded by Col. Frederick West Lander in 1857. See Volume VII of this series, p. 282, for another reference. The best study of the survey of western roads is W. Turrentine Jackson, *Wagon Roads West* (Berkeley, 1953). The best treatments of the Lander cutoff is Peter T. Harstad's "The Lander Trail," in *Idaho Yesterdays*, Fall 1968, Vol. 12, no. 3, pp. 14-28. Lander, Wyoming, is named for this military engineer. Harstad says of the trail that it "spans the plateau south of the Wind River Range, winds its way to the heights of a three-way continental divide, fords swift mountain streams, passes through mountain meadows and tight canyons, and finally rolls out onto the Snake River Plain." p. 16.

night on a small creek where were two small trains that had been so reduced in numbers, by their members going to that gold mine by the Bannock road, that they feared to go farther until others came up, so gladly joined our train. We have climbed the mountains for about eight hundred miles, yet so gradual has been our ascent that we cannot perceive it. Are now nearing the summit. We look southward and see Freemonts Peak. Named for Gen Freemont who explored it. It is 11,000 feet above the sea level, and portions of it always covered with snow.

June 29   Thermometer below freezing point. Eighteen miles and camp at the head water of Sweet Water where we found good supplies of water, wood and buffaloe grass, and an abundance of wood for our camp fire once more. It is no small disappointment when we were deprived of these   when all gathered around our cheerfull bonfire after the days work was done, to rehearse the adventures of the day, mended the numerous rents, washed the childrens faces, dress and tie up the many wounds and bruises and oiled the alkalied faces, hands and toes, while bread, bacon and beans were cooking for the next days travel. To day we crossed the summit of the Rocky Mountains, the dividing lines that nature by her great upheavals has made to divide the the Atlantic and Pacific Oceans. The water is running westward and the altitude so high that we can scarcely fill our lungs. Game is seen here, so we go into camp early when a number go out hunting, returning with one deer, some rabbits and sage hens

June 30   After travelling fifteen miles reach the south fork of Green river, which is a very swift stream with no bridge and on a tare. The snow melting in the mountain causes a rise during the day and lower early in the morning. Here we stop to explore the crossing, its depth, and to make all preparations to ford the river early the next morning.

July 1st   Wagon beds all blocked up nearly to the top of the standards with the beds firmly tied with strong ropes and chains to the axles, one by one was led down the steep bank and plunged in, a guide on a trusty horse going before. At times the water splashed on us and over us, but again we were above, until the opposite shore was reached. After all wagons were crossed, the loose stock was forced in. They plunged, waded, and swam until all got over in safety about noon.

July 2nd   After going eight miles, reached the north fork, where the same process of crossing was begun. It was quite dark before all got over and into camp. Wood being very scarce, we went to bed tired and supperless.

July 3d   We left the Green River valley and began the climbing of mountains again   Late at night before a camping place was announced, which proved to be a lovely little valley along a rocky creek, where good grass, wood and water were abundant. Here we were told was the place where we were to lay over and celebrate Our Nations Anniversary in as becoming a manner as possible. Our patriotism was up to white heat. All we needed was just a little time to give it vent. During the night a son was born to a daughter of our Captain, which event gave additional interest to our fourth of July celebration.

July 4th   This morning was a lovely one, which we hailed with joy notwithstanding we were cuddled down in a lone valley, far from home and all great national festivals. Yet some recognition of a patriotic nature must be observed. The few stars and stripes were raised on top of our tents, a line of men drawn up, and a salute fired from a hundred little guns and pistols. Three cheers were lustily given for "Our Country," "The Soldiers in the field" and last though not least "The Captains new Grand baby"   After an extra dinner made of the same kind of provisions, baked beans, & soup, instead of half cooked ones, and some warm bread instead of burned hoe cake, was our bill of fare. All had a "go as you please time" Some hunted or fished, others lounged around camp, while the children had a picnic under the bows of a large pine tree. Two more trains came up today and camp with us greatly enjoying our celebration.

July 5th Still in camp A hunting party goes out and also a fishing party The streams seem to abound in trout but few have fishing tackle, and fewer know how to fish for trout. The hunters hope to kill a bear, but they are as ignorant of bear killing as the fishers are of trout hooking. So both parties return emty handed.

July 6th After due consideration, our company reorganizes a portion of our teams unite with the two trains that joined us here, and others with Capt Smith who remained behind a few days, being satisfied that we had past the most of the hostile tribes of Indians. As now under the leadership of Capt Spearman we started out.

July 7 We traveled through a narrow deep rock bound canon about fifteen miles and opened up at the base of the "Bear river mountains". One mans wagon was brokeen coming through the canon so we had to wait until repairs were made. Are camping to night at an old demolished adobe Fort.[14] Also an old burying place, which some of us busied ourselves looking over while the wagon was being repaired

July 8th We began the climbing of the Bear river mountains No longer the dull, sameness of barren hills and sandy plains, but mountains and canons & trees of eternal greenness are spread out to our view. We wind around great rocky towering mountain sides until a summit is reached, and then gaze through the tall tree tops into the precipitous caverns below, then twist around another steep mountain,

---

[14]We are at a loss to identify by name this old fort. One must remember that we are in rendezvous country, where rough hewn forts were to be found everywhere.

and reach another higher summit, and then look out at another of natures panoramas of evergreen mountains, and dark chasms. We listen to the sound of deep down waterfalls, where the suns rays have never pierced, nor the foot prints of men never have been made. On the top of one of these mountains we saw a small band of Indians, but they were evidently afraid of us, as they bounded of from us like deer

July 9th   Early to day got down into a beautifull fertile valley beside a clear cold stream of water where an abundance of grass, wild strawberries currants and blooming flowers and strange to say the ice froze one half inch thick at night. We were delighted to stop for awhile in such a delightful place as this but all too soon we heard the order "get into line"   After going eight miles, reach "Independence valley" on the same stream and from thence to Big Meadow and camp   This large and fertile meadow is twenty miles long, and five wide. Grass grows in abundance and the stream is full of fish

July 10th Sunday   remain all day at this beautifull place to rest our stock and ourselves   The lovely place made it a real Sabbath.

July 11th   To day we go into another twenty miles of canon   soon reach Salt Springs. There are acres of beautifull white pure evaporated salt beds from an inch to one foot deep. The lake is brackish and distastfull because of its saltiness. Saw here a number of Indians, but they were apparently afraid of us. We hastened on to get out of this canon before dark. Reached a camp at the western base of the "Bear river mountains."

July 12th   After repairing a broken wagon, Started out shivering with cold. Reach Big Lake and camp   This is low marshy valley all covered with water, willows and dark swamp grass. Wild geese and ducks were very abundant but having neither men or dogs that knew how to get them we got none. Our boys spied the tracks of bear, but like the ducks and the geese there was no bear captured. At night we reach a beautiful mountain stream and camp about dark. A man and his wife and three children in a wagon came rushing into our camp in an exhausted and badly frightened condition. It proved to be J. D. P. Hungate[15] a baptist missionary having been sent out by the American Mission board to labor in Oregon   He having in some way become dissatisfied with his train and learning that our train was about ten miles ahead, pulled out and drove all day alone. He had seen Indians following him as he supposed, which gave him a fearfull scare   He said he believed however, that the Lord brought him through all right, but as I looked at his crying wife and children his steaming and jaded horses and a large whip in his hands, I doubted if the Lord had much to do in that case. Afterwards he did not trust in the Lord to take him through the Bear River Mountains.

July 13th   We only travelled a short distance when we reached a small stream literaly alive with fish. We stopped and made a seine of blankets and old sacks which the boys dragged catching bushels of fish. Hurried on to Blackfoot where we dressed our fish and lunched and then on six and eat them. Our camping place is old Fort Brid[g]er,[16] used

---

[15]The Rev. James D.P. Hungate, a native of Indiana, had graduated from Franklin College, Franklin, Ind., in 1854. Now he was on his way to Oregon, having been sent out by the American Baptist Missionary Society. In Oregon he stayed for only three years, with short pastorates in Forest Grove, West Union and Salem. In 1867 he moved to Petaluma, California. He spend the rest of his life in that state. C.H. Mattoon, *Baptist Annals of Oregon*, I (McMinnville, OR, 1905), p. 175.

[16]This was not the Fort Bridger farther south on the Oregon Trail, but one Jim Bridger had built in 1841 on the Green River between the mouths of the Big Sandy and Black's Fork. For a discussion of the famous trapper's four forts and a map of their localities, see *Fort Bridger, Island in the Wilderness* by Fred R. Gowans and Eugene E. Campbell (Provo, UT, 1975), pp. 2 and 10.

only as a trading post   Two men have a small ranch where we get a small supply of vegetables

July 14th   Good roads. Going through another long canion. Find abundance of currents to day but our sugar is growing short so we can use but few currents. Travel ten miles through a sandy waste and reach Snake river and camp.

July 15   Go down the river two miles to the ferry. More traders cabins, and Indian wig wams, all together. We sold them flour for $3.00 per hundred, and paid for ferriage $3.00 per each wagon and eight cents per head for all stock including the oxen and horses attached to wagons. Leaving only one yoke to a wagon, the others with the loose stock were swimed across in safety. Our road led us down the river a mile to Fort Hall, where we remained for a few days, resting our teams before we cross the desert and make some changes. Part of our company go to California, and other places, leaving only three families to go on to Oregon. We here sold one wagon and all of our cattle and some more flour. After making all preparations for crossing the the thirty three miles of desert which is much lessoned by taking Landers cutoff

July 17th.   We move on, where soon we came to a parched sandy waste where not a sign of animal or vegetable life is seen, only rocks and sand. Our eyes soon began to pain where was nothing to rest upon but bleaching sand. We stoped at noon, gave our horses a small bit of corn meal and about one gallon each of water carried from the Fort in a gallon keg. We had been directed to go to a certain large Butte which became visible in the after noon. At its base was a large spring. On and on we slowly went but the butte seemed to get but little nearer, yet we *must* reach it or suffer. At twilight we got to the butte, and to find the spring with thick darkness coming on was the first consideration. After groping about we discovered a trail leading up to the side into a ravine where we supposed was the spring   My husband mounted a trusty horse, well armed started. After going about one half mile, saw a campfire around which he could see some men and horses. He came back and took every man (five) and all the horses and started out again finding the men to be white and seemingly very accommodating. The horses had water and some brought back in demijohns for us but we were too much frightened to stop to cook, believing that the men seen were "land pirates" aiding the Indians, so we went a short distance and found some dry grass for our horses, made no fire or light, crouched in our wagons and watched all night by turns. Our good horses were all taken back this morning for water before starting out on another hard day's travel. We go in the direction, and soon reach Lost river, which rises and sinks because of its running through a volcanic region where great piles of molton rock and black sand have intercepted the river bed, turning it hither and thither and often causing the absence of any river at all. No vegetation was visible except an occasional parched up bunch of sage brush. An occasional lizard could be seen darting into a hole of a rock as we approached. The whole scene could only remind one of the black valley of death. We were compelled to remain at night in this uninviting place where a few sprigs of dry grass were gathered and water from a pond among the rocks was found

July 19   We were glad to leave this place of barrenness as soon as we could see to travel. The road bed is only known by the rocks and lava being crushed by the many teams passing over it. Another twenty five miles of this road is before us, so all day long we slowly creep along lacerating our horses feet and threatening wheels, axles or some portion of our outfit. All along were pieces of broken wagons which had met with such accidents. At sundown we reach water on a mountain side dripping down from the constant melting of snow on the mountains at this season of the year.

July 20.   At day break this morning, a large train came into camp, having travelled all night in search of water and grass for their almost famished stock. This proved to be far the hardest part of our travel, and yet we *must* go [on] or perish by the road side   Every man, woman and child must walk in order to lessen the weight on our axletree to prevent breaking. We finally reach water, grass, rest and sleep.

July 21   Once more on good roads and plenty of grass and water   Our boys killed a number of sage hens. Met four suspicious looking men with a drove of horses. They were not at all communicative and seemed to be in a great hurry.

July 22.   This morning four other men came up in hot pursuit of the men and horses met yesterday, who on inquiry had stolen the horses at South Boise and were driving them into the distant mountains where Indians, or worse, white men, would keep them in hiding until it was safe to dispose of them. We had heard of these horse thieves, was why we were so alarmed at Big Butte. We are now entering Camas Pararie, a large and fertile valley rich in bunch grass. We camp at night. Large droves of Indian ponies are grazing in this valley, herded by bands of peaceable Indians, yet we watch them. We have found that all the harmless Indians so far are the dead ones. The wolves on the neighboring hills make the night hideous with their howls, but like the Indians are peaceable because they have to be.

July 23   Still passing through Camas prarie

July 24 Sunday   lay by part of the day   A number of wagons with families are here also resting   Rev. Hungate preached while all sat down on the grassy banks of the stream and sang from memory some familiar gospel songs   In the afternoon we, with two other wagons bound for Oregon started out. It is now safe to travel in small companies and much more speedy. We however made only a short drive to Quaking Asp Grove and camped   During the night a thunder storm strikes but after so many days of drought through Alakli beds, salt beds, and black sand and lava dust, it was really enjoyed by both man and beast.

July 25   A number of Indians came to our camp this morning while we were preparing breakfast, seeming very friendly, but they are so treacherous as to demand constant watching, while some of them were begging around the campfires with pretended innocence, others were trying to capture some of [the] horses staked out to feed, not seeing the guard, who yelled out at them causing them to run off. We had been instructed all along not to kill or harm an Indian if it were not necessary. Yet one of our party did one day when out hunting kill one, covering him up with grass and leaves. It caused us much uneasiness for several days, and a man a *Severe* reprimanding. Reach to day Little Camas, where are some Indians and half civilized white men ranching

July 26   Again climbing mountains. Meet to day a large pack train carrying into the mines all manner of camping outfit and general merchandize   Twenty five mules & small horses are packed with the goods. One mule following another in single file a   before and one behind forms a pack train   So many camp at the same places now that we are compelled to take our stock some distance from camp to get good grass. They are securely picked [picketed?] with long ropes, attached to iron rods driven into the ground, and well guarded all night. This affords an opportunity some times for Indians or white men to get them —   Last night while my husband and men were on guard duty about midnight he saw in the semidarkness a man creeping up to one of his

horses   He immediately jumped drew his gun would soon
have sent him to the happy hunting[ground] had he not

July 27   Met this morning an expressman carrying mail to
and from Boise City, and the mining districts   He gave us a
copy of a small paper published in Boise City[17]   Reached at
noon Massacre Creek, a beautiful green grove on the banks
of a small stream   It seems that a large emmigrant train was
in camp here a few years since, when in the night the whole
train was massacred, leaving not one to tell the tale. Of
course it was charged on Indians, but investigation proved
that it was done by a band of so called "destroying angels" of
the Mormon Church[18] at Salt Lake not far off in revenge for
the sever persecution of their church and the murder of their
prophet Joe Smith at Nauvo Illinois some years since by a
party of masked men. It is a beautiful place with rippling
water falls and songs of birds, yet such a sense of sadness and
loneliness comes over me while penciling these lines that the
orders to move were welcome words. This afternoon go down
the creek a few miles to the junction of our road and the Salt
Lake road, We going in a northwesternly direction leaving
Salt Lake to the south. Here is a ranch where a number of
emmigrant teams were in camp going to California.

July 28   A hard days tramp has brought us to Squaw Creek.
Other wagons are camping here at a ranch of a Mr Davidson,
once a Methodist minister but is certainly on a leave of
absence. He seems a gentleman however and treated us well,
supplied us with some green vegetables

---

[17]Boise's first newspaper was the *Boise News*. The first issue had come out on Sept.
29, 1863. Annie Laurie Bird, *Boise, the Peace Valley* (Caldwell, ID, 1934), p. 154.

[18]This is a confused reference to the infamous Mountain Meadows Massacre, which
took place, not in Idaho, but in the southwestern corner of Utah in 1857. A party that
attacked a non-Mormon wagon train was made up of a strange mixture of Mormons
and Indians, led by Mormon John Doyle Lee. Some 120 overlanders were killed. A
balanced account of the event is in Leonard J. Arrington and Davis Bitten, *The Mormon
Experience* (New York, 1979), pp. 167-8. A detailed study of the career of Lee is Juanita
Brooks, *John Doyle Lee* (Glendale, CA, 1962).

July 29   Traveled nineteen miles to day, reaching Boise river. It was easily forded, and always muddy owing to the placer mines at its head waters where gold is washed   Here is a rich fertile valley susceptible of cultivation for small grains

July 30.   This morning go into the City which is only a city in name, just a small mining town the people mostly transient keeping all manner of supplies for miners, and the emmigration to Oregon, at very exorbitant prices. Our rolls of "Greenbacks" which had been tucked away for three months because there was nothing to buy, was now brought forth. We however had more flour that we would use, sold it in exchange for gold dust receiving for it $16 hundred   One of our party sold a featherbed for $1.00 per lb.   his wife refused for awhile to give up her feather bed but they must have something to eat and money to pay ferriage, so the feather bed went

July 31   Camped on "Dry creek" last night and would be glad to remain here to day (Sunday) but for lack of grass, and good water must move on. At night reach Payette river, named for a certain tribe of Indians. A beautiful stream and abundance of grass and wood. How we would like to remain a week here to rest, fish, wash, cook, and clean up generally, but must move on in the morning.

Aug 1st   This dates the fifth month since leaving home, and yet we are far from our place of destination. After fording the river we travel down it all day   we are meeting long lines of pack animals, also large covered wagons called "prararie schooners" drawn by six mules or six yokes of oxen to each wagon all laden with provisions and merchandise from The Dalles, Oregon, going to Boise City, and other places.

Aug 2nd   Still going down Payette river   Met to day a circus from Oregon going to the mining towns.

Aug 3d   Warm weather. Are now on a stage line and get
news occasionally. Noon at Snake River, the same stream
that we crossed two weeks ago. It is quite a large tributary of
the Columbia and the eastern boundary line between Oregon
and Idaho. We go down it thirty miles before crossing. Camp
to night at the Ranch of Mr Poindexter, formerly of the
Willamette Valley, Oregon. The place of our partie's
destination. He of course had to "pose" as a question
answerer as one after another came at him by turns. He
however was much more obliging with his answers than he
was with his supplies.

Aug 5th   After passing over one day at Poindexter's we
again move. Going seven miles we reach the ferry. It took all
the fore noon to get our party across, only one wagon at a
time, with one span of horses or one yoke of oxen, for which
we paid $2.00 in gold dust, or $4.00 in Green Backs.   but
with plenty of patience and still plenty of money we finally
crossed. When the ferriman said, "here you are in a land of
rain, grain, and big red apples," yet neither was realized only
in anticipation. We go five miles, leaving at last Snake river
and came to Burnt river, a small stream winding through
mountain gorges and narrow ravines, the latter so narrow as
to only be room for a wagon to pass through. The grass so
scarce that men take all the horses and blankets and go
through narrow paths to a mountain side where is plenty of
grass, and sleep all night in the grass while the horses feed. A
number of miners camp here to night going home from the
mines, loaded with the precious dust.

Aug 6th   This morning we came to a very steep hill where
some men were grading a new road, claiming a Charter right
to demand toll. We doubted the truthfulness of their demand
yet paid $1.00 for each wagon and tumbled down the
hill   At night reach a stage station in a small mining district

where some men are taking gold at the rate of $5.00 daily to the man

Aug 7.   Sunday we travel about twelve miles, and go into camp for the day. Rev Hungate preached at night again at a ranch.

Aug 8th   Weather good. Ranches are being opened all along these little valleys where all kinds of fruit and vegetables are grown by irrigating the soil. Make eighteen miles over a rough country and reach a muddy spring at dark, no grass or wood, except a little green sage brush. The wind was driving great clouds of sand into our eyes, victuals and bed. Our horses tied up until morning and we eating a little hard tack, lay down and waited for day. It seemed that Paul's shipwreck on the Island Melitas was not so bad as this for he had *dry* sticks when he got ashore and they bundles, while we only got green sage brush growing and too dark and stormy to find it. True he found a snake, and we did too.[19]

Aug 9th   This morning all is quiet, sun shining, the sand piled into shapeless heaps, every crack or crevice in rock or road smoothed over. Our wagon wheels were buried almost to the hubs. After a hasty breakfast, dig out our wagons, pack up and hurry on to find some feed for our animals. Twelve miles and a ranch where we met the Harkleroad brothers[20] who went out from our town two years since in search of gold. In the afternoon we pushed on to Wards ranch[21] on the Powder river slough where we rested and grazed our almost starved horses. At night we had a genuine thunder storm,

---

[19]Acts 28: 1-10 tells of the visit of the Apostle Paul to the island of Malta.

[20]Samuel and Henry Harkleroad were cousins not brothers. They were all over the West and really didn't settle down for a long time anywhere. They took part in the California, Colorado, Idaho, and Powder River gold rushes. Fred Lockley, "The Journal Man," interviewed Sam's son, George J. Harkleroad and recorded the story of these Pennsylvania Dutchmen in the *Oregon Journal* of Portland on May 3 and 4, 1937.

[21]Henry and Joseph Ward were brothers living near the Powder River in eastern Oregon. Henry is listed in the 1870 census as a teamster, and Joseph as a miner.

but did not complain since we expect something new and novel all the way through each day

Aug 10   Blue Mountains in sight for first time   The highest peaks are snow clad, and they rise in their majestic whiteness far above the dark green foliage of tree tops covering the surrounding mountains. The scene is grand and picturesque. Our next point reached is Powder river, a small stream as a duck puddle, owing to the mines

Aug 11   At noon we reach the top of the hill over Grand Ronde Valley. As we approach it we view a complete panorama of the beauty and grandeur of natures handiwork. This is a large and fertile valley nestled down at the eastern base of the Blue Mountains. Water from its icy beds in the surrounding mountains comes rippling down into the valley in every direction giving life, beauty and perpetual greenness. Beautiful grass six feet high is being cut and vegetables and small fruits in great abundance. The little town of Lagrande with 200 inhabitants is located in the valley. We leave this place after dinner, climbing a steep hill a mile in length, take the old emmigrant road to Grand Ronde river and camp for the night.

Aug 13   We are now climbing the Blue Mountains, winding around, and climbing up craggy peaks and narrow passes to deep ravines made dark and sunless by the heavy growth of tall cedar, fir and laurels. But beautiful as it seems, we hasten through it for no grass grows in these mountains, and *grass* is the chief commodity in demand every day.

Aug 14   This is too nice a place to leave on a Sabbath morning, but we leave it and travel over the same kind of roads and scenery as yesterday, until we come to a long divide which is covered with huckleberries. All halt and fill our wagons full of the bushes loaded with the best of blue huckleberries   Go on to Lees encampment,[22] a catchpenny ranch out in these mountains, where emmigrants wont have feed for themselves and beasts, no matter at what the price may be   Panthers and wolves made the night hideous with their screaming. To ward them off we kept fires burning all night.

Aug 15   Start at sunrise going down grade all day reaching the Umatilla valley at night. This is a place where is an Indian Agency, and a large reserve set off by the Government for the Umatilla tribe of Indians.

Aug 16   Move out at nine o'clock going down the river all day.

Aug 17   Our next point is to be Birch Creek, but we wander around all the forenoon.   finally to our surprise came back to our last night's camp   After straightening up found the old emmigrant road that we missed in the morning, went eighteen miles to the Umatilla again, as it winds its course to the great Columbia river.

Aug 18   To day we must make another "dry stretch" to Butter Creek, a small valley stream, which at this season of the year is almost dry, but a ranch near by furnishes water for the families. The vegetation badly parched.

Aug 19th   Our route to day has been over high lands of sandy soil. We reached "Well Spring"   The name sounds nice but what a day, burnt up country all around it, nothing to eat or burn except we pay for it at at the ranch

Aug 20   We are told that we must make fourteen miles before reaching water — so over rocks, gravel and sand we plod along all day. Nothing indicates life except an occasional Juniper tree. Where it gets soil or moisture was to us a question. We reach Willow Creek late in the day and camp

---

[22]John Lee is listed in the 1870 federal census of Oregon as living near the little town of Eldorado. He was a miner.

when another heavy wind and sand storm was in evidence.
After a hard day's work, we of course were hungry but to
cook with a fire made of green sage brush with the sand
driving into your eyes, ears and mouth, being mixed in our
dough, meat and coffee was a task that we seldom want
repeated. We finally abandon the fire part and crouch into
our wagons and nibble hard tack. There was a band of
packers who understood this sand storm better than we.
They got their coffee and bacon all right, one held his old hat
over the fire while another an old black coffee pot and a
frying pan partly grease and part sand. After straining the
coffee through an old dish rag, had supper all right

Aug 21   To day reach Rock Creek where we got a fine view
of Mt. Hood, grand old sentinal of the Cascade Mountains
Our guide tells us it is 16000 feet above sea level[23]

Aug 22   Our teams are generally in need of good grass and
rest, so we lay by all day. Indians brought Salmon for sale but
we, having never seen Salmon refused it because of its color,
believing it to be soiled. They tried to tell us in their
language that the fish was good, but we were as ignorant of
their language as of the Salmon

Aug 23   To day travel up Rock Creek, five miles to John
Day river quite a large stream and beautiful valley, all being
taken by ranchers. After noon go up a steep hill three miles
long, or rather up. There we reach the junction of the two
roads leading to the Willamette Valley, one going over the
Cascade mountains through "Barlow Pass" the other to The
Dalles then by boat to Portland.

Aug 24   This morning our party is separated after months
of toil and hardships, dangers and difficulties freely helping
to bear each others burdon, begets a friendship not easily
severed. All of the wagons go over the mountains except our

[23]The altitude of Mt. Hood is 11239 ft.

own. We start alone toward The Dalles, and camp alone at a ranch.

Aug 25th   Start down a long canon three miles and reach the Deschutes river, a rapid mountain stream dashing into the Great Columbia. There is, happily, a new bridge over it   Toll $1.00 in gold or its equivalent in green back. As we had nothing but "equivalents" it took a number of them to get us over. Camp at night near The Dalles, where we lay by to rest and clean up

Aug 26   Mr L goes into town to day to look after fares, boats &c and to meet N. Loughary[24] who is expected to be at the place from Polk County, Oregon

Aug 27   This afternoon go into town. Here is a portage railway to Umatilla Landing.[25] An old fort no longer in need, the navigation buildings, and a few business places, and fewer residences, makes up the town

29   Still in town waiting for transportation

Aug 30th   At 5 A.M. we drive on board a small Columbia river steamer. Our fare to Portland was $40.00 which of course we had to pay in "equivalents" again at the ratio of 40¢ per dollar, being its gold value   We go forty miles and then the railroad portage around the Cascades five miles. Here we looked with wonder and amazement at the mad waters of the greatest of American rivers as they went seething foaming, dashing, and roaring over rocks, playing hide and seek in the deep cuts between great smooth washed boulders, then down over projecting rocks, making beautiful falls and cascades, throwing great white sheets of mist into the air, then down into a great seething cauldron at the bottom when the water soon resumes its placid course toward

---

[24]We have been able to identify a number of Lougharys in early Oregon, but have found not one with the initial "N."

[25]The town now called Umatilla was first known as Umatilla Landing and later Umatilla City. Lewis L. McArthur, *Oregon Geographic Names* (Portland, 1982), p. 751.

the sea. There is a history of these Cascades that we have
learned since our arrival. "An old Indian legend," which
bears too much of the elements of truth to be denied. They
say that "Amcutta" which means a long time back there was
great stone "Tomanowas" which means a bridge across the
"big waters"[26] the waters passing through a deep dark
narrow passage, through which the Indians paddled their
canoes in safety and that the Great Spirit got angry with
them and shook the earth crashing the bridge to pieces
making these six miles of Cascades. Men familiar with the
legend have carefully studied the story and investigated all
the circumstances and the surroundings, think that at some
time the said great volume of water passing through a
subteraneous passage, increasing its passage way until the
rocks and earth above became weaker and some of the many
volcanic eruptions caused the earth to shake down the bridge,
thereby producing the wonderful phenomena of nature   The
scenery all along the Columbia both above and below the
Cascades are said to be the most beautiful of any on the
Continent which cannot be fully described by other than an
artists pen. Great perpendicular smooth rocks rising out of
the water looking like old grim castles partly demolished,
beautiful waterfalls precipitating down craggy mountains
spreading their silvery veils which the suns rays meet,
forming most beautifull mist and rainbows, then dashing on
through wooded ravines studded with green foliage trees of
fir, cedar and laurel where traling vines and mosses and ferns
are in kept in perpetual greenness by the spray. Then on and
on the same varying, beautiful and picturesque scenery is

[26]The *Bridge of the Gods* myth was based on a fictionalized tale written by Frederick
Homer Balch (Chicago, 1890). The stone bridge, according to Indian legend, was
supposed to have spanned the Columbia at the location known as Cascades Falls. Later
Bonneville Dam was built near the site. This long entry in the diary was probably added
later, after Balch's book came out, when Harriet Loughary revised her original diary.

spread out before you. In the after noon we board a lower cascade steamer and soon touch at Fort Vancouver on the north bank of the river   This is the second oldest place on the coast, Astoria at the mouth of the river named for John Jacob Astor, the oldest. Vancouver is named for an English man of this name, one of the earliest explorers of the North Pacific Coast. Mentioned by Lewis and Clark, the American explorers sent out by the Government in 1804. There is a full force of U. S. Soldiers kept here, with well fortified barracks. Nature has done nobly in the Site of this pretty place. A little farther down we reach the Willamette, one of the largest tributaries of the lower Columbia river. We turn into it and go twelve miles and reach Portland. There is but little in this place yet but in anticipation   It is a sea port town and will in the near future be a great commercial city. Now it has a very poor wharf, a few small wooden business houses along the water front, a row of residences and shops with a little wooden hotel on first street   A forest of large fir trees through which the townsite is laid out, where busy hands are felling these great trees, hauling and burning bush, trees and stumps, make up the residue of Portland   It was with some difficulty that we found a smooth place among the stumps and fallen trees to drive our wagon and pitch our tent beyond the limits of front and first streets. We spent all the following day Aug 31st in sight seeing, replenishing our wardrobes and provision chest. The most attractive of objects was the lucious fruits in the market, large apples of all varieties, pears, peaches and plums. We met Mr J Delashmutte[27] a fellow townsman of Burlington, Iowa, now a resident of Polk Co Oregon the place of our terminus. He

---

[27]J. Delashmutte also came from Burlington, Iowa. He, like Harriet Loughary, was a Virginian. He and his wife, Phoebe, (b. Indiana) had been farming in northern Polk Co., Oregon. They are listed in the United States Census of 1860 as the parents of four children born in Iowa and three born in Oregon.

gave us much reliable information   We much regretted that
no Ocean Steamer, or rather vessel, was in port

Sept 1st   Start up the valley, going over a low range of
mountains, and reach Willamette valley proper. Of course it
was not as we had expected to see. Such is never the case. On
both sides of the river are hills, highland, low land, and
valleys, varying in the nature of soil. Yet all productive.
There are streams, brooks, and springs. Along the stream
and lowland grow Ash, Maple, Alder, Dogwood and Hazle,
with a small growth of fir every where. On the hills larger Fir
and Oak. The farther we go, the more extensive are the
valleys. At this season are all heavily laden with their rich
and valuable productions, large fields of golden grain all
being harvested producing from thirty to forty bushels per
acre, and the ready market price was $1.00 per bushel.
Orchards are every where from one hundred to a thousand
trees on a farm, or as they still say "ranch"   The fruit is
very abundant but in a new country like this, little market for
it. Flocks of sheep, herds of cattle and horses, all feeding on
the hills and valleys on grasses, together with the rich and
fertile fields was a scene delightfull and restfull to our eyes.
After five months of weary toil in reaching two thousands of
miles in an ox team, making an average of eighteen miles a
day enduring privations and dangers of Indians, cold hunger
thirst fatigue and loss of sleep, viewing every day barren
plains, sandy deserts rock mountains and peaks, snow clad
and barren turbulent bridgeless streams, storms of wind hail
and sand t'was a rest to look upon something homelike,
something usefull and good. When we think of the earliest
pioneers that did not have so pleasant and comfortable
things to greet them, we feel an untold gratitude towards
them.

A Journal of our Trip, 1864

✺ Lucretia Lawson Epperson

INTRODUCTION

It was on May 2, 1861, that Lucretia Lawson and Brutus Clay Epperson were married in Etna, Coles County, Illinois. They were both Kentuckians, she having been born in Hardin County on November 28, 1840, and he on October 27, 1830, in Estell County. He was a ticket agent for the Illinois Central Railroad.

After the wedding Brutus and Lucretia decided that farming would be more in their interest than working for the railroad. They bought a farm near the little town of Etna with the idea of raising fine horses and mule stock. On March 14, 1862, a baby boy was born to them. They named him Charles and he, as a two-year-old, is mentioned in Lucretia's overland journal as "Charlie."

Brutus Epperson had already been on a journey to California in 1852. He and his brother, C.C., made the trip by sea from New York to San Francisco. They were attracted to the great interior valley of the Sacramento. To the north of the capital, in Butte County, the two brothers settled on a farm near the Marysville Buttes, a dramatic geological feature of the central valley. Brutus returned east by sea in 1859. His idea was to purchase as many fine horses as possible and drive them to California, there to go into the horse, mule and cattle raising business. In early 1864 he and his friend, Henry Reed, traveled to Kentucky and purchased a herd of brood mares and some jacks and jennets.

On April 1, 1864, the Eppersons and Henry Reed began their long journey to the Land of Gold. They reached the brothers' ranch on September 16th.

Lucretia kept a diary, in which she wrote, sometimes

occasionally, sometimes every day on the long journey. What she did not disclose was that she was pregnant the whole way. She did complain that she did not feel well on some days, and at the California end of their journey on the western slope of the Sierra she obtained the services of one Dr. David Gould Webber, who lived on the shores of a lake to which he had given his own name, Webber Lake. She gave birth to their second child, Thurza A., on October 1, 1864. Two more children were born in Sutter County: Mary J., on December 29, 1866, and Bertha Clay on February 15, 1869.

In the autumn of 1868 the Eppersons purchased another farm in western Colusa County, and they moved to that location in 1869. That became the home place. This farm was at the base of the Coast Range of mountains, and in Bear Valley, athwart the easiest route to the beautiful lakes of Lake County to the west. Brutus Epperson was instrumental in establishing the "Bartlett Springs and Bear Valley Toll-Road Company." So, in addition to having a prosperous ranch for his livestock, he had income from the toll-road.

The source for Lucretia Epperson's journal is a grand old book, one of the ego-books of the late 19th century. It was financed by collecting a fee from each of those whose biographies appeared in it's pages: Will S. Green's *Colusa County, California. Illustrations Descriptive of its Scenery, Fine Residences, Public Buildings, Manufactories, Hotels, Farm Scenes, Business Houses, Schools, Churches, Mines, Mills, Etc. From Original Drawings by Artists of the Highest Ability, With Historical Sketch of the County* (San Francisco, 1880). Hereafter it will be referred to as *History of Colusa County*. If there are more footnotes clarifying the stops in the Nevada-California end of their journey, it is because they traveled the Beckwourth Pass route to northern California. It was one of those "ghost trails" described by Thomas H. Hunt in his book, *Ghost Trails to California*. (Palo Alto, CA, 1974).

LUCRETIA EPPERSON
From the history of *Colusa County, California.*
(San Francisco, 1880) page 149

THE JOURNAL

We started on our journey Friday, April 1, 1864, from the residence of Mrs. Thurza Epperson, in Coles county, Illinois. We took with us a lot of blooded stock purchased in Kentucky by my husband and Mr. Henry Reed. Mr. Reed was a pioneer of Yuba county, California. Mr. Epperson and himself had been old acquaintances in California as early as 1852. We camped near the little town of Oakland [Illinois] the first evening, and it commenced to rain about the time we encamped. Our cook, Joe Gaithe, made a good fire by the side of a large dry log, and soon had nice hot coffee, we having plenty of everything in the line of edibles cooked. The bright fire made our surroundings cheerful, and this was the beginning of camp life for me. My husband procured a bed at a house near by for myself and child. The men slept in the wagons.

April 2.   We went about half a mile, when our four-horse

team became fast in the mud. Our men worked hard two hours before extricating them. Mr. Epperson found it necessary to increase the number of horses from four to six the rest of the journey. We had hard traveling all day and only accomplished seven miles, and we camped at sunset on Grand Prairie. We had but little fuel, and our camp was less cheerful than the evening before, men all tired and not in very good humor. Being unable to procure a bed, my husband and myself were obliged to sleep in our wagon.

April 3.   Rained all day, roads very muddy, we plodded on our way until we entered a narrow lane. Here we became fast in a mud-hole that was almost impassable. Sitting on a fence near by was a gentleman who seemed to be proprietor of said mud-hole, as he told us we could not get our wagon through without the help of another team. He had three yoke of oxen with him, seemed to be ready for business, and demanded five dollars for his services. Mr. Epperson and Reed could not see things in that light, and they offered him two dollars to open his fence and let them drive around, otherwise, they assured him they would go through by force. He finally concluded to accept the money, and we went on our way rejoicing.

April 4 and 5.   Had better roads, as we had got into the timber country.

April 6.   Drove into Springfield, Illinois, about noon. Mr. Epperson had rubbers put under the springs of our family wagon. From Springfield, Illinois, we went to Bardstown on the Illinois river. Nothing of interest transpired on the way.

April 10.   Crossed the Illinois river, and took up our line of march to Keokuk, on the Mississippi, and followed up the Des Moines to Ottumwa. Mr. George Reed's family joined us, they coming from Vermont to join our train.

April 20.   Crossed the Des Moines to Eddyville; here we

got a good supply of fresh fish. We traveled almost due west to Council Bluffs. Nothing occurred to break the monotony of rain and muddy roads, until a flock of tame geese came marching along near the road. One of our men thinking no one would see him, seized one of them and threw it into my wagon. Just in the act, he was spied by the owner of the goose, an old Irish woman, who started after our train, minus bonnet or shawl, and vowed she would have the man arrested. Her husband followed and tried to appease her wrath, but all in vain. Mr. Epperson told her he could not help what his man had done, but was willing to make amends by paying for it. She took two dollars and went home. The goose came to life, it being only stunned, so I dropped it in the road after the old lady was out of sight; and no doubt by the time she reached home, the goose had joined the flock and was relating its sad experience to its comrades. Suffice it to say we had the goose for a joke all the way across the plains.[1]

May 5.   Encamped on Missouri river, two miles from Council Bluffs, and laid in our supply of provisions to last for the journey. About dark it began to rain violently, and continued to fall all night. Here we found quite a number of people ready to emigrate for California, Idaho, and Oregon.

May 7.   Crossed the Missouri river at Omaha, and here purchase a few more supplies which had been overlooked at Council Bluffs. We are now in Nebraska, and fairly started on our tedious journey across the plains. Occasionally, we pass a little farm.

May 9.   Crossed the Elk Horn river on a very shaky old bridge. Here I saw the first Indian, a dirty speciman of the Pawnee tribe.

May 10.   Crossed through the little town of Fremont, and camped on the border of a small stream which abounded with

---

[1] It is obvious that the above comment was written at the end of the journey.

fish. Here we saw three Indian lodges, or wigwams. The
country was sparsely settled with Germans, from whom we
purchased corn and oats for our horses.

May 14.   Came to south fork of Platte river[2] and camped
for the night.

May 15.   Crossed the river by ferry, part of the way the
water being too shallow for our boat. We had some difficulty
in getting our teams off the boat into the water, and after
leaving the boat we found we were in quicksand, and thought
several times our wagons would be carried down the stream,
the current was so swift. After getting our stock safe across,
we drove immediately into camp, bought corn, shelled it,
and with it filled the bed of our heavy wagon.

May 16.   Our road seemed more lonely to-day, we passed
but few houses, and began to realize our situation.

May 17.   In camp on Wood river, Nebraska. Heavy timber
grew along the river, the first we had seen for several days.
We found it to be a good camping ground for the weary and
tired. Edward Russell cooked our supper— "our cook" had
gone fishing. When the table was spread, (need not say table
for our cups plates, etc., were placed upon the ground), and
we all sat around and took a hearty repast of bacon, coffee,
and bread.

May 18.   Very warm, and the road dusty. Saw about two
hundred teams on the road to-day, most of them bound for
Idaho. Camped on the Platte, within six miles of Fort
Kearney. Mr. Epperson rode over to the fort, the men are all
off herding the horses, and I am sitting upon a sack of wheat
writing. I am going to be good "old lady" of the house until
time for retiring. This is a beautiful country, and good
farming land. A German told me, this morning, that he

---

[2]Merrill J. Mattes points out that this was probably the Loup fork, not the South
Fork. *Platte River Road Narratives* (Urbana, 1988), p. 575.

raised eighty bushels of oats to the acre. We bought oats and corn here for $1.25 per bushel.

May 19. Camped on Elm creek; the road was perfectly level. A few days ago, a gentleman from Indiana was murdered near where we were encamped. He was murdered by four men whom he was bringing to California. The men told his wife that if she let it be known, they would put her out of the way too. They took possession of his stock, and proceeded on their way as if nothing had occurred. His wife made it known before going far, a man returned to the fort, procured an officer, and had them detained before night. They were made to unearth the remains of the murdered man, which were removed to Fort Kearney, where the murderers will be held for trial. I saw the ground where the remains were taken from.

May 20. Have excellent food for our horses; wood getting scarce. The wind blew very hard all day, and our eyes were very much inflamed by sand into them. Cactus grows to perfection on the plains or valley lands, and on the sand hills a great variety of flowers. I gathered some phlox which was superior to any I ever saw cultivated. We saw no Indians; they took a train here about two weeks ago.

May 21. After a good night's rest, we start again; roads very heavy; pulling through sand all day. The hills are very bare, no vegetation upon them of any kind. The territory was beautiful up to Fort Kearney. On the north side of the Platte, one day's drive from Fort Kearney, brought quite a change. The country perfectly barron, no timber only on small islands in the Platte river. I often thought, if I made the country, I would put timber on each side of the Platte, so that poor emigrants could have a few sticks, at least, to cook with. The sun was intensely hot at noon, but now we are in camp and experience quite a change. The wind blows, and I am obliged to put on heavy wraps.

May 22.   Filled our casks with ice cold water out of boiling
springs. This was the finest spring we had seen thus far on
our journey; it formed quite a stream that ran down the
mountain side and emptied itself into the Platte. We had
proceeded but a short distance when we observed a sand
storm coming with great violence from the sand hills on the
south side of the Platte. We knew it was time to prepare for a
storm; everything was in confusion. We turned our wagons
and drove all the "loose stock" near them. On it came,
seeming to have no pity, but only raged for a few moments
when its fury was spent, and we made ready to move westward
again. The mountains present a grand and imposing
appearance. We crossed two streams with great difficulty,
the beds of which proved to be quicksand, and the men were
compelled to go into the water to get the wagons out. Passed
a new grave — on the board was cut T. Foster of Ohio, aged
64 years, died May 20, 1864. The grave was near the bank of
the Platte, and no doubt, in a short time, the grave will be
washed away. We saw the bones of the buffalo scattered here
and there over the plains, and frequently a note or line
written on the skull of some venerable fellow, which caused a
hearty laugh. We have no wood to cook with to-night; sage
brush, which is something like small willow, is all we have. A
stranger came in camp to-night, who proved to be one of the
men kept on the trail of the murdered man.

May 23.   Started early; had gone but a short distance when
our heavy wagon became fast in the quicksand, while crossing
a small stream. I was driving the family wagon, and felt very
certain that I would have to be helped out too; but made the
horses go as quickly as possible, so they would have no time
to sink, and we came out all right. Came upon heavy sand
hills about noon. Here we met some fine looking Sioux
Indians. They were well dressed in deer skins, and had

enormous brass rings in their ears and noses. We are now above the fork of the Platte. Could see teams on the south Platte from the hills, to-day. I walked over some of the highest points; large holes have been blown into them by whirlwinds. Saw plenty of flowers growing upon the sand; saw only one tree, and that upon an island. I visited a grave near our camp, after supper. On the head board was cut in rude letters Mrs. Mary Brown, buried June, 1863. Oh! what a lonely place to be laid. From the grave I went up a little mountain stream, half a mile from camp, to see a beaver dam and house. I never saw anything of the kind before. It was astonishing what skill was displayed in making the dam. No timber being near, they used a species of willow that grows upon the margin of the stream. The pond, form by damming the river, looked lovely in the bright moon light — quite a "fairy lake," indeed. Mr. Lawrence cut a hole in the dam, so that the "little workers" would have some "repairs" to make the ensuing day. On returning to camp, I found our cook forming the bread into loaves, ready for baking. I told him I would sit up and bake the bread, and let him retire, as he would have to stand guard after midnight. He gladly availed himself of the privilege and retired. Mr. Mitchell (who was Mr. Reed's cook) sat by the "bake" until ten o'clock. One might think that we had poor bread, when I tell you we had no wood for several days; but the "willow brush" cooks finely.

May 24.   Went over more sand hills; weather very warm. The Platte looked beautiful from the mountains, as we could see the river for miles. To-night we had to gather dry grass to cook with.

May 25.   Started at sunrise, when some of our men said they saw buffalo going over the bluffs. Each and every man was anxious to kill one, so they drew lots to see who should go. Mr. Lawrence being the fortunate one, started off delighted with the prospect of such noble game. When he had got nearly two miles from the train, we discovered to our great surprise that our "game" were Indians, and on looking around, saw quite a number lurking around the brow of the hills. The wagons were stopped, and a flag placed on the end of a stick and a man started on horseback to attract Mr. Lawrence's attention. We all shouted at the top of our voices, and he soon turned his horse and made way for camp. We met Indians in little bands all day, but they did not come near us, and did not seem friendly. We found a lovely spot to rest, on a sloping hillside, about one-half mile from the Platte river, with plenty of good feed near the river for our horses, and were preparing for a quiet night's rest, when two shots were fired, and the cry of a stampede was heard on all sides; our horses, jennets,[3] and cattle, that were near, were all gone entirely out of sight in much less time than I can write it. All was confusion, and some of the men were frightened almost out of their senses. We caught one of our fine horses which was in pursuit of the others. The men all started after our stock, leaving but two or three to guard our camp. They all returned by midnight, and the sound of the horses' feet had entirely ceased.

May 26. Of course, I did not retire at all last night, not to mention of being left in a savage country to walk to the end of our journey. Our jennets came to camp about eight o'clock, "poor things," looking much frightened. About noon Mr. Reed's horses were brought to camp by Mr. William Parker (one of Mr. Reed's men), but none of ours. Gloomy were the prospects of ours returning; but near three o'clock, Mr.

---

[3] Brutus Clay Epperson was noted as a raiser of fine horses and mules. Lucretia here does not mention another member of the overland party, Old Samson, a jack, who over some eight years would bring in to his master stud fees amounting to some $10,000 for his services.

Henry Reed came to camp with all our stock, which filled our hearts with gratitude to Him who is ever caring for the distressed. The Indians had them herded in a little valley over the summit of the mountain. Mr. Reed paid one dollar per head for our stock, and they were satisfied. The horses looked as though they had had little to eat or drink. We put them all to the wagons and drove about five miles, and then made a corral of the wagons, tied them all together with ropes and chains to keep out stock during the night. The Indians are quite numerous. Now and again they ride by on their ponies to reconnoiter. I fear we will have trouble with them, but hope for the best. Two Indians are now in camp asking for bread, and I do not feel like acceding to their request. A squaw and an Indian came riding into camp near sunset. They had a little baby, not more than four weeks old, and I offered to take it. The squaw seemed delighted to have me notice her papoose, and handed it to me. I went to our wagon and got some of my little boy's clothes and dressed her baby. I finally put a bright red wrap around it and gave the child back to its mother. She took it with a smile; then holding the little one up, both laughed heartily, and exclaimed "good squaw, good squaw," at the same time pointing to me. All the men stood guard that night, but all seemed quiet.

May 27. We started out early, did not take time to cook much or let our horses graze. We came to a large Indian village; the huts, or wigwams, were made of buffalo hides and are put up with great ingenuity. We met a great number of Indian wariors, all painted and adorned with feathers. They were going to fight the Pawnee Indians. In front of the wariors rode three chiefs, and the squaw and Indian whose baby I had dressed. They rode along slowly, looking intently at each wagon, until they came to the one I was in. They stopped and shouted "good squaw," and held up the little babe. There were, at least, one hundred wagons on the road at the time. Those in front and rear did not know what to make of such proceedings, and thought they were preparing to attack us, but the Indians soon rode on, and many hearts were relieved.

May 28.   Mr. Epperson taken sick with mountain fever. I took a good sleep while we proceeded forward, as I had slept but little for four days, and was nearly worn out in body and mind; and what made our situation worse, Mr. Epperson sick and unable to sit up. We camped near a prairie dog village. The dogs are small and of brownish color; dogs, rattle-snakes, and owls burrow in the ground together. We had been in camp but a few moments when one of our jennets was bitten on the upper lip by a very poisonous snake, and died in less than twenty minutes. This was the first animal we had lost.

May 29.   This is a beautiful morning. It is Sunday. I walked up on a high point to get a view of Chimney rock; could see it quite distinctly, also Pyramid[4] rock. They are both on the south side of Platte river.

May 30.   Saw Court House rock this morning, shortly after sunrise. The mirage looked beautiful, and the rocks before us looked like old ruins. Passed an Indian village; two white men living among them came out and conversed with us. Said they had lived among the Indians seven years, and did not dislike living with Indians.

May 31.   Passed several more Indian villages; saw quite a number of half-breed children, some of them almost grown. Camped near Platte river. A point of the mountain extended near the river which sheltered our wagons and stock from the storm which suddenly arose near bed time.[5]

---

[4]Mattes, *op cit*, suggests that her "Pyramid Rock" might have been "Dome Rock" within the boundaries of Scotts Bluff National Monument.

June 1   Still raining, and very little food for our horses. We started by daylight, without breakfast, in search of feed which we found about two miles from our camping ground of last night. Our cook made a good fire and prepared coffee and toast. Bought Charlie (my baby) a pair of moccasins from an old Indian who had nice bead-work for sale. Very cold all day; camped in a cotton-wood grove, and had plenty of wood.

June 2.   Roads very heavy. Saw two more white men who had squaw wives. Mr. Epperson able to be up and about.

June 3.   Came to Fort Laramie. Mr. Epperson crossed the river and went to the fort, purchased some picket ropes and overtook the train at noon. After dinner we arrived at the Black Hills, found them steep and slippery; encountered a heavy hail storm in the afternoon. Our stock seem worn out, and yet no camping ground in sight; nothing but steep hills covered with rock and small cedar and pine. I must confess I became impatient for a place to halt. On ascending a high point, we descried the grand old Platte about five miles distant and with eager hearts we drove on. At dark we were all seated around a cheerful fire, partaking our evening meal. Our horses have excellent feed, but do not seem to have got over the effects of the stampede. The river is narrow at this point, flows swiftly, and is as cold as ice water.

June 4.   Traveled up a canyon all day; had no water after leaving camp. Late in the afternoon we drove into a little flat surrounded by high hills or mountains, Here we found eight men who had lost all their horses; one white man and two Indians drove them off before their eyes. The horses were grazing, and were started by the cries of the Indians who were soon out of sight. Two of the men walked back to Fort Laramie for assistance from the soldiers, but got none. In a

[5]*Ibid.* Mattes concludes that the "point of the mountain" is a high bluff within present Scotts Bluff National Monument.

few days they had an opportunity to buy a couple of horses, which they did, these they harnessed to their lightest wagon. We made a bright fire where we camped, and after dusk put the fire out and drove back five miles to where we entered the little flat, so that if the Indians attacked us we would have a better chance to resist. Signal lights were on the mountains that surrounded us all night. All the men stood guard over the stock, (which was half a mile from the wagons), driven there on account of the grass for feed, and but three men staid near the wagons. I sat up all night fearful we might be killed any moment.

June 5.   I had prepared breakfast for the men who came driving in the horses, all ate in a hurry, as we were anxious to move from our present camping ground as we considered ourselves in danger. Our unfortunate friends started with us, they being compelled to walk, and carry their coats and guns, the horses they had purchased being unable to carry more than blankets and provision. We are now in a country where we can get no help in case of danger, save from emigrants whom we may perchance meet. We are now in Idaho;[6] the scenery to-day has been grand. On going over the high points of the mountains, we see the Platte winding its way among the hills, far below. Near sunset we came to the Platte again; here we found plenty of grass and wood. There are ten wagons near by. We are all too tired to do anything. I told our cook to make a good cup of tea and I would prepare the rest of our supper. I washed the breakfast dishes, as we started in such a hurry in the morning they were left unwashed, and we prepared no lunch for the men. All

---

[6]This may seem strange, but one must remember that from March 1863 to May 1864, present Wyoming was within the boundaries of Idaho Territory. The news had simply not gotten out about the second date to the overlanders that year. This is well shown in a series of maps in Cornelius J. Brosnan, *History of Idaho* (New York, 1948), pp. 180-81.

partook of a hearty supper, and were soon in dreamland. However, I awoke several times during the night and slipped out to see whether those on guard had fallen asleep.

June 6.   Feel rested this morning, had a late breakfast, traveled near the Platte all day; the wind blew very cold. The hills around us are covered with rock that looks like it had passed through a furnace. These rocks are perfectly bare.

June 7.   I walked over some high points to see the different formations of rock. They look as if skillful hands had chiseled them. To-day it is very warm; quite a change since yesterday. Some of the emigrants who started for Idaho, are going home. Now and then we meet men with pack mules returning to their former homes. They discourage men who are on their way to the mines. We heard to-day from men in charge of a pack train of the drouth in California. Saw snow for the first time on the mountain peaks.

June 8.   I am sitting upon the ground writing; it is growing dark, so I will say good night and retire. Part of the road is quite sandy; passed Deer creek which is on the opposite side of the river, a few log cabins and Indian huts are in view at the mouth of the creek. Saw some very intelligent Sioux Indians. Wm. Munran killed a young rabbit which was the first fresh meat we have eaten for many days.

June 9.   Here the emigrants from South [side of the] Platte cross the river on a good bridge, and join those who traveled on the north side of the river. A little store is kept at the bridge by the toll keeper. Feed scarce. Mr. Epperson has some oats which he feeds to his fine horses when grass is found to be scarce.

June 10.   Rode horseback a few miles; let "Charlie," my little boy, ride a little way, and he now thinks riding in the wagon no ride at all. At two o'clock we bid the dear old Platte a sad and final farewell. I could not but look back with regret to leave this beautiful river in whom the thirsty finds a true friend. No water for our stock to-night, but good grass. No wood, but plenty of sage brush.

June 11.   Started early without breakfast in order to get water for our horses. We drove a few miles and came upon an alkali stream. We had great difficulty in keeping the loose stock from drinking. The ground for several acres in extent is white with alkali. At ten o'clock we came upon a pure stream of cold water. Here we cooked breakfast and let the horses graze for two hours. We stopped at a cold spring and filled our water casks. In looking over a guide book, we learned by digging to a depth of two feet, we would find ice. Some of our men dug the stated depth and found ice, nice and clean, as if put up for use. We camped in a little cove where we were sheltered from the cold winds.

June 12.   Camped on Horse Shoe creek. Good feed and water. Let our horses rest most of the day. Here all of Mr. Reed's men left him with the exception of his cook, Mr. Mitchell, and J.W. Shaddock, a mere boy.

June 13.   Came to Sweetwater river. A few soldiers are stationed here in a little fort. Three of the officers have their wives with them. In crossing the bridge, toll at the rate of one dollar per wagon was demanded of us. Livestock passed through without charge. One of the soldiers came to Mr. Epperson and wanted to buy some lead. Said if he would let him have one pound he might pass free of toll. The lead was forthcoming immediately and we proceeded on our way. At noon stopped, and ate our lunch at Independence Rock. We are now in the spurs of the Rocky Mountains. Met a train of Mormons leaving Salt Lake City; they were disgusted with Mormonism. Passed the Devil's Gate, and camped near Sweetwater river for the first time.

June 14. Up early. Went to the river and bathed my face in its cool waters. The river banks are not more than one foot high. Mr. Epperson and myself rode back to view the Devil's Gate and some of the grandest sights I ever beheld. We undertook to descend the mountain to a pine tree that grew by the water's edge. I soon became dizzy and went back. Mr. Epperson continued on down and soon reached the tree, cut his name thereon, and was at the summit as soon as I. I gathered some flowers that resemble our verbenas. I suffered more with the cold that night than I had since leaving Illinois.

June 15. Came to the crossing of the Sweetwater; could not be forded so traveled around it. Took one day to perform the journey.

June 16. One of Mr. Reed's men, Mr. Kelly, came and wanted to join our train.

June 17. Crossed Sweetwater. Camped near some springs where we found onions. Had some cooked for supper.

June 18. Had plenty of snow to-day. Camped on Sweetwater for the last time.

June 19. Filled our water casks at Pacific springs. Passed over the summit of the Rocky Mountains at ten o'clock. Here the river changed its course. We drove one mile off the road and camped on Big Sandy river. Here we found the best grass which we had had for some time. But few had camped here before, it being off the road. We had just fallen asleep, when a stranger rode into camp. It proved to be our friend Thornton Coleman, from Coles county, Illinois. He was an old neighbor of ours, who started a few days after we left home, and had been trying to catch us for several days; he learned we were only a short distance in advance of him. He now returned and met his train and brought them into camp about midnight. I had supper ready for his family when they arrived; was very glad to see Mrs. Coleman. We had lived near each other for years.

June 20. Gathered some gooseberries and made pie. Left camp after dinner, and camped next on Little Sandy river.

June 21. The wind blew violently; sand and dust covered everything, and by noon the wind had risen to a gale, and we had to remove the covers from the wagons to keep them from blowing over.

June 22. Came to Green river early in the morning. There were so many teams ahead of us we did not cross the river until noon. We were obliged to travel twenty-five miles before reaching water after leaving Green river. We turned our horses out to graze near sunset; let them eat until eight o'clock; we then started to look for water; no moon, and the stars shone dimly; it was anything but pleasant driving. Mr. Epperson was not able to drive, as he was suffering from sick headache, so it fell upon me. About one o'clock we came in sight of camp fires, near Ham's Fork on Green river. We had to descend a very steep hill, which took nearly an hour. Tired and sleepy, we were soon in bed.

June 23. Mr. Epperson shod some of the horses. Had antelope meat for dinner. Camped near Black Fort[7] on Bear river.

June 24. Camped on Bridger's creek, opposite Fort Bridger. Our horses, not being satisfied with their feed, plunged into the water and swam to the other side, thinking, probably, the grass on that side looked more inviting. Mr. Epperson and one of our men had to go down the creek two miles, where it could be forded without danger, and drove

---

[7]This should be "Black's Fork," a branch of Wyoming's Green River. Whether Lucretia Epperson heard it wrong, or she or somebody else copied it wrong from the original we don't know. It was named for a trapper, Daniel Black. May Urbanek, *Wyoming Place Names* (Missoula, MT, 1988).

our horses back to camp. Bridger is quite a little place, about one dozen houses. There are only a few soldiers at the fort at this time. Some had gone with the Mormon train (whom we met) to protect them, and some were fighting the Goose creek Indians, who had stolen some of their stock. Saw the first Snake Indians. After dark several wagons were driven into camp. The parties had a man securely bound, taking him to the fort for trial, he having stolen four horses from the man who employed him (one a valuable race horse), and started for Denver City. He was overtaken in three days and brought back to the train.

June 25. Continues cold; snow on the mountain tops. Camped near a stream of clear water, plenty of wood and feed. Mrs. Coleman washing, men shoeing horses. I made a bed for myself on the ground, in the shade made by our wagon, and saw that the work went on properly. Soon after retiring for the night, Mr. Coleman's horses became alarmed, and started all of ours. I began to fear another stampede; they only ran about one mile when they were stopped and brought back. They were tied for the night, and all was quiet after. Mosquitoes nearly ate us up.

June 26. We are now on the stage route, and our road does not seem so lonely. Pass stage stands every few miles. Mr. Moran[8] killed a large sage hen; had it roasted for supper.

June 27. Came to stage stand early in the morning. Here a family of Mormons resided; they had a nice garden and several acres of oats. Mr. Epperson traded his heavy wagon for a light one, crossed Bear river on toll bridge; paid one-half dollar per wagon. A heavy thunder storm came upon us. The ground was covered with hail; it looked perfectly white. In the middle of the afternoon came to a

---

[8]She spells this name in two ways: "Moran" and "Maran." We suspect that the first one is right, but however the name is spelled, we cannot identify the person.

high mountain, whose sides were so slippery, we would not
attempt to climb. Had a cold, lonely place to camp in, water
so strong with alkali we could not drink it. The tea left in the
kettle from supper was frozen in the morning. No wood; half
dozen bundles of sage brush were all that we could get.

June 28.   Difficult road to climb as we ascend the mountain.
Continued on to the head of Echo canyon, and camped for
the night; weather cold and frosty.

June 29.   Started down the canyon; met a great many
Mormon teams on the way to Omaha, for the purpose of
getting merchandise for Salt Lake City merchants. Came to
Weber river, at the mouth of Echo canyon, one hour before
sunset. Here we found quite a Mormon settlement; bought
fresh milk, butter and cheese, the first we had since leaving
our German friends beyond Fort Kearney. I need not say we
all enjoyed it.

June 30.   Passed few houses; camped near a mountain
stream, which abounded with fine mountain trout. All hands
were soon busy preparing lines and hooks; started out, and
soon returned with a supply of fish, enough for supper and
breakfast. Found a stranger in camp, who proved to be a
Mormon elder, who wished to convert Mr. Epperson. His
efforts were in vain. Mr. Epperson told him he was afraid
they would want him to take another wife. Told him he
could never do that, as his hair was nearly all pulled out by
the one he had, and if he were obliged to take two or three
more, he would have no head left. The elder looked a
moment at Mr. Epperson, then left in disgust.

July 1.   Started early, all eager to reach Salt Lake City. We
passed some neat little adobe houses, all having nice gardens.
We found great quantities of mustard growing by the
roadside. Mrs. Coleman and myself walked along and
gathered enough to make a good mess for supper. This was

quite a treat to us, who had been so long without vegetables. About ten o'clock came in sight of Fort Douglass, General Conner in command. His heavy guns covered Salt Lake City, in order to compel Brigham Young and his saints to respect the laws of the United States, and permit emigrants to pass unmolested. Uncle Sam does not intend to have the Mountain Meadow massacre repeated. Here I will say it is my belief that General Conner[9] was the best man the Government ever sent out to look after Brigham Young and his followers. He will not be forgotten by the emigrants of 1864. Entered the city about noon. Mr. Epperson procured pasture near the city, and we turned our horses out to graze, but kept close watch over them, as General Conner told us they were looking for an outreak among the Mormons, for which reason he held himself in readiness. He said there were a great many good, honest and well-meaning Mormons, who were subordinate to Brigham Young and his disciples. We received letters here, from friends in Illinois and Kentucky, also one from C.C. Epperson of Sutter county, California,[10] informing us of the drouth and hard times there.

July 2.   Mrs. Coleman and I rode through the city on horseback; stopped in front of Brigham's Lion house (so called in honor of a carved lion, couchant in front of the building). We conversed with some of the guards at the gate, who invited us to enter and see Brigham's building inside the

---

[9]Colonel Patrick Edward Conner of California had been ordered by the Federal Government to raise a body of volunteers to go to Utah and keep order in that area. Conner stationed his troops on a height east of Salt Lake City from which he could dominate the Mormons. This did not exactly endear the American army to the Mormon citizens. William J. Ghent, "Conner, Patrick Edward (Mar. 17, 1820-Dec. 17, 1891)" *Dictionary of American Biography*, IV (N.Y., 1930), pp. 352-53.

[10]C. C. Epperson was the brother of Brutus Clay Epperson, Lucretia's husband. He had traveled to California by sea in 1852 and farmed near South Butte in Sutter County. He had met and married a California woman, Miss Sisk, in 1855. They had two children, Josephine, and Fanny. William L. Chamberlain and Harry L. Wells, *History of Sutter County, California* (Oakland, 1879), p. 114.

wall. Mrs. Coleman was afraid to enter; said they might close
the gates upon us. After dinner Mr. Epperson went into the
city to purchase flour for use until we arrived at Austin
[Nevada]. Could get no flour or other necessities, as the sale
of such things by Mormons to emigrants was forbidden by
the "high and mighty Brigham." They would sell milk,
vegetables, butter and fresh meat. An elderly man saw Mr.
Epperson when he was refused flour. He came to our wagon
after dark, and said that he had plenty of flour, and if Mr.
Epperson would go to his house between ten and eleven
o'clock, he would let him have what flour he wanted. Asked
that Mr. Epperson would tell no one, as he was at the tender
mercies of Brigham and his saints. Mr. Epperson paid the
enormous sum of fourteen dollars per hundred pounds.

July 3.   Started forward, crossed the river Jordan, and
camped on the south side of Great Salt Lake.

July 4.   Early in the morning Mr. Epperson took our son
Charlie and a few of the men and went to the lake to bathe.
Mr. Epperson put Charlie on his back and swam out into the
lake near a quarter of a mile; Charlie enjoyed it very much;
the men said he looked like a large toad on his father's back.
Charlie is two years old and very fleshy. We saw a number of
Mormons at work making salt on a small scale.

July 5.   Started early, passed a place where some of our
predecessors had celebrated the Fourth of July. The
programme of the day was written and placed upon a board,
and nailed to a tree by the road side. We stopped, read it, and
felt a little more patriotic. Found a good camping ground for
the night.

July 6.   We now approach the great desert; at noon we
found excellent grass for our stock. Mr. Epperson ordered
the men to cut some for feed while crossing the desert. The
mountains are covered with good "bunch grass," the best we

found so far. Encamped at the entrance of a beautiful canyon; had plenty of company. Quite a number had camped here upward of one week, in order to let the stock rest.

July 7. Traveled until noon and then halted near a stream of clear, cold water. The men are busy cutting grass with their knives and putting it into sacks. Our cook is baking and preparing food for use while crossing the desert.

July 8. Men still cutting grass; our cook filled the casks, kegs and jugs with water. At eleven o'clock dinner was ready, and we all took an extra cup of coffee, as this would be the last warm meal until we arrived on the other side of the desert. Everything in readiness, we started and reached the desert at four o'clock. The sun shone bright and warm in our faces as we traveled westward, and the alkali dust filled the air like fog. Just before sunset we came to the foot of a mountain; here we took some grass and water from our wagons, gave some to each of our animals, and took a cold supper ourselves; after resting an hour we prepared to start. Our little boy fell asleep; I put him in bed and told Mr. Epperson I would walk forward with Mrs. Coleman. We proceeded up the mountain half a mile; perceived a trail which seemed to cut off quite a distance, and concluded to follow it. The wagons were behind us; we chatted and walked along, thinking we would soon come into the road again. It grew dark rapidly, and we were getting anxious to see the road. We hurried on, and very soon it was quite dark. We listened for the sound of the wagons as the wheels jolted over the rocky road, but could hear them no longer. Mrs. Coleman said, Mrs. Epperson, we are lost! We can never find the train, it is so dark. We shouted at the top of our voices, but received no answer. She proposed going back; I was unwilling; told her to follow me, I was going forward, as I felt certain we would come to the road soon. It was now so dark we could not see the trail. We continued on up the moun-

tain side for some time; at last I stepped into the dust, and I
felt convinced we were on the road. We were almost exhausted
I assure you. We were afraid of wagons were beyond the point
assure you. We were afraid of wagons were beyond the point
where we came into the road. At last we heard sounds like
the loose stock coming; so we sat down by the roadside and
waited for the coming of the train, and meanwhile vowed we
would not undertake to travel by "short cuts" again. I was so
fatigued, I went to bed in the wagon immediately and slept
until we began to descend the mountain; the road was rough,
I could not sleep, reached the foot of the mountain about two
o'clock. Just before daylight we came to a stage stand, could
get no water for our stock; water had to be brought from a
distance of sixteen miles for the stage horses.

July 9.   About nine o'clock we gave our horses water from
the supply we carried with us. We partook of a slight repast
ourselves and then drove on through heat and dust, arriving
at another stage stand about two o'clock. Here we found two
ox teams, some of the oxen almost worn out. The owner was
trying to buy water from the man at the station. Soon after
the man left, Mr. Epperson produced a flour sack containing
some choice tobacco. This he passed among the station
hands, who pronounced it excellent. One of the men who
seemed to be manager, told Mr. Epperson to go into the
shed where the water barrels were kept and give each of our
animals a bucket of water. Mr. Epperson gave each man a
good supply of tobacco, and we drove on our way. Just as the
sun was sinking in the far west, we drove into Willow
Springs. Our stock looks tired and worn. The cook soon
prepared a good hot supper, which we enjoyed more than
any meal since leaving home.

July 10.   Let our tired stock rest; had good feed; all day
teams kept coming in; everything was in confusion; every

train that arrived, everybody would rush to see who it was, and if they had met on the road. When night came I was as weary as if I had been riding all day.

July 11. Started early. All feel this morning like the most difficult part of our journey was over. In camp on Deer creek. Indians in camp asking for bread.

July 12. Drove eight miles and camped for the day. Cut grass for our horses as we have to cross a desert twenty-two miles in width.

July 13. Drove across the desert by three o'clock; camped near stage stand. There was a little fort here and a few soldiers. Some Indians came and wanted to take our horses a distance of two miles to graze. The soldiers said they were to be trusted, so we permitted them to go with our stock. Some of the guards remarked that they would sleep well to-night.

July 14. Early this morning our horses were brought to camp. Mr. Epperson paid them for their work, gave them something to eat, and soon after we were on our way.

July 15. Did not feel well this morning; drove only a few hours, and camped in a lovely canyon; found plenty of feed and mahogany wood.

July 16. Started early; came to a little village, only five or six huts. The name of the village is Steptoe [Nevada].[11] Passed into Egan canyon. Mr. Epperson found some California miners at work, tunneling the hill. They think it is a rich mine. The soldiers told us to-day that Salt Lake City was under martial law.

July 17. Camped at Butte springs.[12] About twenty wagons left camp, intending to travel all night, it is so very warm

---

[11]Steptoe, in White Pine County, lay between the Egan and Shell Creek ranges, in Steptoe Valley. It was named for Captain Edward J. Steptoe, who led a military unit to the Pacific Coast in 1854-1855. Helen S. Carlson, *Nevada Place Names* (Reno, 1974), pp. 223-24.

[12]There was a station here for the Pony Express. *Ibid.*, p. 65.

during the day. A Californian trader pitched his tent here, with emigrant supplies. Only asked one dollar per pound for cheese, and one dollar and one-half for coffee, and everything else in proportion.

July 18.   Traveled over a rough mountainous road, and camped in Ruby valley.[13] Here we found quite a little settlement, grocery store and fort. The soldiers are going to give a dancing party to-night. They have a wagon in camp now, to take the ladies of our train to the ball. There are a great many camped in the valley. We have to make certain drives to obtain water and feed. This causes the camping place to be crowded. I am very tired to-night; will sleep soon, knowing we are in no danger.

July 19.   Have a dusty drive before us to-day, but I console myself with the thought that every day brings us nearer home. How glad I will be when this toilsome journey is at an end. Had but little water for our stock to-day. Camped on Diamond mountain.[14]

July 20.   This is the steepest mountain we have encountered so far. Met a number of teams on the road to Salt Lake. Camp at Diamond springs. I counted forty wagons near us. The stage has just passed. The sky is cloudy and everything has a gloomy appearance. Gave Charlie a bath, and covered him in bed. I am alone at the wagon, sitting on the tool-chest writing. Ponto, my dog, seeing me alone, came up, wagging his tail, as much as to say he was still on his way to California, and hoped to find a better country than we were now in.

July 21.   There was so much noise in camp last night, I slept but little. Traveled all day, and camped near a mountain stream. Thirty wagons near by, and enough of crying children

---

[13]Ruby Valley came by its name because early travelers found red garnets there. It was established as a postoffice from 1862 to 1869. *Ibid.*, p. 206.

[14]Diamond Springs, Diamond Valley, Diamond Mountain were all named for Jack Diamond, an old pioneer. Diamond Springs was an overland stage station. *Ibid.*, p. 95.

to disturb a camp meeting. After it was quite dark, a wagon came into camp from Austin. Mr. Epperson went to the wagon, and found one of his old California friends, Thomas Andrews, former Sheriff of Nevada county, California. Mr. Epperson brought him to our camp. I soon prepared a good supper for him, and we all sat around a cheerful camp-fire until quite late. He was taking a mowing machine to Ruby valley, to cut his hay. He gave us a supply of sugar, our's being almost out.

July 22. The men came into camp with three horses; said the others had wandered off, and they could not find them. They soon found them and brought them to camp. Mr. Epperson gave them powder and caps for their trouble. The Indians here can be trusted to some extent; they are kept down by the soldiers. An old Indian is now walking around camp with an old plug hat on, which hat constitutes the principal part of his clothing. You can imagine how comical he looks.

July 23. We traveled alone to-day for the first time, the rest stopping to recruit their stock. I was thinking we would have a lonely camp, but by evening we came to a beautiful canyon, where we met a number of teams on their way to Austin [Nevada].[15] All camped together, and quite a jolly crowd camped around the fire before retiring.

July 24. When the men were bringing the horses to camp this morning, one of our mares started back on the road we traveled yesterday. She was caught by some men at a stage-stand, eighteen miles from our present stopping place. Mr. Epperson started after her, and did not return until nearly night. It was a lonely day for me.

July 25. Started early. I rode horseback up the canyon.

[15] Austin was the site of a famous silver camp. William M. Talcott, an Overland Stage agent, stumbled over a rich silver load in May 1862. *Ibid.*, p. 43.

Looking down on the little valley below, I saw we had a very steep hill to descend, I dismounted and walked. The men tied a tree to each of our wagons, to keep them from rolling forward too quickly. I was somewhat alarmed, but we arrived at the bottom safely. This afternoon we passed "Simpson's Park."[16] It was enclosed by stretching strips of raw-hide from post to post. This was the first raw-hide fence I had ever seen. We met a man to-day looking for his wife; said he with his team started for Virginia City after provisions; while absent his wife sold the ranch, purchased two horses and a wagon, and started for Illinois, her former home. He wished to know if she had been seen by us. After giving a description of her, we assured him we had met her over fifty miles from this place. He sighed and said "well, I will let her go, as I could not overtake her before reaching Salt Lake." I pitied him, but could not help laughing when he told his doleful story. He turned about and started westward. We camped at Emigrant springs,[17] the dustiest camp that we had during our journey; were obliged to drive the horses two miles to feed.

July 26. William Maran is herding the horses. Mr. Epperson and his men are gone to Austin, about four miles distant. There is a small party encamped near by, so I have company. Charlie and Ponto (my dog) are playing around our wagon. The mountains near are perfectly bare, no vegetation; those more distant have a few small pine and cedar. Mr. Epperson came to camp in the afternoon, bringing with him Mr. Gabriel Stickley, an old California friend. He told us that he owned a wood ranch about six miles from Austin, and at that place we would find good feed and water for our horses, and insisted that we take our stock there and

---

[16]Simpson's Park was a pony express and an overland stage station. *Ibid.*, p. 217.

[17]There were several "Immigrant Springs." Across Nevada the immigrants traveled from spring to spring, and names such as this were very fluid as to location.

camp as long as we wished; he also proposed to go with Mr. Epperson and show him the place. His kind offer was accepted with gratitude.

July 27. Mr. Epperson and his friend Mr. Stickley, started early on horseback to see the ranch. Another lonely day for me. I occupied myself by writing letters to friends at home. At intervals, teams pass whom we had met before on the road, and so the day passed. Mr. Epperson came to camp about dark, well pleased with the proposed change.

July 28. Started early for our new camping ground, arrived safely there about noon, and soon after the men had a brush shanty made for me, which I occupied with great pleasure. The sun was very warm, and no shade but that made by the wagons. We turned the horses loose, thinking they would not stray off, but before dark the men went to drive them close to camp, and three were missing; and were not found to-night.

July 29. Bright and early our men started to find the missing horses. Soon after the men were gone the horses were driven into camp by a wood chopper, who camped near us. He was looking for some horses he had lost, when he came upon ours. In the afternoon, a gentleman rode into camp very much excited, and wished to know who owned those jennets branded with the letter "B" upon the jaw. Mr. Epperson replied, "they belong to me." And then asked "where, and of whom did you buy them?" Mr. Epperson said, "I purchased them in Bourbon county, Kentucky, of old uncle Ben Bedford, last February." When he heard that he jumped from his horse and shook hands with us all, as heartily as if he had known us for years. He told us Mr. Bedford was his uncle, and that he had left Kentucky before the commencement of the war, and had not heard from there for quite a length of time. Mr. Epperson told him of many

changes that had taken place since he left his home. He
stayed all the afternoon at our camp, made Mr. Epperson
promise to take our little boy and myself to Austin, so that
we might occupy one of his houses until we started for
California. He said we should have it free of charge. I
thanked him very much for his kindness, and told him I had
been in camp so long, I would as soon remain in camp for the
short time we expected to remain. He would not listen to my
refusal, but turned to Mr. Epperson and says, "I shall
expect to see you in Austin to-morrow; will show you the
house I wish you to occupy, as I shall be absent for three or
four days after to-morrow." After bidding good-bye he rode
off, and I felt we had found a true friend, although an entire
stranger. Be assured we appreciated his kindness. I was not
feeling well. Had it been necessary for us to rent a house we
had not the means to pay rent, we had left but one dollar and
fifty cents. Mr. Epperson had written to his brother, C.C.
Epperson of Sutter county, California, to send us one
hundred and fifty dollars. Mr. Epperson could not go to
Austin to-day, as I was feeling very badly.[18] Our stock
seem contented and do not require such close watching.

July 31.   Mr. Epperson started for Austin. William Maran
stayed at camp and took charge of Charlie and prepared
dinner. Our men are all off prospecting, hoping to discover a
rich silver mine. It is amusing to see them coming into camp
loaded with rock; never saw a silver mine until they went
into Austin a few days ago; they would not know a valuable
piece of ore if they should find one. We are in camp some
distance from the road, and can see nothing but black hills,
most of them entirely barren. Occasionally a raven may be
seen flying overhead chattering a doleful tale.

---

[18]When Lucretia says she was "feeling very badly," one must remember that she was
pregnant and had every right to feel badly. See introduction above.

August 1.   Up early and hurrying around preparing to move into Austin. William Maran went wth us to take the horses back to camp; he will be alone in camp as the men have gone to work. Austin is quite a little place, everything stirring. Our house is made of adobe. We put our bed and trunks in the house, had lunch, and Mr. Maran started back to camp. He appeared somewhat lonely, but will have neighbors, as there are men only a short distance from our camp chopping wood.

August 2.   After a good night's rest, I feel like preparing our breakfast, which I have not done for some time. Breakfast ready, Mr. Epperson and I sit down alone (our table is a pine board two feet wide and four feet long) for the first time since leaving our home in Illinois. One year ago to-day I was with my mother; I wish she could see me in my little mansion, dirt floor, bedstead made of pine posts, stools for chairs, and our trunks; these are all that our furniture consists of. Many of the houses are covered with canvass. Our friend Mr. Stickley called and wished us to go with him to Mrs. Hick's, where he boarded, and take supper. I found Mrs. Hicks very pleasant. She had one room with plank floor, of which she was very proud, as but few could afford plank floors, lumber being very scarce, and worth two hundred and fifty dollars per thousand. Saw for the first time the Chinamen in their washhouses.

August 3.   Mr. Epperson found quite a number of Californian friends and acquaintances in Austin to-day, among them was Mr. Robert C. Murdock, who is a resident of Colusa at this date. Also George W. Thomson, from Colusa county, a well known stock-raiser, but now interested in the hardware business in Santa Rosa, Sonoma county, California.

August 4.   Mr. Epperson found another friend, Mr. James

Rooker,[19] formerly of Sutter county, California. He was
engaged in the butcher business. Informed Mr. Epperson he
had married since they last met, and had the biggest boy of
his age in Nevada Territory. Mr. Epperson asked him the
age of his boy. Said a little over two years old. Mr. Epperson
told him he also had married, and had a boy a few weeks
younger than his, whom he would like to weigh against his;
and it followed that they weighed them next day.

August 5.   After breakfast Mr. Epperson, with our Charlie,
started for Mr. Rooker's shop, and quite a crowd gathered
around to see the children weighed. Mr. Rooker's son
weighed forty pounds, and Charlie forty-four. Those who
witnessed the weighing told Mr. Rooker not to boast of his
mammoth infant any longer. Charlie was brought home with
his hands full of candies, very much pleased indeed.

August 6.   Mr. Spurgeon and family drove into town and
camped near our house. I was glad to meet them again. They
had been delayed by sickness, and two members of his family
not able to sit up at this time.

August 7.   Mrs. Hicks spent the afternoon with me;
together we called upon a sick man camped quite near; he is
not expected to live.

August 8.   Started to walk about the town and see some of
the quartz mills, but soon tired and returned home.

August 9.   Attended an exhibition given by the pupils of
the public school. This was the first exhibition given in
Austin. Nothing of interest transpired for the next nine
days.

August 19.   Wm. Mason[20] and Mr. Stickley brought our
stock to town, we loaded our wagons again and were soon in

---

[19]General James E. Rooker of Austin, was for a time the head of the Nevada militia
and owned a ranch on the Reese River. *Calif. Hist. Soc. Quarterly*, XXI (1929), p. 379.

the Reese river valley.[21] Mr. A. C. Chalmers drove the loose stock. It was nine o'clock before we found a desirable place to camp for the night. The wind blew extremely cold and chilly.

August 20.   Had breakfast ready by the time the sun rose, anxious to get on our road early. I must confess I really enjoyed camping again. We crossed a barren alkali flat, that was so white when the sun shone upon it that it was almost blinding.

August 21.   Camped in a deep canyon, no feed near by; had to send the stock off about two miles to graze. Mr. Epperson and I are alone.

August 22.   Camped in the greesewood, bought feed for our animals, and had quite a shower which laid the dust.

August 23.   Our horses strayed off into the woods which caused us some delay, crossed the Carson desert, in going about twenty-two miles I counted sixty-five head of dead horses and cattle; camped at Salt Wells.[22] Here we found the water very salt, our stock would not drink it. From the salt lake here, they make tons of salt, which is shipped in great quantities to Austin and Virginia City. The salt is used in the quartz mills. Saw several camels carrying packs of salt. Several in camp to-night, are having a dancing party; made so much noise until midnight we could not sleep.

---

[20]This was probably a mistaken reference to O.S. Mason, who arrived in Colusa in 1864 and was elected sheriff soon after. He went on to be a member of the bar, served as superintendent of the county hospital, and as a justice of the peace. Will S. Green, in *History of Colusa County* (San Francisco, 1880), has a short blurb telling of the life and career of O.S. Mason and says, "Judge Mason is the happy father of nineteen children, who have received the best of care and instruction from him." Never in the article is one mention of a woman in the family. Such neglect of women is often characteristic of the ego books of the time.

[21]The Reese River arises in the Toiyabe range south of Austin and flows directly north, past that city, through Lander County, until it reaches the Humboldt.

[22]Helen S. Carlson, in her *Nevada Place Names*, lists nine localities containing the word "salt." This is probably the one in Churchill County. Lucretia's description of it is classic.

August 24. Camped in the sand; no wood, bad water, bought or hired pasture for our stock; every little oasis is claimed by some one; we have to pay dear for the grass we get. This is the most desolate looking country we have yet seen. Now and then we pass a little hut, cannot imagine how the occupants exist. All the money in Nevada Territory would not induce me to live here.

August 25. In the afternoon came to a little ranch, where we saw a fine garden. Mr. Epperson bought vegetables, also a nice large watermelon. This place looked so inviting after traveling through such a dreary part of the country, we concluded to encamp here for the night. We are near the Carson river.

August 26. Passed Ragtown this morning.[23] The town resembles Truckee. We crossed a desert twenty-five miles in width to the Truckee river. This is altogether desolate. The ground looked as if a fire had passed over it. Near sunset we came near the Truckee river and were thankful for good drinking water. The Indian agent and wife came to our camp and chatted until bed time.

August 27. Traveled up the Truckee river, passed several ranches, bought new potatoes at five cents per pound. Camped near a neat little village, where they were making butter and cheese. Had plenty of milk, which was a great treat.

August 28. Came to Truckee Meadows, a lovely place thickly settled.[24]

August 29. Passed a great many encamped recruiting their

[23]Ragtown was so called because the emigrants tended to drop off excessive clothing there. Their arrival at the Carson River meant also that they could wash their clothing and hang it out to dry on surrounding bushes. Late August was not really the ideal time to travel in such desert country. Carlson, *op. cit.*, p. 197.

[24]The valley in which both Sparks and Reno are located is Truckee Meadows. Carlson, *op. cit.*, p. 235.

stock. They can have good pasture very reasonable. I felt very badly all day.

August 30. Was taken very sick during the night. Mr. Epperson thought best to remain in camp, but I was so anxious to reach home insisted upon going forward.

August 31. Passed through Beckwith[25] into the Sierra valley. Drove to Mr. Ead's ranch, where we got good pasture, and the use of a little house where I could be made more comfortable than in our own wagon. Mrs. Ead did all she could for me. Mr. Chalmers rode thirty miles to procure the assistance of Dr. Weber,[26] who was absent. Left a message to have him come as soon as he returned. Was sick for several days; finally Dr. Weber came and gave me some medicine which soon gave relief. He refused pay for his visit; we were thankful to him and hope some day it will be my privilege to pay him tenfold. We remained here until September 10th; left all our stock in care of Wm. Maran, except three horses and four head of choice stock, which we left upon Mr. Jones' ranch.

September 11. Traveled slowly all day and camp near Weber Lake.[27] I have a view of the lake from the wagon,

---

[25]They are now traveling over the Beckwourth Pass, named for the first person to explore the area, James Beckwourth. If Lucretia is in error in spelling it, so were members of the family and friends of the notorious mountain man. In the 1860's the trapper built a trading post at the western side of the trail in the Sierra Valley. The prime reference on the Beckwourth Route is Thomas H. Hunt, *Ghost Trail to California* (Palo Alto, 1974) pp. 247-57, and Map #28. The main reference to the life of Jim Beckwourth is the definitive biography by Elinor Wilson: *Jim Beckwourth, Black Mountain Man and War Chief of the Crows,* (Norman, Okla., 1972). Mrs. Wilson has an appendix giving information about the Beckwourth Ranch. The main trading post is still there on the property belonging to Mrs. Guido Ramelli. *Ibid.,* p. 192.

[26]Dr. David Gould Webber traveled to California in 1850, settled and mined near Downieville. In 1864 he was living on his ranch near Loyalton, some ten miles from Beckwourth's trading post. *History of Plumas, Lassen, and Sierra Counties.* (Oakland, 1882) p. 267.

being unable to get out and walk around.

September 12.   Traveled through heavy pine and fir timber; enjoyed the scenery very much. Camped at Middle Water.[28] it was very cold. I went into a house and sat by the fire until bed time.

September 13.   Enjoyed my ride to-day very much; had very good road all day.

September 14.   Started early, arrived at San Juan.[29] Here we purchased fresh beef. Passed through French Corral,[30] crossed the Yuba river on Rice's Bridge, and camped at Woods' ranch. Got some fresh fruit, the first I had eaten in California. Mr. Epperson killed a dog that was stealing our meat.

September 15.   Gathered up our camping utensils for the last time and started for Yuba City, where we arrived that night about eight o'clock, and stopped with our old friends William P. and Lydia A. Hanson.

September 16.   Friday we drove out from Yuba City to Mr. Epperson's ranch, south of the Butte mountains,[31] where he had resided before our marriage. Here we found his brother, C. C. Epperson, whom he left here when he started back to Illinois on a visit, or after your humble servant.

---

[27]Formerly Little Truckee Lake, was renamed by Dr. Webber after the good doctor had purchased the lake and its surrounding land as a place to raise livestock in 1852. His place of residence was known as Webber's Station. Edwin G. Gudde, *California Place Names* (Berkeley, 1969), p. 360.

[28]Middle Waters is the name of a creek in Sierra County. *Ibid.*, p. 201.

[29]San Juan, Nevada County, was the locale of a rich gold deposit. One of the miners, Christian Kientz, had fought in the Mexican War. He named it for San Juan de Ulloa in Mexico. The town became North San Juan in 1857 when a post office was established to distinguish it from other San Juans in California. *Ibid.*, p. 224.

[30]French Corral, Nevada County, was named for the corral of a Frenchman after the finding of gold in that locality in 1849. *Ibid.*, p. 115.

[31]The Marysville or Sutter Buttes form a noteworthy landmark in the Sacramento Valley. They are in Sutter County.

The 1864 Journal $ Mary Ringo

INTRODUCTION

When Mary Ringo on Wednesday, May 18, 1864, began the entries in her overland journal she was expecting the birth of her sixth child. Not once did she mention this fact in the record of her journey. It was on this date that the Ringos left family and friends in Liberty, Missouri, for the long trek to California.

This is a very special diary written by a woman of remarkable inner strength. A daughter, Mattie Bell, wrote years after the event, "I think she was the bravest woman I ever heard of..."

Mary was the wife of Martin Ringo (b. Oct. 1, 1819), a Kentuckian who had served during the Mexican War as a mounted infantryman at Fort Leavenworth, Kansas.[1] He was discharged on June 21, 1847, and settled down as a farmer near Weston, Missouri, just across the Missouri River from Leavenworth. He met a young woman named Mary Peters (b. Nov. 13, 1826) and on Sept. 5, 1848, they were married. Immediately after the marriage ceremony the Ringos moved to Washington, Wayne County, Indiana.

Their first two children were born in Indiana: John Peters (b. May 3, 1850), and Martin Albert (b. Jan. 28, 1854). The family later moved to Gallatin, Daviess County, Missouri, where three more children were born, all girls: Fanny Fern (b. July 20, 1857); Mary Enna (b. May 2, 1860); and Mattie Bell (b. April 28, 1862).

At the time of the first entry in her journal, May 18, 1864, the ages of the children were John, 14 years; Albert, 10; Fanny, 7; Mary Enna, 4; and Mattie Bell, 2. Mother Ringo had a very busy journey.

That first entry (May 18) in the diary was made in Liberty,

Cass County, Missouri. They had relatives in that town just north of Kansas City, and there was a tearful parting for the start of the journey. The next day, May 19, they were ferried across the river and camped out near Leavenworth on the Kansas side. They followed the Leavenworth Trail, as it was called, across northeast Kansas, to join the main trail along the Platte at Ft. Kearney, Nebraska. From there they took the usual trail along the Platte, turned south to Salt Lake City on the Mormon Trail, then they went on westward by the stagecoach road to Austin, Nevada, on the Reese River. They eventually continued west to San Jose, California, where they were met by Mary's sister, Augusta, and her husband, Coleman Younger, a well-known breeder of fine cattle. Mary and the children settled down to live in San Jose. The 1870 Census listed their address as "Santa Clara Co., California, Alviso P.O., City of San Jose, 1st ward."

There are two dreadfully tragic events that marked the Ringo journey.

The first of these is summed up in Mary's diary entry for Saturday, July 30: "And now Oh God comes the saddest record of my life for this day my husband accidentally shot himself and was buried by the wayside and oh, my heart is breaking. . . . "

We have published as an "Epilogue" to Mary Ringo's journal a letter written by a fellow traveler, William Davenport, to the Liberty, Missouri, *Tribune*. Davenport was mentioned many times by Mary, once, even, as "Dr. Davenport." His letter is dated August 1, 1864, sent from "the Platte River." It was published in the *Tribune* on September 16. Here are some of the key lines:

> Just after daylight on the morning of the 30th ult. Mr. Ringo stepped on top of the wagon, as I suppose, for the purpose of looking around to see if Indians were in sight, and his shot gun went off accidentally in his own hands, the load entering his right eye and coming out the top of his head. At the report of his gun I saw his hat blown up twenty feet in the air, and his brains were scattered in all directions.

---

[1]Much of the detailed information about the Ringo family has come from *Ringo Family History Series*, Volume V, *Line of Descent from Major Ringo* (Alhambra, CA, 1980), pp. 11-34.

GRAVE MARKER OF MARTIN RINGO
Near Glenrock, Wyoming
Courtesy of Randy Brown of Douglas, Wyoming

Martin Ringo was buried alongside the overland train. Aubrey L. Haines in his book, *Historic Sites along the Oregon Trail,*[2] tells of the site as having a marker of native stone incised with the words, "M. Ringo." He says the location is two miles west of Glenrock, Wyoming, 150 feet north of the old U.S. Highway 26/87. A new marker was set up by the Oregon-California Trails Association at the behest of Randy Brown of Douglas Wyoming, who has given much help to the editor of this series, with verbal and photographic information about the setting. The new marker was set up in the summer of 1987. It has a quote from William Davenport's letter to the *Tribune:* "He was buried near the place he was shot, in as decent a manner as was possible with the facilities on the plains."

But there was a second tragic event that marked the exodus of this family. On October 8 Mary Ringo wrote, "We remain in Austin, Nevada." This was her last entry in the diary. There is

[2](Gerald, MO, 1981), p. 178.

appended to the journal a conclusion written by the youngest of the three daughters, Mattie Bell (Ringo) Cushing, saying that in Austin a son was born. She writes, "Fortunately it was still-born for he was terribly disfigured from mother seeing father after he was shot. Even my brother [John] who was fourteen years old noticed it and said he looked just like father did."

After "a week or ten days," Mattie says, they went on with one wagon pulled by mules over the Sierra to San Jose, where they settled permanently. They were welcomed by Mary's sister, Augusta, and her husband, Coleman Younger.

Now as to the diary itself. We learned that Frank Cushing, son of Mattie Bell Cushing, and a printer by trade, had published the diary of Mary Ringo, his grandmother, in 1956. We learned also that Frank Cushing had died, but had given a copy of the diary to several friends, among them Herschel C. Logan of Santa Ana, California. Mr. Logan sent us his copy of the book, and we were able, with his permission, to make a photocopy of it. Of the rare journal Frank Cushing had printed only 45 copies, and had copyrighted it so that it could not be copied promiscuously. There is a note at the beginning of the book saying that it had been copied from the handwritten original which had become almost illegible over the many years since 1864. In this note Frank Cushing said, "We have followed the original spelling, punctuation and capitalization."

We wrote the Register of Copyrights in Washington, D.C., and learned that under the law as it was used in 1956, the copyright had run out fourteen years after October 24, 1956. The book is now in the public domain. We hope the present publication of the precious diary in *Covered Wagon Women* would have met Frank Cushing's approval.

NOTE ON JOHN RINGO

There was one person mentioned by Mary Ringo from time to time in her journal. That was John, her oldest son, age fourteen. She fondly called him "Johnny" or "Johnnie." Johnny spent most of his time as a cowboy, handling the oxen and horses and mules. He observed the two traumatic experiences of the family's long journey: the death of his father, and the stillborn child with the disfigured face, born in Austin to his mother.

Now it is known for a fact that this young man grew up to become the notorious cattle rustler, Johnny Ringo.[3] There are songs about him, movies, television programs, and countless western articles and books. He was the man behind the myth. To sort fact from fiction is virtually impossible.

He was listed by the census taker in San Jose in 1870 as John Ringo, age 20. Some time after that date he made the long journey on horseback to Mason County, Texas, where he worked driving cattle. He was supposed to have been involved in several killings during his Texas years, but the historical record is quite confused. He did serve for a period as sheriff of Mason County in the late 1870's.

He made his first appearance in Arizona in 1879, and lived out his life in the Tombstone area. There he was involved in cattle rustling, both from American ranches, and from Mexicans just across the border. A major problem for John Ringo was that he often drank too much to assuage times of moodiness and despondency. This led him into quarrels with other cattlemen. One day early in July 1882, Johnny Ringo's body was found near the side of a road leading to Tombstone. There has been much disagreement as to how and why Ringo met his death, whether he had been murdered, or was it suicide?

A statement of a coroner's jury dated July 14, 1882, seems to solve the problem.[4]

The undersigned reviewed the body and found it in a sitting posture facing west, the head inclined to the right. . . There was a bullet hole in the right temple, the bullet coming out on top of the

---

[3]Much of the material on Johnny Ringo we have gleaned from an excellent study of both the man and the myth in Jack Burrows, *John Ringo: The Gunfighter Who Never Was* (Tucson, 1987), *passim.* Burrows study is a definitive biography of John Peters Ringo.

[4]This coroner's report on the death of John Ringo has been published in several sources. We have used the version published in Allen A. Erwin, *The Southwest of John H. Slaughter, 1841-1922* (Glendale, CA, 1965), pp. 203-4.

head on the left side... Several of the undersigned identify the body as that of John Ringo, well known in Tombstone... His revolver, he grasped in his right hand, his rifle rested against the tree close to him — He had two cartridge belts, the belt for the revolver cartridges being buckled on upside down.

We agree with Jack Burrows, the major authority on the life and death of Johnny Ringo that death was by suicide. Gunfighter buffs have a term, "man-tally," to describe the number of deaths that could be attributed to gunfighters as they drew on each other. Burrows succinctly says of Ringo, "For the record, his man-tally stands at one: himself."[5]

THE JOURNAL

May 18, Wednesday. Left my family and started on my long trip across the plains, went 10 miles, had some trouble with the oxen and camped for the night and here I took my first lesson in camp life, cooked my supper and went to bed but couldn't sleep until after the chickens crowed for the day and after a short nap I awoke.

May 19, Thursday. I got up and prepared breakfast and started again. We traveled two miles and come to the Missouri river at Leavenworth[1] and here the children have the pleasure of seeing a steamboat. We were detained a short time waiting for the Ferry-boat being on the opposite side we got across in safety. A gentleman by the name of Owen drives the mules up in the city for me while Mr. Ringo helps Johnny with the oxen here. We get our groceries and other necessities for our comfort and then drive about four

---

[5]*Op. cit.*, p. 197.

[1]Merrill J. Mattes, in his *Great Platte Road* (Lincoln, 1969), describes one of the "Jumping-off Places" as WESTON-FORT LEAVENWORTH. The Leavenworth Road lay from Leavenworth, Kansas, to Fort Kearney, Nebraska. Mattes' section on "The Fort Leavenworth Road and the Pony Express Route" (pp. 149ff) is of inestimable value to students of the overland trail.

miles and camp for the night, prepare our supper and go to bed and slept much better than I did last night, we got a stable for our mules and both the oxen for which we pay fifteen cents a head.

May 20, Friday. We remain here waiting we have our family wagon tires cut and by noon Mr. Tipton and Mr. Cirby's families overtake us, we then hitch up and travel out as far as the eight mile house and camp for the night. Mr. Tipton was so unfortunate as to get their wagon wheel broke which will detain them a short time and just after we get into camp Dr. Moores family came up.

May 21, Saturday. Still in camp repacking and repairing. Nothing occurred worthy of note.

May 22. Sabbath morning we hitch up and travel through Mount Pleasant — eighteen miles.

May 23, Monday. Travel 20 miles and have a hard storm near Lancaster a small town in Kansas.

May 24, Tuesday. Travel 5 miles could not go any farther on account of the mud.

May 25, Wednesday. Still at Clear Creek waiting for D. Gatty.

May 26, Thursday. We started again and got to a little town called Kinnekuck stayed their most of the day having the wagons repaired. In the evening we moved out two miles and camped on a creek called Grass Hopper.

May 27, Friday. Our cattle scattered, we only traveled 7 miles and camped at Walnut Creek.

May 28, Saturday. Started early this morning and traveled 18 miles and passed through a little town called Grenado and camped 4 miles this side.

May 29, Sabbath. Start to travel 20 miles today and would have done it had we not stopped at Senica — traveled 15 miles and camped on a little trail.

May 30, Monday.   We traveled 20 miles and camped quite early,   we passed through a town. I knew no name so called it Uncle John's store.

May 31, Tuesday.   Traveled 13 miles today and camped at Maryesvill.

June 1st, Wednesday.   We laid by today on account of the rain. The gentlemen went fishing and caught a great many fish. We have quite a nice evening,   some gentlemen who are camped near us came and played on their violins, which is quite entertaining to California travelers.

June 2, Thursday.   We travel 17 miles and camp and have very poor water.

June 3, Friday.   We travel 20 miles and camp at Rock Creek,   here we have such a beautiful camp,   large rocks are here with numerous names, some of them handsomely carved and conspicuously on a nice little square is a Seces [Secesh] Flag. I know by this southerners are ahead.

June 4, Saturday.   We camped at Big Sandy   traveled 20 miles today,   nothing worthy of note transpired.

June 5, Sunday.   We travel 18 miles and camp at Little Blue   Lay by to wait for Mr. Guthry,   while here I washed up all of our dirty clothes,   at night our camp friends came and we had some more music. *(Stayed here two nights)*

June 7, Tuesday.   Left and traveled 18 miles. Today Johnnie got his foot hurt quite badly by the wheels running over it,   it seems to have been a day of accidents,   a little boy was run over by a wagon and killed and a wagon master by the name of Hase killed one of his teamsters, shot him through the head. The murdered man leaves a wife and children.

June 8, Wednesday.   We lay by for the gentlemen to go buffalo hunting,   they stay all day and until one o'clock at night,   they came back very much elated having killed a nice buffalo, the meat is very tender. Johnnie goes along not withstanding his foot is very sore,   he says they saw a great many Elk and Antelopes.

June 9, Thursday.   We travel 18 miles over what is called the "Nine mile prarie"   it has been the hardest drive for our cattle that we have had,   some places you could hardly see the men in the wagon for the dust,   I was glad indeed to camp,   we had good water and plenty of wood.

June 10, Friday.   We traveled 22 miles and camped on thirty-two mile creek,   we had a very refreshing shower while camped here that settled the dust and cooled the air.

June 11, Saturday.   We traveled 15 miles and camped three miles from Platt river,   we have to drive our stock to the river,   this place is almost destitute of grass,   the soil is sandy,   we find the cactus and prickly pears grow here and we see numerous little lizzards sliding through the grass and one extremely long snake gliding down in a hole. Our camping neighbors again give us some nice music.

June 12, Sunday.   We travel 10 miles and camp at noon,   we pass through a town called Doby Town, most all of the houses are built of dirt,   the prarie here is very level,   we have excellent grass for the stock. In days gone by it must have been a great place for Buffaloes as we see a great many skeletons some of them extremely large. From here I write a letter to my sisters Mrs. McCown and Mrs. Miller.

June 13, Monday.   Start early and travel 19 miles. We pass by Fort Kinney [Kearney],   we are not allowed to go through the Fort. Mr. Ringo walked up to see if we had any letters from our friends and was disappointed as we did not receive any,   mailed my letters here and go on. About two miles from this place is a small town called Kerney City. It is a right promising town. I buy myself a dress here,   we find the goods about as cheap as they are in the states. We camp tonight on the Platt River, it is very wide here, we think a mile and a half. The wind is very high and tonight is quite rainy.

June 14, Tuesday.   It is still raining,   we hitch up and travel 5 miles and camp as it will not do to drive our oxen while it is raining. Johnnie has a chill when we stop and now seems quite sick   I hope it may not be anything serious. Johnnie remains quite sick tonight. This evening Dr. Guthries train over take us. I am glad they have as they seem to be very gentlemanly.

June 15, Wednesday.   This morning is cloudy but we are going to drive some 19 miles,   we find the road very muddy,   camp about 5 o'clock,   make a corrall with Dr. Guthrie. We find some beautiful cactus in bloom today.

June 16, Thursday.   Its a foggy, misty morning — we drive 17 miles,   camp late this evening but on account of having stopped on Plumb [Plum] Creek so as to lay on a supply of wood — nothing of note today.

June 17, Friday.   We start late and drive 19 miles and camp about sun-set. I do not like to travel so late.

June 18, Saturday.   We get an early start this morning,   we pass fewer ranches than any day yet,   stopped at one and got some excellant water. Near this place is a dead Indian Scaffold. We drive up near so as to see how it is fixed,   it is not straightened as we straighten our dead but the feet are doubled round most to his head and it is tied up in blankets   its a strange looking way to put away the dead. We travel some miles and camp near the river,   some of the cattle give out almost and fall down. We ladies wade over a slough and go over to the river and we have a nice time. There are some ducks swimming,   the Dr. killed one and gave it to the children,   we saw another large snake.

June 19, Sunday.   This is a beautiful day and I am glad to say we lay by and this evening we have a good sermon by the Rev. Mr. Hodge and an exhortation by reformer by the name of Ewel. We are all thankful to have a preacher in our outfit.

June 20, Monday.   We are up very early   make a cup of coffee and start and travel 25 miles. We pass through a small town called Cotton Wood Springs,   this is a military post, they stopped every wagon to examine if we had any United States goods, horses and etc. We think they would have taken Mr. Tiptons horse as he had a U.S. brand on him but thought he was too old to be of much service. We camp about two miles from town and have most excellant water.

June 21, Tuesday.   We lay by here so as to lay in a supply of wood. Mr. Ringo, John and Allie take the wagon and go up a canyon some 2½ mi. and get plenty of good dry Cedar,   they tell me it is a most beautiful place in those mountains, every variety of flowers. We hitch up at noon and travel 10 miles and camp on a lake called Fremont,   it is a beautiful place   to look at it you would not think any ways deep but it was over the cattles back,   we had a laughable time driving them across the lake,   some of them would jump in and go under as though they enjoyed it very much.

June 22, Wednesday.   We traveled 21 mi. and camped where there was good grass,   at noon we watered in Fremont lake and now leave it and are near the North and South Platt. To day for the first time I see some Antelope,   they are beautiful. We are getting along very well.

June 23, Thursday.   This morning the cattle are scattered very much and we get a late start. Nothing of note today except we cross what is called Offallins Bluff and have a heavy, sandy road. We see some Indian Wigwams and two Indians came and offer two ponies for [space]   travel 17 miles.

June 24, Friday.   We only travel 10 miles and camp at noon so as to make enquiries about the boat.

June 25, Saturday.   Several outfits going in and buy the boat and this evening we camp some 4 miles from where we camped last night and its now raining hard,   I hope we will not be detained here long — the rain increases and we have quite a storm but not near so severe as it was some two or three miles up,   it blew so hard there that it turned wagons over that were heavily loaded.

June 26, Sunday.   We are still in camp,   I was in hopes we would have a sermon but Mr. Hodges was helping to cross over the boat, as we are anxious to get away and it was essential to be crossing.

June 27, Monday.   It is a bright morning so I wash all our dirty clothes and in the evening have a headache. We have another light shower. Nothing of interest today.

June 28, Tuesday.   A very warm day and I am getting very tired of lying by, would much rather be traveling. I made myself a bonnet today and am quite tired this evening.

June 29, Wednesday.   I walked with Mr. Ringo down to the river,   the water does look so swift, they are crossing wagons quite fast. Several Indians came to camp this morning,   one of them had a saber,   we asked him where he got it,   he said he killed a soldier and took it. I have cut myself a dress and am going to try and make it this week.

June 30, Thursday.   I did very little work today — we have a shower this evening.

July 1, Friday.   We do nothing,   we are getting so tired of camp and tonight we had quite a storm,   such vivid lightning and loud thunder.

July 2, Saturday.   We hitch up once more and start,   we have quite a time for the first few miles, three teams mired down, we travel some eight miles and camp for the night.

July 3, Sunday. The boat has been towed up to this point and we are crossing slowly, very slowly, today we cross seven wagons and as it is cloudy we think best not to cross any tonight. Today Mr. Forbuses train came up, they are to have the boat 6 hours and we are to have it at noon and use it 6 hours.

July 4, Monday. Mr. Forbus is crossing wagons and we are resting, the day is very pleasant but no one is talking of celebrating Independence Day — this evening we continue crossing our wagons. Nothing worthy of note transpires today.

July 5, Tuesday. It is very warm, we ladies walk up on the river and have a nice bath and this evening the mosquitoes just swarm all over the prarie, no one can sleep for them scarcely and we are all getting very tired — we have been lying by now some 12 days and nearly all the emigration seems to be going on ahead of us.

July 6, Wednesday. We cross over the South Platt quite safely, got on a sand bar and had hard pulling for awhile to get off, the river is over a mile wide but it is not swearving many places. We are so glad to get over.

July 7, Thursday. It is a beautiful morning and as we expect to start early I wash all of our dirty clothes this evening. Mr. Moors and Mr. Tiptons families came over and at night we have some more rain with a great deal of wind.

July 8, Friday. We get up our cattle and hitch up and once more start on our journey, we are all so glad to get off of this river as we have been lying by on this river 14 days, we traveled 10 miles today and camp at the old California crossing. We have another slight shower with wind enough to blow our wagons on like as if they were pulled by mules.

July 9, Saturday.   This morning we leave the river and cross over to North Platt and I had such a nice walk over the bluffs and through the canyon and gathered mountain currants and we saw some beautiful flowers and when I came up with the wagons we were on the top of a very high hill and when we went down we had to lock the wagons and then the gentlemen had to hold back on the wheels and when we got down in the valley we are in what is called Ash Hollow,   here we find the road very sandy. We travel some 25 miles today,   most of the road is very good.

July 10, Sunday.   The morning is warm and sultry,   we hitch up and after having gotten up enough wood to last us some two weeks we travel some 14 miles and this is the hardest day we have had on our cattle,   there is so much sand on this route and some such jump offs that it makes it dangerous. Mr. Moors wagon wheel was crashed in coming down a hill,   we travel some 14 miles and camp.

July 11, Monday.   This morning we have to mend the wagon and I take a long walk and climb to the top of the highest bluff,   on one of them is the grave of a man by the name of W. Craner who was shot by accident. We have several Indians to come in our camps and trade for buffalo robes and antelope skins,   there were also two gentlemen from Clay Co. who are returning to the states and who live near my uncles,   one of them, a Mr. Johnson says he will tell them of seeing us and I was glad to have an opportunity of sending them some home messages. This evening we hitch up and start and have quite a storm,   only travel some 5 miles and camp. In the night the wolves come in and howl and scares me a good deal at first. I hope we will not have the plagues to visit us again.

July 12, Tuesday.   We get an early start and travel some 20 miles and camp at a large spring of as good water as I ever drank. Nothing else of note today.

July 13, Wednesday.   It is eight weeks today since we left home and we ought to have been 200 miles farther on our way but we have been detained some 22 days since we left Missouri. Well today we pass the great Courthouse rock and its certainly a great curiosity. I would have been delighted to have gone up close to it but it is some 3 miles from the road at the nearest point. Some of the gentlemen rode up there and said it was surrounded by mountain currants of the largest size — near the rock is another large rock called the Clerks Office,[2] tis certainly a grand natural curiosity. We camped late, traveled 22 miles,   had a stream called Laurence Branch of North Platt,   this is a bad crossing on account of quicksand, three wagons mired down in it,   we have had a tiresome day.

July 14, Thursday.   Last night Mr. Tiptons horse and our Kate mule run off and Mr. Ringo was out all day hunting them and found them some eight miles down the road, going back the picket pin had stuck in her leg and she is quite lame. Today we pass Chimney Rock   this is another grand edifice,   you can see it for some 20 miles,   it is a 150 feet high, the chimney or cone being some 70 feet in heighth. The young ladies walked up to see it and brought me some specimans of the plants,   they describe it as being beautiful. I have been riding behind the ox wagon all day as we had to tie our wagon tongue under our large wagon. Its much pleasanter than I thought it would be but not like having our mules. We travel some 18 miles today and camp on the river where there is plenty of fish.

July 15, Friday.   Our mule is too lame to work today and we will have to ride tied to the other wagon — we traveled about

---

[2]This was one of the terms used for a smaller formation near Court House Rock, now called Jail Rock. It was occasionally called "The Clerk," meaning probably the clerk of the court.

10 miles and reached a telegraph office,   here they tell us
that the Indians were committing depredations on the
emigrants but we did not think much of it and had gone on
some 2 miles when they attracted two of our wagons. Mr.
Gouly and one other gentleman had turned out at the wrong
road and we drove on knowing that they could see us and
would cross the prarie and come to us,   whilest we were
looking at them we saw the Indians manouvering around
them and then rode close enough to shoot the arrows through
their wagon sheets just missing their heads,   they fired at
them and the Indians ran as fast as their horses could
go,   they crossed the river and attacted another emigrant
train killing one man and wounding another. As soon as they
attacted we went back to the ranch, correlled, and prepared
for a fight but they will not fight if they think you are
prepared for them. I do not think I ever spent such a night
for I could not sleep a wink. All of the families in the train
stayed in the telegraph office and anxiously waited for the
morning. We sent back for another train to come up with us
and here Mr. Morrices train join us and we now have in our
train 62 wagons and are very careful to keep out our guards.
July 16, Saturday.   We hitch up and travel some 18 miles
crossing the Scotts Bluff,   this is a bad road but grand
scenery. I could have enjoyed it very much but I was so afraid
the Indians would attack us but we got over safe and camped
at a beautiful place on the river,   there is an alkali slough
here and some of the cattle drank of it and it killed them. Mr.
Hoge loses some of his best oxen.
July 17, Sunday.   We travel 18 or 20 miles and camp near
the river,   nothing of note transpires today.
July 18, Monday.   We travel 19 miles and camp,   our
correll is very large as all of Mr. Forbuses has fell in with us
tonight. Mr. Hoge lost another ox.

July 19, Tuesday.   We got an early start and travel 10 miles
by noon,   we have quite an exciting time, correlled twice
thinking the Indians were going to attack us but we mistook
friendly Indians and one of our train fired at them,   we are
fearful that it will cause us more trouble as the Indian has
gone to the Fort to inform against us,   tis noon now and we
have stopped for the purpose of having some blacksmithing
done,   while here Mr. Davenport[3] came around to see
me,   he and the Mr. Morrisons are in our train and I am
very glad as they are very excellent men,   several persons
from Clay Co. are here. Rock Stone, Lincoln and Beachem
and I am partial to Missourians. I write a short letter home.

July 20, Wednesday.   We travel 13 miles and would have
gone farther but were detained at the Fort on account of
having shot at that friendly Indian and had to recompence
them by paying them some flour, bacon, sugar and coffee and
were glad to get off on those terms. We camp late,   had
quite a shower and ate our supper in the rain. Today I
received a letter from sis Mattie, the first I have had since I
left Mo.

July 21, Thursday.   We do not start early and only travel 9
miles over a very bad road and stop at a good place to grass
the stock. I wash some clothes today. Nothing of importance
transpires.

July 22, Friday.   We get in to what is called the Black Hills
and no one ever saw such bad roads as we have traveled and
this is only the beginning of what we will have for the next 75
miles,   our stock gave out and two belonging to the outfit
died. We travel 20 miles today and camp after night. I am
very tired and we only make a cup of coffee and go to bed.

---

[3]This was William Davenport whose letter is published at the end of Mary Ringo's
journal. She calls him "Dr." in her entry for August 22, below. He was of great
assistance to the Ringo family during the journey. He was from Liberty, Missouri.

July 23, Saturday.   We remain in camp and I gather such
nice currants and make some nice tarts for dinner,   there is
no grass here and they drive the cattle over the river where
they get good grass.

July 24, Sunday.   We start at day break and travel some 6
miles to a ranch and here we leave the train that we have been
traveling with and join Calon Morrices. I hated to leave the
family but they are traveling with freight trains and only go
ten miles a day and have camped now to remain some days
and Mr. Guthrie advised us to go on,   their cattle are dying
so fast, the road is strewn with dead cattle. We travel some 14
miles and camp near a spring and do not herd the cattle,   we
have not the men to spare from camp so we only keep camp
guard.

July 25, Monday.   This morning early some emigrants
came to camp who had a man killed by the Indians last
night,   they report sad times ahead. I pray God we may get
along safely. Today we discovered our ox was sick and
bleeding at the nose,   we turned him out and he was dead in
about an hour after we unyoked him. Dr. Davis cut him open
to find out what disease was killing off so many cattle and
pronounced it bloody murrin [murrain],[4] all the entrails were
full of blood and no one can tell of anything that will cure
them. Salt is said to be good but they will not lick salt in an
alkalie country. I am sorry to lose him but hope we wont lose
anymore. Today we travel 15 miles and camp on a creek. I do
not know the name of it. It is very brushy,   the grass is
scarce and we drive the cattle out to the bluffs. Some of the
gentlemen kill a black tail deer and we have very nice steaks.

July 26, Tuesday.   The cattle are scattered in every direction
and we will get a very late start — we only travel some 5 miles

---

[4]Murrain was the name applied to several cattle diseases, the most likely one being
anthrax. See introduction to Volume V of this set, pp. 15-16. It could also have been foot
and mouth disease.

and correll and send the cattle some 2 miles where they get good grass. We have a large spring but the water is callaciate. Mr. Forbs called to see me this evening and several gentlemen from the States came around. Mr. Summers from Platte. I think we are all going to travel together through this Indian country.

July 27, Wednesday. We got up at two o'clock and got breakfast and travel some 15 miles and stop on a creek, plenty of good water and fine grass. We find posted on a tree a notice that the Indians have killed six men near here. We hear they have had a fight ahead of us. I do hope and pray God that we may get through safely, it keeps me so uneasy and anxious.

July 28, Thursday. We do not get an early breakfast as we only think of traveling 10 miles to reach this place, a nice creek and correll and have good grass and water. Nothing of importance transpires today, above here 3 miles the Indians killed some men and took the ladies prisoners.

July 29, Friday. We do not get an early start and after traveling some 5 miles we see the corpse of a man lying by the side of the road, scalped, had been buried on top of the ground and the wolves had scratched it up. I think we ought to have buried him. We pass the Durlock ranch and camp some two or three miles this side on a beautiful grassy spot and about dark Mr. Ravel went out to bring in his horses when a man shot him through the arm, in a short time all lights were extinguished and every man to his post expecting to be attacked by Indians but we do not think it was the Indians but a band of robbers.

July 30, Saturday. And now Oh God comes the saddest record of my life for this day my husband accidentally shot himself and was buried by the wayside and oh, my heart is breaking, if I had no children how gladly would I lay me

down with my dead — but now Oh God I pray for strength
to raise our precious children and oh — may no one ever
suffer the anguish that is breaking my heart, my little
children are crying all the time and I — oh what am I to do.
Every one in camp is kind to us but God alone can heal the
breaking heart. After burying my darling husband we hitch
up and drive some 5 miles. Mr. Davenport drove my mules
for me and Oh, the agony of parting from that grave, to go
and leave him on that hillside where I shall never see it more
but thank God tis only the body lying there and may we only
meet in Heaven where there is no more death but only life
eternally.

July 31st, Sunday.   We are up and start early. I could not
sleep but rested tolerably well. I and Allie drive our
mules   they are very gentle and go so nicely. This has been
the longest day I ever spent. We travel about 14 miles and
camp — we keep out a strong guard but I was uneasy and
afraid all night.

August 1, Monday.   We travel 10 miles and cross Platte
River bridge, it is a nice bridge. There is a company of
soldiers here who seem to be very fearful of an attack from
the Indians. We camp about 2 miles from the Station.

August 2, Tuesday.   We remain in camp having some
wagons repaired. I am so anxious to be moving,   time seems
so long to me. This morning quite early a good many of the
Rappahoes tribe came in to camp but seemed quite friendly.
Several ladies called to see me and every one is very kind but
I am so lonely and tonight Fanny has an attack of
cholremorbus and after she gets easy I rest better than I have
any night since the death of my dear husband. Oh God help
me to bear this hard trial.

August 3, Wednesday.   We travel 10 miles over a hilly
country and camp on Platte River,   tolerably good grass.

We meet a good many returning to the States who report no grass ahead. I fear we will make slow progress through. Nothing of note transpires.

August 4, Thursday.   We are detained in camp waiting for some young men who got their wagon wheel broke and had to go back to the bridge station and buy them another and when they came up we start and go about 200 yards and break another wagon,   we correll and remain in camp for the rest of the day. Late in the evening Bovey's [Beauvais] train pass us. I was sorry to see them leave as they had some such kind friends   among them is a Mr. Kella and Mr. Summers, they were particularly kind.

August 5, Friday.   The cattle were scattered so it takes all day to get them together,   we keep them in correll all night so as to get an early start in the morning.

August 6, Saturday.   We get an early start and go some 10 miles — correll and grass the cattle,   there is no water here,   we do not tarry longer than to get dinner. Travel on some miles to find a good cool spring. Today we make some 14 miles and camp at Willow Spring. We find good springs here,   our cattle scatter very much. I feel so sad and lonely.

August 7, Sunday.   We get a late start on account of the cattle scattering. The Mr. Morrices leave our train and are traveling by themselves. I feel sorry for any one to leave as I feel safer in a large company. We noon at what is called Fish Creek and tonight we correll on Home Creek,   the water is very clear and full of fish. We drive the cattle 1½ miles to good grass. We have no wood but sagebrush. The wolves howl all around our camp even after daylight. We travel 14 miles.

August 8, Monday.   We start at five o'clock and drive to Sweet Water by noon where we are now nooning. There is a great deal of alkalie through this section, many places the

water is crusted all over with beautiful white crust. We cross
Sweet Water and camp at a sandy camping place. We passed
Independence Rock and it is a grand sight, many names are
carved there, some few of them I knew. We have good grass
for our stock but there is a great deal of alkalie here.

August 9, Tuesday.   We get a late start and drive to a point
called Hell's Gate (I do not think it an appropriate name for
the grand and sublime scenery). The pass is very narrow and
perpendicular walls on either side. We heard that a gentleman
had fallen from the top of them and was killed instantly. We
travel 14 miles and camp at Plantes Station,   have a nice
camp.

August 10, Wednesday.   We travel 12 miles and camp
below Split Rock,   nothing of importance transpires today.
Some of the cattle die and we travel slowly.

August 11, Thursday.   We travel 13 miles and camp near
three crossing at a beautiful place but everything seems
lonely to me. I hate to see night coming and do hope we will
soon get through to Salt Lake.

August 12, Friday.   Our cattle scattered and we get a late
start and traveled some 10 or 12 miles by noon. We hitch up
and start at 4 o'clock and travel till 9 o'clock at night and
camp at Ice Spring,   its very cold,   we keep our cattle in
the correll so as to get an early start in the morning.

August 13, Saturday.   We start early and come some 14
miles and rest our stock and then travel some 4 miles and
camp on Sweet Water. The stock have good grass tonight.

August 14, Sunday.   We pass a ranch at the foot of Rocky
Ridge. We leave Sweet Water here and travel over a hilly
country with scarcely any grass,   we rest our cattle till late
and then travel till 9 o'clock. We make some 20 miles and
camp on Strawberry — the night is beautiful. We pass
several trains and their campfires look so cheerful.

August 15, Monday.   We start by sun-up and travel some 3 miles here. Mr. Morris train passes us. Mr. Davis comes to see me   I am always glad to see him for he is the last one Mr. Ringo ever talked to. Oh God thou hast sorely afflicted me — give me strength to bear this heart tryal. We traveled about 11 miles and camp on Sweet Water near a ranch. Nothing of importance transpires today.

August 16, Tuesday.   We come over South Pass and camp at Paciffick Springs,   these springs are very cold and its quite mirey. We travel 15 miles today.

August 17, Wednesday.   We get a late start and noon on dry Sandy — here the cattle have no water and but little grass. We travel some 6 miles and camp where there is neither grass or water,   correll our cattle and horses.

August 18, Thursday.   We start very early and travel to a station on Little Sandy where we have fine water but little grass. We are nooning now — we hitch up and travel some 7 miles farther and camp on Big Sandy — grass very scarce and one of my oxen gives out and we unyoke him and let him rest.

August 19, Friday.   We get breakfast and start — have traveled 10 miles and are now nooning,   tis very windy and we have a sandy camping place — we travel very slowly and camp 4 miles from Big Timbers and our camp is far from water,   we correll our cattle to keep them from scattering.

August 20, Saturday.   We start early and drive to Green River some 16 miles and correll after dark. I do not get any supper for I am too tired — we have had a sandy hilly road. Mr. Dewey drove down some of the long hills for me.

August 21, Sunday.   We remain in camp today,   our stock are on good grass and they are going to let them recruit for a few days. This is the most beautiful river I ever saw — tis very rapid and the water looks green and is very clear. I have not spent my Sabbath as I would like to — I have been cooking and first one thing and then another. I did not read any.

August 22, Monday.   We cross Green River and camp on this side. We separate here from Forbuses train and we go with Mr. Davises, Mr. How and Mr. Campbells train. We only have seven wagons in all and I am afraid to travel with so few but no one seems to apprehend any danger but me. Dr. Davenport stays in our correll and writes a letter to his wife. He has been very kind to me since the death of my husband and I am sorry to separate from their train. Mr. Forbus and family were more than kind. I hope they may do well.

August 23, Tuesday.   This morning we start our train for Salt Lake and have traveled some 16 miles and camp on Black Creek Fork. I do not think we have much grass and its raining and very disagreeable,   do not get any supper as its raining too hard.

August 24, Wednesday.   We start our train out at ten o'clock and noon on Black Fork,   we then start again and travel some 11 miles by traveling in the night,   our mule is a little alkalied and seems quite sick and I walk several miles pass Church Buttes,   the sand hills are grand looking domes — we find tolerable good grass for our stock and camp near a mail station,   I am glad we are once more in the mail line, it seems more like civilization.

August 25, Thursday.   We passe Millesville and camp some three miles this side,   have good water and grass. Tonight we keep up a guard as we are in Indian settlement.

August 26, Friday.   We get a late start this morning and have only come 6 miles   are now nooning in sight of Fort Bridger. My ox team has come and I am going some three-quarters of a mile beyond the Fort and camp. I go to the Post Office and mail one letter only there is no Eastern Mail, the

Indians are too bad for the coaches to run. We camp this side
of Fort Bridger and have fine grass.

August 27, Saturday.   We travel 13 miles today,   are
traveling the new cut-off,   so far the road is very good,   we
are camping on Muddy Creek   we find the government
corrells here,   a Mr. Bently comes and takes supper with
us. Mr. Donly also comes round to see us. I am so lonely and
sad and I wish I was at my journeys end.

August 28, Sunday.   We lay over today as it is the Sabbath.
I am glad that we do. I do not think it is right to travel on the
Sabbath. I have the headache today   Mr. Buell and family
leave our party and go back to the Fort, they were very
pleasant people.

August 29, Monday.   We start early and travel 19½ miles
and camp on Willow Creek,   here we see potatoes growing
and buy some turnips for 25 cts. a dozen,   we also get some
cheese at 50 cts. a pound, it is very nice. This is a good
camping place and I sleep better than I have for a long time.

August 30, Tuesday.   We travel on 8 miles and correll for
the night. It is rainy and we do not cook supper, have
crackers and cheese.

August 31, Wednesday.   We start tolerably early but fall in
behind the Government train and have to travel very slowly.
At noon we pass them and travel but a short distance as tis
raining. We stop for the night having made only 6 miles
today.

September 1, Thursday.   We lay by and wash. I wash most
all of my dirty clothes,   we have another shower, it has
rained every day this week. I was quite tired but rest very
well tonight.

September 2, Friday.   We start late and have come 4 or 5
miles,   have passed Huffs ranch where I see the first corn
growing I have seen this year. I sent Johnny to see if he could

buy some potatoes and he has not caught up with us yet,   he does not get any potatoes but gets some nice turnips.

September 3, Saturday.   We travel some 18 miles and correll on Silver Creek where the canyon is so narrow that we hardly have room for our wagons.

September 4, Sunday.   We lay over till afternoon and would not travel now but we have no place for our stock so we hitch up and travel some 6 miles where we have a good camping ground and nice grass.

September 5, Monday.   We travel some 20 miles and camp near a station where a Missouri lady comes to see us,   she is stopping here for the winter, her name is Hueston.

September 6, Tuesday.   We start early and have reached the great Salt Lake City. I have not been up in the City   are camping on the Emigrants Square. Expect I will go up in the morning. I received two letters from sister Mattie and one from Mr. Halliday and no tongue can tell how sad I feel for each letter was written to my dear husband for they know not that he is dead.

September 7, Wednesday.   I wait for Major Barron[5] to come down and as he does not   I go up to see him and present my letter of introduction,   he receives me very politely and promised to assist me in selling my outfit and procuring me a passage in the coach for California but took good care not to come down. I am at a loss what to do. Mrs. Belt called down awhile this evening to see Mrs. Davise. This City is handsomely laid out, every house has an acre of ground ornamented with trees and flowers but I would not live here if the whole city belonged to me among such a class

---

[5]We checked all of the soldiers named Barron listed in J. Carlyle Parker's *Personal Name Index to Orton's "Records of California Men in the War of the Rebellion, 1861 to 1867,"* (Detroit, 1978), and found only privates. A careful check with Orton's original work (Sacramento, 1890) listed no officers by that name.

of community. I haven't seen a handsomely dressed lady since I have been here. Morman communities are poor excuses to me and there are more dirty children running around begging than a few,   we buy some nice peaches but they are 25 cts. a dozen. I tell you you have to pay high for everything you get here.

September 8, Thursday.   I sent up for Major Barron to come down as I did not know what to do,   he came down looked at my wagons, oxen and mules and seemed to think they were worth so little that I thought I had better not try to sell them and have hired a Mr. John Donly to drive my oxen and am going to try to go through in my wagons. We leave Salt Lake City about noon and travel some 15 miles and camp near a ranch where they have a large spring but the water is salty and makes us all sick.

September 9, Friday.   We lay over all day.

September 10, Saturday.   We hitch up and travel some 12 miles and camp at a village called E. T.   here the water is very salty as well as the grass,   our mules come very near dying from the effects of it.

September 11, Sunday.   We leave Mr. Davises family and travel on to a small town,   I do not know the name of it and here we get some hay for the stock and buy some nice peaches. We drive out about a mile from town and Mr. Davises family come on and correll with us.

September 12, Monday.   We drive some 10 miles and camp by some fine springs and our stock has fine grass,   we stay here for the rest of the day.

September 13, Tuesday.   We hitch up and go through a settlement where we buy some excellent Irish potatoes. We drive some 21 miles and my mules give out,   we have poor grass and I buy hay and oats for the mules for which I pay $6.00.

September 14, Wednesday.   We travel some 5 miles and camp near a mail station and we have to drive our stock 6 miles to grass,   we stay here the rest of the day and I buy some most excellent mutton. Mr. Davises overtake us again.

September 15, Thursday.   We go some 10 miles to a station called Look-out,   stay here all night.

September 16, Friday.   We travel 12 miles and camp at Government Springs and have excellent grass for our stock.

September 17, Saturday.   We lay over here and I wash our dirty clothes,   they cut some excellent grass for the stock as we will soon cross the great desert and will need all the feed we can haul for them.

September 18, Sunday.   We lay over here as our stock is improving so much.

September 19, Monday.   We leave this place and travel some 10 miles to Indian Springs, here we again lay over for the rest of the day so the stock may all fill up.

September 20, Tuesday.   We remain here until one o'clock and then start for the desert. We travel all this evening and all night and have come some 36 miles and are now resting in the desert.

September 21, Wednesday.   We travel some 10 miles and noon at Fish Springs Station, our Bet mule is a little sick and we fasten our wagon under the ox wagon and go to the next station   from here we move up some 2 miles to a fine spring and camp for the night. The grass and water here are quite salty.

September 22, Thursday.   We hitch up and start again, the stock seem rested and we have traveled some 10 miles and are now nooning but there is not a sprig of grass for our teams. We travel some 24 miles and camp at Willow Springs — good water and grass.

September 23, Friday.   We start before day and travel some

30 miles and camp at Deep Creek,   this is a narrow stream but very deep, grass good.

September 24, Saturday.   We remain here until noon and then travel some 6 miles and camp as this is the last good grass we will have for some miles.

September 25, Sunday.   We start early this morning and travel 28 miles and camp but find very little grass,   our mules are very tired as well as the oxen and we camp for the night,   it rains very hard and is very windy.

September 26, Monday.   We start early and travel 16 miles,   we find some good bunch grass and stop and let the stock grass.

September 27, Tuesday.   We travel 16 miles and camp near a station and have good grass,   the water here is quite warm.

September 28, Wednesday.   We travel 25 miles and pass through Egan Canyon,   here we see a good many emigrants stopping here for the winter to try their luck in the mining process,   tis thought that these are rich mines. At night when we camp we have a fine camp fire,   near us is camped a woman who is confined and gives birth to a son, her name is Richardson.

September 29, Thursday.   We travel 27 miles and have a very tiresome drive   our mules and cattle both give out and we do not get into camp till almost midnight. I am very tired.

September 30, Friday.   We start as early as we can and go some 10 miles to Ruby Valley,   we stop here and rest our stock,   we find everything very dear, I buy some coffee at one dollar a pound and give them my tin can to pay for it.

October 1, Saturday.   We start early, travel 24 miles and camp at the foot of Diamond Mountain,   this is a very high peak, the highest I have seen yet — our mules give out again and we haul our wagon with the oxen,   it is a very cold night.

October 2, Sunday.   We hitch up and climb the high hill,   we get up safely and then descend to a beautiful valley and remain there the rest of the day and night and have a very windy evening and night.

October 3, Monday.   We get an early start and have traveled very well but our mules are tired and I am getting so tired traveling. This evening we have a great time climbing to the top of a high hill and are very glad to get to the top,   we then camp near a ranch and buy some hay for our oxen — we taveled 24 miles today.

October 4, Tuesday.   We travel 20 miles   have no grass and poor water.

October 5, Wednesday.   We travel 22 miles and have good grass and water — camp in a canyon.

October 6, Thursday.   We travel 20 miles over a very bad road,   had a very bad hill to climb and a worse one to descend. I walk down which brings on a spell of sickness for tonight I am very poorly. We camp in Simpson's Park.

October 7, Friday.   We travel 10 miles and reach Austin,[6] Nevada, where I have the pleasure of seeing cousin Charley Peters and my old acquaintance Mr. Ford from Liberty, Mo. They are very kind to me and assist me to dispose of my oxen and wagon.

October 8, Saturday.   We remain in Austin, Nev.

IN CONCLUSION: Written by Mattie Bell (Ringo) Cushing, daughter of Mary Ringo.

---

[6] Far and away the best reference to this silver mining town is Oscar Lewis' book with the attenuated title: *The Town That Died Laughing, The Story of Austin, Nevada, Rambunctious Early-Day Mining Camp, and of Its Renowned Newspaper, The Reese River Reveille* (Reno, 1955). We have used the 1986 edition with a new foreword by Kenneth N. Owens.

That is the last Mother wrote in her diary so I will have to finish the best I can from things she told us at different times. I think she was the bravest woman I ever heard of — left as she was with five children to look after and to have everything else to attend to and in the condition she was in. In Austin she had a son born, fortunately it was still-born for he was terribly disfigured from mother seeing father after he was shot. Even my brother who was fourteen years old noticed it and said he looked just like father did. On the way out when we reached Fort Laramie, Wyoming, the government offered her an escort of soldiers to go back to Missouri but she said she was as much afraid of the soldiers as she was of the Indians and besides it wouldn't seem like home without father.

I don't know how long we stayed in Austin, probably a week or ten days and I don't know how we made the rest of the trip. We took the mules and one wagon to San Jose and she told of stopping in San Francisco, California, and how high up the beds were, my sister had to climb on a chair to get in it.

We finally reached San Jose where Mother's sister lived. My aunt and her husband had a very large place and Mr. Younger raised blooded cattle. They had a small house on the place that had formerly been a carriage house and had been made into a house. We lived there a year as mother was not able to do anything for some time but she paid our living expenses as of course she had some money but it was confederate money and she lost 36 dollars on the hundred.

We moved to San Jose and lived on Second Street where mother began the task of providing for her little family, the way was rough but with her sheer determination she raised her family unaided.

EPILOGUE: LETTER OF WILLIAM DAVENPORT
From the Liberty, Missouri, *Tribune*, September 16, 1864

From the Plains
Platte River   Idaho Ter.
August 1, 1864

Mr. R.H. Miller — Dear Friend. I write to give you the melancholy information of the death of Martin Ringo. Owing to some difficulties we had with the Indians below Fort Laramie at Scott's Bluffs the emigration formed themselves into large companies. Our company consisted of the Morris brothers and Jas. Reed of Clay county, Forbes, Irvin, Lucas & Co., from Platte and Buc[h]anan counties — Beauvais & Co. from St. Joseph with Mr. Ringo and family and others, making in all about 70 wagons, have been traveling together for mutual protection. We passed through the Black Hills, where the Indians have committed most of their depredations this season without being molested, and camped the night of the 28th July about three miles this side of Deer Creek, and about twenty five miles from this point. Shortly after dark a gentleman by the name of Davis, from Kansas, went out about fifty yards from the camp to look after his horses that were picketed out, and an Indian shot and wounded him in the right arm and side, making a painful tho' not dangerous wound. The Indian succeeded in stealing three horses — one from Mr. Davis, one from Mr. Irvin and one from David Morris. There was only one Indian seen, and I think his only object was to steal horses. The shooting of Mr. Davis created considerable excitement in camp, as we expected to be attacked by Indians in force. The whole company stood guard during the night so as to be prepared in case we were attacked. Just after daylight on the morning of the 30th ult. Mr. Ringo stepped on top of the wagon, as I suppose, for the purpose of looking around to see if Indians were in sight, and his shot gun went off accidentally in his own hands, the load entering his right eye and coming out at the top of his head. At the report of the gun I saw his hat blown up twenty feet in the air, and his brains were scattered in all directions. I never saw a more heartrending sight, and to see the distress and agony of his wife and children was painful in the extreme. Mr. Ringo's death has cast a gloom over the whole company, and his wife and children have our sympathy. The ladies in our company are very kind and attentive to Mrs. Ringo, and every gentleman in the company is disposed to do anything in his power to make her comfortable, or promote her interests. Mr. Ringo was a very mild, pleasant and unassuming gentleman, and was duly appreciated by our company — all of whom esteemed him highly. He was buried near the place he was shot in as decent a manner as possible with the facilities on the plains.

Mrs. Ringo thinks of going to Salt Lake and of disposing of her outfit at that point and taking the stage from there to California. There is a portion of our company that are going to California via Salt Lake, the larger portion are going to Idaho via the South Pass, and a portion of them are going by Bridger's Cut Off, sixteen miles from here.

We do not anticipate any further Indian troubles on our journey, as there is no report of their committing any depredations beyond this point. We are going to travel in sufficiently large companies to protect ourselves, and by keeping strict guard we do not expect to be molested — their only object being to steal horses.

Our company are all enjoying excellent health.

Your friend,
Wm. Davenport.

HARRIET ADELLE HITCHCOCK
Courtesy of Mrs. Catherine J. Webb of Albany, California

Thoughts by the Way, 1864-1865
♪ Harriet Hitchcock

INTRODUCTION

"Thoughts by the way. And why not!"

With the above words Harriet Adelle Hitchcock, a delightful 13-year-old began her story of a journey to the Pikes Peak country and return in 1864-5. She was one member of a family traveling to Colorado to scout out the mining possibilities. Her father's fascination with gold mining was a paramount reason to take part in the Colorado gold rush. Years later, after the death of his wife and the breaking up of the family when one after another of the three daughters were married, he went to Colorado and spent his last years there in the Leadville area. Harriet's mother, Emily, also traveled to Colorado with the family wagon train, two sisters, Lucy and Bell, whom she mentions many times. They hired two young men to handle the livestock. She tells us nothing about them but their given names: Dick and Harry.

We find Harriet's age by reading the diary entry for January 25, 1865: "My 14th birthday." Hence, her birth date was January 25, 1851.

The diary covers the round trip from St. Joseph, Missouri, to Denver and return, from June 2, 1864, to February 15, 1865, when they arrived in Nevada, Iowa. Their journey from there would be by railroad.

Harriet lived for several years more in North East, Pennsylvania, her hometown right on the shore of Lake Erie, then it was off to Oberlin College, Oberlin, Ohio. There she met a young man training for the Congregational ministry, Oramel William Lucas, (b. December 22, 1849, Pittsfield, Ohio). He liked to call himself "a genuine Forty-niner." The two were united in marriage on June 27, 1883, in North East.

Fifty years later in an "Autobiography" written for the 50th reunion of Oberlin's class of 1883, Oramel William Lucas reminisced about a meeting he had with a young girl who would later become his wife:

> At the age of fifteen I united with the Congregational Church in Pittsfield — a time ever memorable. Just at that time the wife and three daughters of a Colorado miner on their way home from a year in the Rocky Mountains visited our home. It was maple sugar season and a batch of syrup fresh from sugar bush [a grove of sugar maple trees] was at hand. This was put in the big, brass kettle in the fireplace and sugared off. The youngest of our visiters, a girl of about my age, and myself with others were helped to hot sugar and we two gravitated to the lounge in the corner and chatted as we ate our sugar. It was literally a sweet time and thus began a friendship which eventuated in marriage. After sixty-four years of acquaintance and most helpful and loving companionship, that beautiful girl of fourteen, grown to almost seventy eight fruitful years, passed on, leaving two sorrowing and lonely ones to carry on in the home.

The new minister's first church was Pendleton, Oregon. They traveled by train from Pennsylvania to Pendleton and reached their new place of service on October 3, 1883. While in Pendleton the first of their children, Ethel Eudora Lucas, was born on January 20, 1888. A son, Arthur LeRoy, was born on September 11, 1888, but tragically he lived only two years.

There followed a succession of pastorates in Oregon and in California: Oregon City, San Bernardino, Oakland, and Pacific Grove. After retirement the Lucases moved to Berkeley, where they lived out their lives. Harriet died on December 16, 1928, and Oramel on May 12, 1935.

We learned of this overland journal when we received a letter from Mrs. Catherine J. Webb of Albany, California. She is the kind of family historian who has published the diary along with many letters in a large photocopied book, *A Family History of*

California, in 1975. She had heard your editor tell of this series over a San Francisco radio station, KGO. She wrote a letter telling about the Hitchcock diary. She has been most cooperative and provided us with numerous other documents and photographs relating to the life of Harriet (Hitchcock) Lucas and her minister husband. Through the years we have had numerous telephone conversations, and her words of encouragement are priceless.

She provided us with both a typescript and a photocopy of the original handwritten document, which we have reproduced as carefully as we could.

THE JOURNAL

Thoughts by the way.   And why not! Others think and why not I! And what is the harm in simply penning a few thoughts now and then by the way side or by the side of the way, for it is a new and strange way that we are going to travel. True we have already travelled over 1000 miles but it was the same way other people travel by railroad and steamboat and of course saw the same that other people see when they are bewildered and see nothing. But now after crossing the Father of Waters and its greatest tributary we find ourselves in a new and strange place, with our faces toward the setting sun (for it is afternoon) and the tongue of our wagon is the same direction. And as thought is ever busy I will make my hands help a little by scratching them down on paper, for my diary is too small for the purpose, and memory too short. Of course it ise'nt a Journal and no one will ever see it only a thought now and then.

Lucy will think me a thoughtless silly girl for she always remembers every thing and in her quiet way, will in future years convince us that her memory is sufficient for any emergency, and Bell who always speaks her thoughts before

she thinks them will undoubtedly advise me to admire the
beauties of nature as she is doing and even now she is telling
me that I had better note down where we came from and
where we are going lest I should forget. Which I will now do.
My two elder sisters and myself concluded to accompany Pa
on his annual trip to Colorado.

Our home is in a pleasant little village far to the east
situated not on the banks of a river but in a beautiful tract of
country with a long range of hills onto the south, and the
clear blue waters of one of our Great Lakes on the north.[1]

Well here we are on the 2nd day of June 1864 in this great
state of Kansas, ten miles from St Joseph, doing as all other
travellers are doing, camping out. We have two wagons and
two span of horses. Pa drives one team and Dick and Harry
(two men who have joined our company) drive the other
team. Lucy my oldest sister is cooking our supper for the first
time on our new stove in the open air. This new mode of life
seems very strange and I can hardly realize that we are here
but as I gaze for miles on the rolling prairie I begin to think
of a reality

June 3rd   Here we are after another days travel camped by
the side of a beautiful little stream, and for a change I have
been wandering around among the bushes until I found a
birds nest, with five blue eggs in it looking for all the world
just as birds eggs look at home and being in quite a practical
mood I seated myself on a log and composed a hymn
addressed to the mother bird who sat perched over my head
which I will note down for fear I shall forget it.

        As wandering forth mid shrub and tree
          In quest of something new to see —
There, I have forgotten all the rest, but never mind. I wont

[1]Harriet Adella Hitchcock was born in the town of North East, on Lake Erie, in the
northwestern county of Pennsylvania, Erie County.

let Bell know it and I can have the good of thinking that I did compose a long hymn.

June 4th   Are we truly going farther and farther away from our old home. But it will pay to see these vast plains the home of the red man   Here and there an enterprising white family are settled on a spot of ground which they call a ranche.

6th   We stopped to feed this noon where a woman with three small children were waiting alone   Her husband had gone in search of his oxen which ran away last night probably in search of water.   she was very glad to see us as there was no human habitation in miles   nothing to be seen but a vast plain bounded by the horison. A hen coop was attached to the rear end of the wagon containing about a dozen nice specimans of poultry of the Shanghai order. She had roasted some eggs over a few coals made from dried grass which she had gathered   I pitied the poor little children and gave them what few apples we had. After dinner we were obliged to go on and leave them.

7th   Crossed the Big Blue and are now in Nebraska Territory. Bought some Buffalo meat. We do not see any Buffalos as they are all driven south by the Indians.

June 13th   This afternoon we reached the great thorough-fare from Nebraska city to Denver. The road is filled with emigrants and my eyes ache with looking at the long trains of wagons which we can see for miles ahead some of them drawn by six and eight yoke of oxen. We are in sight of the Platte river which we shall follow the rest of our journey. It is a very wide river but shallow and singular in its appearance being filled with islands of sand. The water is very muddy. There are no fish in it. It is navigable for mules only   their ears are serving for sails.

14th   Here we are at Kearney city. We stopped two miles east

of here at Fort Kearney. After camping we sent to the Post
Office and to our great joy received six letters from home.
while perusing them an officer came riding very fast on horse
back and informed us that no travellers were allowed to camp
on the Military Reservation, so we came on to this place. A
large number of soldiers are stationed at the Fort, which
makes it a lively place. The Fort is built of sods several feet in
thickness and over it waves the flag of our country. Here we
find eight or ten sod buildings each one containing about as
many occupants, with nearly the same number of dogs
around the doors who were trying to exercise their lungs by
barking most furiously at us but as adventurers are not to be
frightened by quadrupeds of that order we gave little heed to
them

16th   The road is filled with emigrants. I suppose that they
are all bound to the same place and for the same object. Most
of them have ox teams and of course we have plenty of music
such as it is. Some nights it is not quite as agreeable as we
would like. We are now camped near the river   fifteen
families on one acre of ground. There is a man just taking the
census. I think he will need to understand the first rule in
Arithmatic in order to count all of the children for they are so
thick they can hardly tell to which wagon they belong. It is
quite amusing to look around among the different families,
some are churning others are baking bread and preparing
supper, while others are scolding their children and probably
would use the rod of correction if they had any, but as we are
getting out of the region of bushes and trees it is hard to find
a rod and they are obliged to use threats instead.

17th   Dear me I am tired of counting. We have passed two
hundred ox teams today and met fifty going east. The road is
wide enough to accomodate us all   We have not seen a fence
since leaving Missouri,   Killed a large rattlesnake. We were

kept awake last night by the constant roaring of thunder   It was truly terrific

18th   After supper Lucy Bell and myself accompanied by Dick and Harry took a walk to the Bluff, about a mile. Here is the highest point on the whole route. We managed to reach the top of it with some difficulty as it was rather steep. Here we had a fine view of the plains in all directions. Harry said we could see 95000,000s of miles which I very much doubted but he explained it to my satisfaction by saying we could see to the sun   We have seen the manner in which Indians bury their Chiefs, which is to wrap them in large red blankets and fasten them at the top of four high poles   They can be seen a great ways off. We have seen quite a number of Indians today   they appeared friendly but they are an ignorant miserable race of beings

19th   The railroads in this country differ from those in the east in many respects   There is no artificial work needed Natures work is perfect. The roads are always in good condition. The cars are built similar to eastern cars except they are roofed with cloth and are furnished with sundry culinary appendages for the convenience of passengers as the power of locomotion is of such a kind that they are obliged to camp at night and cook their food. Each one is prepared for luggage, passenger and baggage car which renders it very convenient. Instead of being propelled by the iron horse they are propelled by oxen. The manner of raising the steam is by the use of a whip about twenty feet long with the voice raised an octave higher than when Moses sounded the trumpet to lead the children of Isreal out of the wilderness and using the monosyllables Whoa, Haw, Gee, and when one wheel is out of sight in the mud drawn by the attraction of gravitation towards the centre of the earth, the application of more steam and a more vigorous use of the lungs, soon brings it back

again and equilibrium is restored. Wood and water are quite
as necessary as on eastern roads, although they are used in a
different way. Each car has its own conductor who also fills
the part of engineer and brakesman, except those cars that
are propelled by mules in which case they sound the whistle
at their own option which is quite an improvement   There
is no danger of collisions as each train measures its own time
and distance and the speed with which they move enables
them to see each other in time to pass.

20th   Arrived at Cotton Wood about noon where we mailed
some letters. Saw a great many soldiers there. Bought several
large sticks of wood which we think will last us to Denver as
we shall not have another chance to get any —

21st   We are camped near a stage station   Such stations
are about fifteen miles apart   A man is now sitting on the
top of the house watching his horses while they are feeding
on the plains three or four miles away. Saw some bipeds
resembling birds that are called Snipes and I think they are
rightly named for they look as though the wind had blown
here from some distant clime   They do not sing at all
perhaps the wind has blown the music all out of them.

22nd   Passed through a large settlement of Prairie dogs and
indeed the whole country seems full of them. They are very
small resembling a squirrel except the head which is shaped
like that of a dog. They are very shy and keep near their
holes and commence barking as soon as they see anyone
coming near. The rattle snakes and the white owl live with
them under the ground. We undertook to get a Prairie dog
by pouring water into the hole   After we had poured several
pails of water in we heard a great commotion underneath. We
were all provided with gloves   Harry held a bag ready to receive the stranger   Lucy was bending over the hole to watch
its coming when suddenly she jumped and screamed as a

large animal came rushing out with glaring eyeballs looking fiercely at us   we were all frightened and the animal seemed no less so as he slowly walked away the water dripping from his sides, probably he had never received such treatment from girls before. It proved to be a Rocky Mountain Badger   a very savage animal when attacked.

23rd   I am wondering where we are   day after day we travel and still we seem to be "Nowhere" although the road is filled with teams. I wonder if any of them know where they are.   no one appears to care   We keep jogging on and camp where night over takes us. We are now where the sand is so deep that we are obliged to double our teams to get through as is often the case while crossing this desert. There is but little grass here But its ground is covered with cactus which grows spontaneously in the sand. It has a beautiful blossom and makes this desert region look much pleasanter than it other wise would. It is said that the Prairie dogs subsist on the leaf of the cactus. The weather is very hot and water scarce   The river water is very poor and there are few wells and fewer inhabitants. The only thing to remind one of civilization is the Telegraph which the poor Indians can not understand. They call it the whispering spirit   Although wood is very scarce yet a white man dare not cut a post down for its penalty is death. The scenery is very mountanus, but sun and sand day after day   A vast level plain bounded by the horison on all sides.

24th   Arrived at Julesburg.[2] A city on the plains is composed of one solid building called a stage station, two hay stacks, a few sticks of wood which perhaps has been brought a hundred miles, a tame antelope and five or six ant

[2]Julesburg, also known as Denver Junction, is where the first telegraph and later the railroad stations came into being. Telegraph messages in the 1860's addressed to Denver were received in Julesburg, then carried by pony express to Denver. J. Frank Dawson, *Place Names in Colorado* (Denver, 1954), p. 28.

hills   The principle streets are laid out by the ants which
are by far the most enterprising part of the population. They
greet me very cordially wherever we stop and are particularly
fond of forming an acquaintance with our provision boxes.
This city is more thriving than most of the cities as there are
eight or ten buildings here   Here is also the upper crossing
on the Platte for the California emigrants   a large number of
our company has crossed today—Fare ten dollars per wagon.
The method of crossing is to run the wagons on a flat
boat   the horses and mules are made to swim across. We
received letters from home among which was one from Ma's
sister in which she imagines me "as hoopless and shoeless
standing with arms akimbo, mouth extended, tongue
protruding, nose contracted, surveying the wonders of this
wonderfully wonderful world["]. Just as though I couldent
cross the plains without looking like a squaw. And then to
cap the climax she says My Dear Niece Eda do be careful
and now swallow a live Buffalo. Dear me I suppose she thinks
that I belong to the Arabs by this time but never mind she
will see when I get home that I am the same light hearted
Eda that I ever was.

25th   A heavy thunder shower. Saw some Indians. The
road is lined with carcasses of horses and oxen which have
died by the way. Last night while Dick and Harry were
watching our horses they got frightened and ran away. They
called for help and Pa after fastening the lantern to the top of
the wagon, as the night was very dark, hastened to their
assistance. They found them before morning and returned to
camp. Such stampedes are very common   some nights large
droves of horses are frightened and run off together.

26th   This part of the world abounds with Musquitoes of
an enormous size   some nights the air is filled with them.
Our Musquitos bars are the blue skies   I should think that

all of the musquitoes in the world had got inside of the bars and were awaiting further orders, if I was Colonel of their regiment I would drive them into the river on double quick. There are also a great many large bugs which are drawn at night by the light to the camp fires and can be gathered up by the bushel (or in a bushel basket)

27th   Saw a man who was taking some Cashmere Goats to California. They were quite a curiosity. We stopped this noon near a house where there is a dairy kept. We went in to buy some milk and found the woman making cheese. As she had no timber to make a cheese press, she hung her cheese in a bag by the door and as we came near we found the air filled with a strong odor from the bag. There were pans of milk standing on the ground in one corner of the cabin. In the other corner lay a pile of sundry articles which I suppose they used for a bed. We soon lost our appetite for milk and bidding the woman Good Bye we proceeded on our journey.

28th   This morn just as we had got our breakfast ready there was a severe thunder shower. We were obliged to leave our wide spread table and carry our food into the wagons and eat as we best could. Our crockery is made of a material that does not easily break. We reached the junction at noon and left the Muddy Platte river to go on what is called the cut off to Denver. We are about buried in the sand   no grass for our horses and the men have taken them two miles away to feed. We have no water only what we carry in our firkin.[3]

29th   We are now in sight of the great mountains   they are nearly one hundred miles from here and look like white clouds. Saw a few stunted trees by the side of a place that is called a creek, but there was nothing but mud in it with a few poles laid down to cross on.

---

[3] A firkin is a small wooden tub, usually used for butter or lard.

30th   Bought some Antelope meat very nice and tender. We can see a great many Antelopes every day. The men often hunt them but they are too quick for them.

July 1st   Camped at noon where there was a family killed two weeks since by the Indians   I did not relish my dinner much on account of fear, but we were not molested. We are camped by the toll gate within nine miles of Denver. Here we are called upon to pay for the privilege dragging ourselves through the sandy desert for two dollars per wagon. There is a well here but the water is so poor we cannot drink it. But we are getting accustomed to live with out water.

2nd   Here we are at Denver the great metropolis of the west. The sight of some decent buildings is very cheering after our long journey through a barren country. Here we find ten thousand people from different parts of the world. They vary in their looks and appearance from the well dressed lady to the bare footed beggar. Some of the buildings are made of sods with board fronts some are very nice brick buildings. There are several nice churches   most of the principal streets look very nicely but the whole city is built on the sand. It is situated at the mouth of cherry creek. We are now by the side of our good old friend the Platte river again, which has supplied us for the past month with one of the greatest necessities of life

3rd   Sunday   attended church   heard a very good sermon.   How good it seems to hear the bells ring and attend meeting.

4th   We were awakened this morn by the firing of cannons. Saw two balloon ascensions. No great doings in the city.

5th   We are still in Denver   Mr. Young who has traveled with us invited Bell and myself to attend a concert given by the Colorado band as he had read the advertisement. We looked in at the window before entering and found it was a colored band instead of Colorado. So we walked around the city instead of going in.

13th   having completed our preparations for a tour up the Rocky Mountains we started this morning with renewed energy   Crossed the Platte river at ten oclock on a ferry boat. Then road [*sic*] ten miles through a kind of weed resembling sun flower   Passed through the table lands they look very green and nice. At three oclock arrived at the Pennsylvania house where we called for a drink. Here we found the first pure water we have seen since leaving Missouri river. Bear creek at this place comes down the mountains and an excellent water. There is no bridge and we forded the stream. We are now camped in an empty house or rather it was empty of every thing but dirt before we came into it.   We do not expect to make long drives in a day as our horses during our stay in Denver were suddenly transformed into an animal not very much unlike in shape but more clumsy footed and furnished by nature with horns. They seem to have an inclination to go in any direction but the right one and as we cannot guide them by reins we resort to more vigorous use of the whip and free exercise of the lungs. We think the old way of "slow and sure" better than going up by steam. Perseverance will accomplish more than steam in such a place as this. We are trying to furnish ourselves with a good supply of that material but find it quite a costly article in this country. Its value increases according to the length of transportation which is the case with nearly every thing brought from the states.

14th   This morning we commenced our first experiance in climbing mountains. Having hitched our three yoke of oxen forward of our wagon we started up Bradford Mountain leaving the other wagon at the foot with Ma and Bell to guard it. Lucy and I took turns riding our little cream colored Indian pony which we purchased in Denver. It is a very gentle animal although but three years old and seems to understand that we are not very well skilled in horsemanship and carries us very carefully over the rocks and stones.   after a long and tedious pull during which time our teams were obliged to stop often to breathe we reached the top of the mountain in safety   the road is very winding and we travelled nearly around the mountain before getting to the top. Here Lucy and I staid while the men went back with the teams after the other wagon   We amused ourselves the meanwhile in wondering where we were. There are not many trees here and we can stand and look back on to the plains perhaps for a distance of a hundred miles   It was a grand sight.

18th   Forded the Platte river twice this afternoon. The current was very swift water up to the wagon box. We got across it first time with out much trouble but the second time Pa went ahead with the freight wagon and called to Harry to follow. When we were about half way through our horned steeds following the example of an animal owned by Balaam in ancient times refused to move forward or backward or side ways. The first wagon had reached the opposite bank in safety and Pa was looking back and giving orders to us which we would gladly of obeyed were it in our power but there we were immovable Harry using every effort to make the team move and Dick on the pony at our side trying to help each whipping until their whips were used up. The pony and his rider were carried down stream several times by the current then he would make his way back to our help again but all in vain   our team was not to be coaxed or drove. At last Pa came from the other side with another team and after a vigorous effort we succeeded in gaining the shore which instead of being terra firma proves to be water filled with bushes where we are now camped for the night as the teams

are too much exhausted to go farther   The men have built a
large fire on a stump by which they are drying their wet
clothes   a few poles hold up the stove so that Lucy is
cooking our supper. What is underneath us I can not tell and
do not wish to know as long as I can keep on the poles.
Around and above us are piled rocks as high as our vision
extends excepting a narrow strip of sky between them.

19th   Last night three of our oxen ran away   Dick and
Harry started at day break and returned with them at ten
oclock. We have rain every afternoon. Saw some wild
cats   There are no birds here to greet us with their morning
song   the croaking of a tree toad would even be music to our
ears.

July 20th   We are now in the middle park   It is a valley
between the mountains extending three hundred miles in
length and varying from five to fifty in width   There are a
few small groves on it. Antelopes appear to be the only living
inhabitants of the park. They can see us at a great distance
and are sure to keep out of the reach of our guns. It seems
quite a refreshing change to ride over level ground one
day   The Ute Indians have lived here but we do not expect
any improvements made by such a race of beings.

21st   After all our level ground di[d]nt last long in a place
for today we have rode over the red hills which are situated
nearly in the centre of the park from east to west and are so
named because of the redness of the soil. We camped early
and I have picked up some handsome red stones.

July 22nd   While the oxen were feeding this noon we
improved the time in slicking up a little as we were soon to
enter the city of Fairplay [in present Park County] where we
expected to meet some of the Rocky Mountain Aristocracy.
This is the first city we have seen since leaving Denver. Here

are six or eight pine log cabins about six feet high with poles laid on for roofs covered with dirt. They each have one door and one window. On the top of our house is a large deers horn which is a sign for a hotel. There is one store also a school taught here but I should judge that there are but few literary characters in this place. I entered the city on my pony by the side of the wagon — I conclude that we created quite a sensation for one young lady with red curls pink dress and white apron stood gazing at us with mouth wide open. My pony pranced and bowed very gracefully through the street. As we were making our way along one of our party recognized an old friend of his quite a dignified young gentleman who offered to assist us in crossing the Platte as the water is unusually high. As I could not go through on horse back I gave up my pony to Dick and I got into the wagon. The banks are very steep and water up to the wagon box. After we were safely landed on the opposite bank we missed our stove pipe and water pail   on looking back we could see that they were caught in the bushes where we first entered the river and the young stranger kindly offered to take our pony and go and get them for us. While he was gone we camped and took possession of a shanty near by. He soon returned with the lost articles and invited Bell and myself to attend a party this eve but we did not accept the invitation.

July 23rd   We are staying where we camped last night because one of our oxen died this morning. Pa has just bought another one. Three men have just stopped and put up with us who are bringing goods into the mountains packed on mules. The manner of packing is to fasten boxes of equal weight to each side of the pack saddle. One mule is often made to carry three hundred pounds in this way. It is quite amusing to see them swim across the rivers. Saw some string beans for sale today which have been brought one hundred miles priced twenty five cents per pound. It is raining hard.

24th   We left this forenoon and entered the mountains again. While we were on the first mountain we could see the clouds below us. The sun shown in the clouds which made a very beautiful sight. We are in an empty house tonight. We often find deserted houses where we can camp.

July 25th   This morning we commenced to climb the snowy range. We made extra preparations for cold weather as we are coming into perpetual snow   blankets and mittens are at hand and we soon found that the tug of war in our journey was only just begun. We could see the top of one hill and think that was the last but when we gained that others still kept rising before us. To look back in retreat seemed utterly out of the question. To look forward was to look directly upwards as the ascent seemed nearly perpendicular but remembering our motto "Perseverance" we doubled our teams and went on. At last when all hope had nearly left us we found ourselves on the top of the range. After skillful management climbing rocks alternately on foot, horse back and in the wagon. When we were afraid to ride up a rock we could climb up and then coax or pull the pony after us. We then stopped for dinner   set our stove by the side of a snow bank and cooked our dinner. We had a merry time playing snow ball and picking flowers in the snow. We felt that we were "Monarch of all we surveyed"   Just before reaching the top we came to a beautiful lake. It was a splendid sight. On the opposite side of the lake and on another mountain we could see two men prospecting. After resting awhile we began to study the best way to get down the other side of this range. After mature deliberation we hitched one yoke of oxen to the rear end of the wagon in order to hold it back as the descent was very steep but as they had become so

strongly impressed with the idea of going ahead we were
obliged to adopt some other method. We then cut down a
large pine tree which we chained to the wagon   This seemed
to answer our purpose entirely. Pull backs in life are generally
considered a calamity but today they seemed the very thing
we needed. Had the teams gone on according to their own
impulse our wagons would all have been upset and the
precious freight would have been — nowhere —   We are
now camped at the foot of this range and feel that we have
accomplished quite a hard days work.

26th   After traveling up hill and down until after noon we
came into the valley of the great Arkansaw. Here we could
not help but admire nature. This is a beautiful river running
in a south easterly direction. On its banks we find excellent
grass for our cattle. Its current is very rapid the water so deep
that it is hardly fordable but we have reached its western bank
in safety and are now on the dividing line between the waters
of the Atlantic and Pacific[4]   After following it eight miles
we came suddenly down a steep mountain into our gulch
called Young America. This gulch is two miles in length.
Our cabin stands near the foot of it and so near the Arkansaw
that the roarings of its waters can be plainly heard from the
house. It is very pleasant here but quite retired there being
no family with[in] one half mile of us. As is usual in new
countries we were cordially welcomed. Our first greeting was
from a little bare footed boy who brought us some fresh fish
for our supper.

27th   Our house has but one room in it and that is now full.
In one corner stands a rude concern made for a bedstead. In
another stands our stove. We found a table here and four
rough shelves fastened to the legs answer for a cupboard. Our
melodian three boxes and a few three legged stools make up

---

[4] Actually they were still some six mountainous miles east of the Continental Divide.

the list of our furniture. Two dripping pans and a spider[5] hanging against the logs answer for pictures. Although the back ground is rather dark yet the features of Bonapart are distinctly visible in one. Daniel Boon the hermit in another. There are two mountains within steps of the door on both sides of the house covered with wormwood. Towards the upper end of the gulch is a grove of pine trees. The ground is full of particles of yellow ore which fools mistake for gold but the more wise have learned that all is not gold that glitters.

28th   A gentleman from Cache Creek (which is four miles from here) called to engage a school teacher and Bell after hearing his offer of seventy five dollars a month and board was induced to accept the situation   There has never been a school taught in that place.

29th   Although we are out of sight of the snowy range yet the mountains around us are covered with perpetual snow. We have had a hail storm today. As there is no vegetation here a hail storm does no injury. Dick and Harry saw a bear in the woods nearby but as they had only one revolver with them they did not dare to fire at it.

30th   Variety is the spice of life. Today we could see the rain pouring down in torrents on one mountain at the right   At the left on another mountain. While here and south of here the sun is shining pleasantly.

August 1st   Bell started this morning on my little pony full of ambition to commence her labors in school teaching. Pa accompanied her to bring the pony back, and brought several letters from friends at home. Lucy had quite a feast reading her letters. I think she has more than her share.

2nd   The miners around us as well as ourselves are feeling quite alarmed on account of guerillas who are prowling

---

[5] A spider is a small frying pan with legs attached for use over an open fire.

around doing all of the damage they can. We are obliged to observe the utmost caution. We keep our pony in sight and our revolvers in readiness. A party of them recently passed through Cache Creek and stole three ponies.

4th   Dick Lucy and myself went fishing   There are very many speckled trout in Lake Creek half a mile from here. They are often caught in a dark night with a spear by building a fire on the bank towards which they are drawn by the light. We caught seven in a short time. It is quite an amusement for us and they are very delicious.

5th   Rode to Cache Creek on my pony to visit Bells school. This is a city composed of ten or twelve log cabins   It is the largest city on the western side of the snowy range. Population this summer one hundred. Should the census be taken of the quadrupeds it might be called a thriving city. Mining is the principle occupation of the inhabitants. They go down to the foot of the mountains to winter as the climate is too cold to winter here   On the principle street (which by the way is the only one) there are two hotels and one store containing a few yards of calico plenty of flour and whiskey. Bread is considered the staff of life. Whiskey the life itself. I found Bell in the upper story of the only two story building in the place. But what a place for a school room   A few rough benches and standing against the logs on which are seated about twenty rougher specimens of the rising generation and Bell in the middle of the room presiding with matronly dignity. A school here is quite a novelty and of course perfect order is not to be expected. A Mr Brown also a visitor was sitting near a window and a boy sitting near him was improving his time by trying the point of a pin through Mr Browns coat sleeve. Another boy near him seemed in danger of swallowing his fist. There are no books without sending one hundred and fifty miles to Denver — So Bell teaches them what she knows (and perhaps a little more) by word of mouth. After the usual exercises Bell in order to show to her visitors the improvement made in school asked one of her brightest scholars Who was the first man! When a prompt answer came, Abraham Lincoln. Feeling a little chagrined she thought it time to dismiss school.

8th   This morning in my rambols along the banks of the Arkansaw I found some singular looking bushes containing berries resembling the goos berry though inferior in size And while I was busy gathering them I chanced to look on the opposite bank of the river and to my surprise there stood a bear gazing intently at me as if to say Pray! to what race do you belong   He soon showed signs of attempting to swim across the river evidently to form an acquaintance with me but as I was not disposed to make his acquaintance I started on double quick for the house running through the weeds stumbling over and between rocks and upsetting things in general. I was very much exhausted but was soon able to relate my adventure.

9th   I have been down into the pit helping men wash gold. We were twenty feet below the surface of the ground   The water is brought two miles in a ditch to a reservoir and then let down into the pit through a gate with such a force that the ground caves off on both sides and as it runs through the flume the gold dust settles to the bottom and is caught in the riffles. The bottom of the boxes are then scraped out into pans and taken to the reservoir to be washed again and then as the dust is a fine particles we use quick silver to save it. The flume extends to the Arkansaw river. The water makes such a noise that it is difficult to hear each other talk. When I go to call the men to dinner I am obliged to throw a stone down to make the men look up as they cannot hear me call. To get into the pit we are obliged to go down the bank to the

river side and then climb over the rocks that have been dug
out till we get back to where the men are at work.

10th   I thought I would shorten my walk into the pit this
afternoon by sliding down the bank onto a rock which
projected from the side of the cave but as I struck it with too
much force it gave way and carried me to the bottom and a
plenty of sand following me. Not a very pleasant ride at the
time but when the men found I was not seriously hurt they
had a hearty laugh at my expense.

11th   Have been over to Mrs Camerons our nearest
neighbors   Crossed Lake Creek on a foot bridge. She gave
me some reading in the shape of old smoky pamphlets which
looked as though they were published in Adam's day and
hung in the corner of a log cabin ever since. I brought them
home with me and on examination found them to be novels
and laid them on the shelf till I make her another call.

13th   Lucy, Bell, and myself went fishing with Mrs
Cameron. Had a pleasant time   caught a fine lot of fish.

15th   There are two beautiful lakes called the Twin Lakes
about one mile from here. We have been to see them this
afternoon. One of them is three miles long the other four.
They are full of speckled trout. There has never been any
bottom found to the upper one. There is no inlet into it.
Lake Creek is the outlet which empties into the Arkansaw.
There is an artist there today taking a picture of the Lakes
and the scenery around them. It will make a nice picture.

17th   Dick Lucy and myself have been raspberrying. We
put our dinners in pails and took our pony on which we took
turns riding. We went a mile and a half where we found
several acres covered with red raspberries on the side of a
mountain. They grow on low bushes not more than one foot
and a half in height. We picked until noon, then spread our
dinners on a huge flat rock and sat by it to eat. We are

obliged to keep a good look out for bears as they are very fond of berries. But we did not see any. We laraetted our pony and he fed on grass while we picked berries. We wandered until we lost sight of him and hunted a long time to find him   At length we filled our pails and started home leaving plenty for the bears to feast on   Picked twenty quarts.

18th   Had to heat a boiler of water to thaw out a tub of frozen clothes. It freezes every night   In the middle of the day it is quite warm   Morning and evening we need a fire to sit by. We use pine wood entirely. This afternoon one of Bells scholars (a little boy nine years old) was buried. The neighbors made a box for a coffin and he was buried without any funeral cerimonies   There is no minister nor physician near here.

August 19th   Had a severe thunder shower this afternoon The lightning looks terrific. It strikes the ground mostly every time drawn by the metal in the earth. Towards night it cleared off and is now quite pleasant. We can not see the sun rise nor set here in the mountains.

20th   Reports say that the Indians are murdering the whites on the plains at a rapid rate. It is sad news but we hope they will soon be drawn to the Pacific coast and then pushed in.

21st   Heard of the brutal conduct of the Guerillas   a band of twelve attacked the stage last week a few miles below Fairplay on its way to Denver. Robbed the mail bag of its contents which was several thousand dollars in gold dust, and threatened to shoot the driver if he ever drove the stage again. A large number of miners have turned out to hunt for them and it is hoped they will be found   This is Sunday and as usual has been a lonely day for us as there is no meeting within one hundred and fifty miles of here. If we could hear our old church bell ring it would be charming music but all we can hear is the cowbell. It seems almost like a heathen country.

29th   Last night we were disturbed very much by the howling of wolves. They often come near the house nights but our dog frightens them away. I have been in Cache Creek on my pony this afternoon.

30th   New discoveries are being made in Red Mountain twenty miles west of here and great excitement prevails. Two companies from Central City are prospecting there now. It is thought that the mountain is rich with gold. Pa and Harry are prospecting there this week.

Sept 6th   I went fishing   caught seven fish and then lost my hook. Just as I arrived home a traveler called and offered me one dollar for them which I accepted.

8th   Visited Mrs Cameron   found them eating dinner Mr & Mrs Ca sitting at the table eating fish and bread. The three children sitting on the floor around a spider of hot bread and milk each one busy in getting her share. During the afternoon Mrs Cameron gave a history of her life in Colorado. She has endured many hardships and privations. Says "she has been struck dead twice by lightning" and her brother had been kicked by a horse and was dead as a stick for three hours. Their cabin had been surrounded with bears and wolves and numerous other adventures which I do not remember. I started home early out of pity to her tongue.   she must be tired talking.

10th   Pa came home from Cache Creek this morn and said he had got my pony in his pocket. I looked up amazed as he took out three ounces of gold dust from his pocket and said he had sold it for so much. I shall miss my little pony very much as I have fed him regularly with salt and meal.

12th   There are some prairie dogs here in the Mt's resembling those on the plains   Lucy and I have caught one and got it in a cage. In order to tame it I take it out every day and feed it with meat.

14th   We were invited to join a fishing party at Lake Creek. There were several from Cache Creek. We caught a fine lot of fish and had a pleasant walk. We cannot walk very fast here as the air is so light it is difficult to breath freely.

20th   Bell has closed her short term in school and I suppose her pupils have all graduated with high honors. Wonder if they can tell who the first man was. She is quite elated with her success.   whether it is the weight of character which her scholars have acquired or the weight of her purse I do not know.

26th   It is snowing hard and has been for several days and we are making preparations to leave the mountains as there is danger of getting snowed in for the winter if we stay much longer.

28th   Sold our cow this morn. We shall miss the nice milk and cream which we have enjoyed although we have not had it regularly as our pasture extends from Behrings strait to Cape Horn (I guess) and she comes home whenever her conscience dictates as when ever we hear the bell which is as apt to be at midnight as any time our milk pail is at hand and we soon have a pail of fresh milk.

29th   We bade our affectionate adieu to Young America gulch and started for home. At ten oclock we started up the mountain back of the house. The oxen had become so much attached to their mountain home that just before reaching the top of the mountain they suddenly turned, (probably to view the gulch once more) and upset the freight wagon. Ma's rocking chair was crushed to atoms. The pail of milk for our dinner spilled and our poor little prairie dog went rolling in his cage to the foot of the mountain. After an hours hinderance we were again on our way. Arrived at Colorado

Gulch at dusk   here we shall stay for a few days for the purpose of prospecting   I will not attempt to describe the road as it is past description   This is a desolate looking place

Oct 1st   We are stopping at the house of Mr Miller. They have a little girl named Colorado. I suppose because of their attachment to the country. I think there is a striking resemblance.

3rd   Snow is so deep that prospecting is out of the question and we started this afternoon on our long journey. Are now camped at the foot of the snowy range—

4th   We have crossed the snowy range again. Snow eighteen inches deep. On the top of the range the wind blew very hard and the snow was blowing into drifts   But "will stand the storm   it wont be long"   We are now camped at the foot of the range in a deserted house   The occupants have been frightened away by Guerrillas.

5th   High winds. Saw a great many deer. We are now at Fairplay. Here we find a few vegitables that have been brought up from the valley. We bought some nice onions for dinner.

6th   Passed a place that has been smoking and burning ever since whites first came to this country. It is thought there will be a volcanic eruption there at some future day. Crossed the red hills   Camped in a thick forest of pines   Have plenty of wood for fires.

11th   As we descend we find warmer weather. Gathered a small bag of pine cones and some Kinikinick berries. This is a plant which was used by the Indians for medicine.

12th   Reached the Junction. Took the road for Central City.

14th   Crossed Clear Creek fifteen times and then payed toll,

75cts per wagon. Have at last arrived at the far famed city of Black Hawk. Why it is so named we cannot tell. I am sure no birds of that name or any other name would hover or sing near such a looking place. It is built on the sides of two mountains   streets are laid out in a very singular style.

17th   Visited several quartz mills in Central City. They make a wonderful noise and are kept running night and day. Also went into a tunnel by the light of a candle. Saw three buckets of quartz drawn up out of a shaft three hundred & fifty feet deep.

18th   Started for Denver. After riding three miles we met a train two miles in length loaded with quartz mills. As we cannot pass we were obliged to camp for the night. The coach is behind the train and as it cannot come by, the passengers have come on afoot and are now warming by our fire, which is quite a luxery to them.

20.   We are now back to Denver again. Rented two small rooms for a few days on Cherry Creek. While we were making preparations to cross the plains.

25th   Sold our melodian.

28th   We had nearly completed our arrangments when to our great surprise we find that our money was stolen this morning. Pa immediately started the Sheriff and several others in pursuit of the Thief   also sent telegrams to the states, Salt Lake and Santa fe. We are feeling very sad. We shall probably remain here a while longer.

29th   Snowing hard.

31st   Snow two and a half feet deep. The air is so full of snow that we can hardly see the Mts

Nov 6th   Lucy Bell and myself attended church also the Sunday School. It is an interesting school. Mrs. Charles is my teacher.

24th   Thanksgiving day. We have attended church   heard a good sermon preached by Mr Day.

Dec 2nd   Moved into a large building called the Common wealth from the name of a paper which has been printed here.

11th   Have attended church and Sunday School.

14th   Lucy and Bell attended Judge Fillemans funeral. The services were held in the Episcopal church.

22nd   The third Col Cavalry came into Denver riding four abreast displaying their flags in honor of their great victory over the Indians in the late battle at Sand creek. The band rode out a few miles to meet them. It was quite a sight.

25th   Attended the Sunday School festival. Received a present of a pin cushion from off the Christmas tree.

27th   At the late battle at Sand Creek Col Shivington destroyed a village of 1000 Cheyennes[6]   The next day while the soldiers were burning the wigwams three little Indian children were found hidden under some Buffalo robes. They were nearly frightened to death. The soldiers brought them here and are getting clothes made for them. Bell has made a dress for the little girl and I have made her an apron. She is very shy and afraid of white people but seems much pleased with her new clothes. The man who took her intends sending her to the states to be educated.

Jan 4th   Have had a feast better than a christmas dinner

----

[6]The Sand Creek Massacre was one of the most dreadful slaughters of Indians by the American military. The battle took place on November 29, 1864. The commander in charge was Colonel John M. Chivington, whose command was the Third Regiment of the Colorado Cavalry. Numbers of Indians dead have been estimated from 100 to 800. "The soldiers scalped the dead, cut up and mutilated the bodies, and took back to Denver over a hundred scalps, which were exhibited in triumph between the acts of a theatrical performance one evening." George Bird Grinnell, *The Fighting Cheyennes* (Norman, 1956), p. 173. See also Stan Hoig, *The Sand Creek Massacre* (Norman, 1961), *passim.*

We received fourteen letters from home. They have been
around by California   Although they are old still we are
glad to get them.

12th   All communication across the plains is now stopped
as the Indians are again on the road murdering and driving
off stock

15th   Started for our home in the old Keystone state.[7] A
long cold dangerous journey lies before us but the thought of
home and friends is a strong motive to urge us to brave
dangers. According to report we are to meet four thousand
warriors but every preparation has been made for such an
event by our brave captain   Our train consists of one
government and two merchants outfits making in all 150
wagons, and six hundred men. We have a military escort of
one company of Artillery with a cannon and one of cavalry.
We are now camped at Fort Lupton. We form a correl in
camping that is the wagons are driven into a circle and those
that contain the families (which number seventeen) in the
middle of the circle   We have a small sheet iron stove in our
wagon.

16th   The bugle sounded at four oclock this morning for us
to get up. Fires were started all over the camp ground, and at
seven we were again on our way. We do not stop at noon.
Soon after camping tonight the bugle sounded for every man
to appear in the middle of the correll when captain Wanless
issued the following orders.

    Order 1st   Every mans name will now be taken and any
        man found without his name in the book in the morning
        shall be turned out of the train.
    Order 2nd   Twenty eight men shall be detailed to stand as
        guard each night consisting of four reliefs   The bugle

---

[7]Pennsylvania.

will sound four times during the night when as the roll is
called the men will form into line and proceed to their
duty 100 yards from camp. Eight men shall also be sent
out one half mile as pickets. If any man fail to do his duty
on guard or picket he shall stand twice the length of time
the next night

Order 3rd   In case of an attack in the night the bugle will
     sound when every man will stand by his own wagon ready
     to fire as soon as our pickets are all in

Order 4th   There shall be no firing across the correll.

Order 5th   No man shall get out of his wagon to walk
     without his gun in his hand.

[January] 17th   This afternoon several guns were fired at a
Jack Rabbit which came bounding past the train. Our
advance guard and scouts came rushing back supposing us to
be attacked. After we had camped tonight the captain addressed the men as follows. Gentlemen you are not aware of
the harm that may result from the firing this afternoon. The
Indians without doubt are aware of our position and probably
are now pursuing us as we can see hay burning a few miles back
of us   After one or two false alarms if the train should be
attacked the cavalry would not return supposing it to be only
a Jack Rabbit. To the five orders given last night I will now
add another one.

Order 6th   There shall be no firing while the train is
     moving. Should this order be disobeyed, I pledge my word
     and honor the offender shall be strapped to the cannon and
     ride there one day.

19th   Passed the American Ranch which was still burning.
The bodies of two Indians were lying in the fire supposed to
have been shot by the woman in their efforts to capture her.
The family were all killed.

21st   At three oclock this morning we were all aroused by

the firing of guns from our guard at some indians who came prowling around but they did not dare to attack us   Great excitement prevailed throughout the camp until morning.

22nd   At ten oclock this morning two of our scouts brought in two indian ponies saddled without a rider. Passed a ranch which was burned yesterday Valley Station which was well fortified with sacks of government corn. Passed Julesburg The indians nearly destroyed the place last week. They fought all day   21 whites were killed and 50 indians   The place looks desolate. After camping the body of Mr Andrews of Denver who fell a victim to savage cruelty two weeks since in the battle at Valley Station was taken up. His remains are to be taken in this train to the river for burial. His body was badly mutilated having both eyes shot out arms broken &c &c.

23rd   This morning a large party of men were sent out to bury a little child who died in camp last night   No funeral ceremonies, no coffins and the heart stricken parents must go on and leave it for the foot of the red man to tread on.

24th   Arrived at Cotton Wood   it is very cold indeed.

25th   My 14th birth day   celebrated it in rather a novel way by riding all day in the cold. Met a train of 100 wagons bound for Denver with an escort   Sent letters back to Denver by them.

26   Crossed Plum Creek   Drove 18 miles

27th   Arrived at Fort Kearney at one oclock and camped for the night

30th   We are now among the Pawnie Indians but they are friendly. This noon we saw several of them. Crossed the Nimaha [Nemaha] river.

Feb 2nd   Arrived at Nebraska city   Crossed the Missouri river on the ice and are now in the United States again. It is thawing and the water was running very swiftly one foot deep on the ice.

13th   We passed through Fort Des Moins the capital of Iowa.

15th   Arrived at Nevada [Iowa] at the end of the railroad Here we bid an affectionate adiew to our wagon horses and driver. As we shall now exchange that mode of traveling for one of more speed

INDEX